Postwar Migration in Southern Europe, 1950–2000

Managing migration promises to be one of the most difficult challenges of the twenty-first century. It will be even more difficult for southern European countries, from which emigration has leveled off and to which immigration has become a significant economic issue. Southern Europe is close to other regions where the pressure to emigrate is intense: These regions have a high level of unemployment, higher than the European Union average, and a large informal sector, often 15–25 percent of their economies as a whole. This book analyzes the southern European migration case using an economic approach. It combines a theoretical and an empirical approach on the fundamental migration issues: the decision to migrate, effects on the country of departure and country of destination, and the effectiveness of policies in managing migration. It also explores the transformation due to migration of southern European countries in the 1980s and 1990s.

Alessandra Venturini is Professor of Economics at the University of Torino, Italy. She previously taught at the University of Florence, the University of Bergamo, and the University of Padua. Professor Venturini won the Saint Vincent Prize for the volume *Microeconomia del Lavoro*, coauthored with R. Brunetta. Professor Venturini joined IZA as a Research Fellow in 1999, the CHILD Research Center in 2000, and the FIERI Research Center in 2002. She has also held visiting positions at Brown University, the Institute of Development Studies at the University of Sussex, and the International Institute of Labour Studies at the International Labour Organization. Her research has appeared in journals such as *Labour, European Economic Review, Journal of Population Economics*, and the *International Labour Review*. Professor Venturini's research interests remain focused on migration studies.

Postwar Migration in Southern Europe, 1950–2000

An Economic Analysis

ALESSANDRA VENTURINI
University of Torino

CAMBRIDGE
UNIVERSITY PRESS

PUBLISHED BY THE PRESS SYNDICATE OF THE UNIVERSITY OF CAMBRIDGE
The Pitt Building, Trumpington Street, Cambridge, United Kingdom

CAMBRIDGE UNIVERSITY PRESS
The Edinburgh Building, Cambridge CB2 2RU, UK
40 West 20th Street, New York, NY 10011-4211, USA
477 Williamstown Road, Port Melbourne, VIC 3207, Australia
Ruiz de Alarcón 13, 28014 Madrid, Spain
Dock House, The Waterfront, Cape Town 8001, South Africa

http://www.cambridge.org

First published 2004

Printed in the United States of America

Typeface Minion 10.5/13 pt.   *System* LATEX 2_ε [TB]

A catalog record for this book is available from the British Library.

Library of Congress Cataloging in Publication Data
Venturini, Alessandra.
Postwar migration in southern Europe, 1950–2000 : an economic analysis / Alessandra Venturini.
p.   cm.
Includes bibliographical references and index.
ISBN 0-521-64040-7 (hardback)
1. Europe, Southern – Emigration and immigration – Economic aspects.   I. Title.
JV7590.V463   2004
304.8′094′09045–dc22   2003055862

ISBN 0 521 64040 7 hardback

To my beloved son Giovanni, husband Luciano, and family

Contents

List of Figures and Tables

FIGURES

TABLES

Acknowledgments

I would like to thank the Aurelio Peccei Foundation, the Giacomo Brodolini Foundation, the Ministry of Education, the Departments of Economics of the Universities of Florence, Bergamo, Padova, and Torino and all the members of these institutions who helped to provide financial and scientific support for my research. The number of people I would like to thank for their support during this long research project is unfortunately too long to list here. However, I must thank my fellow authors, Michele Bruni, Daniela Del Boca, Riccardo Faini, and Claudia Villosio, as well as my colleagues, Nicolas Glytsos, Maria Bagahna, Philip Martin, Roger Kramer, Francisco Ferri, and many IZA Fellows who provided me with invaluable information on specific issues.

Introduction

Migration promises to be one of the most pressing topics of debate in the twenty-first century. Emigrants are leaving from an ever increasing number of countries, and their destinations are equally varied, so that the phenomenon is, using a much abused word, global. The rapid decrease in transport costs, the availability of cheap information, the political and economic upheavals in eastern Europe, and the outbreak of local conflicts have all meant that the number of potential emigrants has multiplied. At the same time, many former countries of emigration have reached an overall standard of living that makes them potential destination areas.

Thus, one of the most difficult challenges of the twenty-first century will be how to manage immigration and emigration. Destination countries would like to control the inflow of foreigners, but their policies risk being ineffective because the flows are changing and becoming more complex as labor immigration is replaced or largely integrated by family reunification (about half of the foreigners in Europe entered as family members)[1] and refugees.[2] In addition, development policies designed to help countries of origin to raise their standard of living will take time to have any effect so that individuals' propensity to emigrate will not decrease in the near term. The political changes that are necessary in many countries of origin cannot be completed easily; consequently, the demand and supply of migrants will not be balanced in the near future.

The southern European countries are a very interesting case to study. If the other industrialized countries find managing migration difficult, it will be much more difficult for the southern European countries. This is

---

[1] See, for example, Table 1.7 in Boeri, Hanson, and McCornick (2002).
[2] The average demands for asylum increased enormously in Europe during the 1990s. In Germany, for example, the average annual flow was 142,000, and in the United States only 83,000. See Table 5.4 in this volume.

because they have recently ended their emigration phase, and they now must learn how to manage immigration in a period of "large" emigration. They are also close to areas where the pressure to emigrate is extremely high, such as North Africa and eastern Europe. There are, of course, inflows from more distant countries, too. These "new" receiving countries are attractive because of their increased level of income. However, they also have high unemployment rate (above the EU average) and a large informal sector, 15% to 25% of the economy,[3] two factors that complicate the management of immigration policy.

This book, the fruit of many years of research, aims to analyze this special case using an economic approach. I am convinced that migration is not only an economic phenomenon but also a social one. However, the economic analyses of its interaction provide a very thorough tool that can help us to understand its dynamics.

This volume tries to cover all aspects of the migratory phenomenon that constitute the economic and not only economic debate. I consider such questions as the determinants of the choice to migrate, the effect of immigration on the receiving country, and the consequences of emigration on the country of origin. I also assess the effectiveness of migration policies, and the policies that involve the area of migration, in managing the migratory phenomenon. In the literature, immigration is not usually divided into these four themes, but such a division makes it possible to separate the various methodological approaches. These approaches can then be combined into a single model so that the causes and effects of migration can be analyzed using a wide range of studies.

These themes have been analyzed within the context of European migration, especially the migratory phenomenon of the southern European countries after the Second World War. The migratory phenomenon in Italy, Spain, Portugal, and Greece, despite national differences, evolved in similar ways. There was transoceanic and, especially in the immediate postwar period, European emigration, while in the 1980s there were new flows of immigration from the developing countries and eastern Europe.

Chapter 1 lays out the main numbers so that emigration from southern Europe can be compared with immigration into southern European countries. The evolution of emigration from the southern European countries in the postwar period and of the recent immigration to those countries is highlighted, showing the similarities and differences between these flows regarding gender, age, activities, professional standing,

---

[3] See, for example, Schneider and Enste (2000).

the direction of the emigration flows, and the immigrants' countries of origin. A survey of the theoretical approaches and the content of the debate follows. Its aim is to facilitate the identification of the four most important topics, which are dealt with in later chapters.

What determines the choice to migrate is considered in Chapter 2. An initial survey of the economic approaches to the choice to migrate highlights a variety of models that question the role played by wage differentials. Other interpretations emphasize, for example, the importance of spreading risks when income is uncertain or the importance of budget constraints and the level of income in the country of origin. The wealth of theoretical models is countered by the limited data available in the case of the southern European countries; thus, the choice of emigration is tested, whereas the choice made by immigrants is left until better information is available. Because of the availability of data, a different approach has been adopted in the empirical analysis. The microeconomic model of an individual's or a family's choice as a function of expected wage differentials is compared with the gravitational model, where distance plays a key role in slowing migration, and with the sociological model, which identifies family and social ties (the *migratory chain*) as the effective driving forces of migration.

The results of the empirical tests show that, despite national differences, the best interpretation of the evolution of emigration from the southern European countries is a combination of the sociological factor of the migratory chain with the traditional economic variables in the form of wage differentials. Thus, although the theoretical models question the importance of wage differentials in explaining the choice to migrate, it is true that overall flows of emigrants respond positively to an increase in wage differentials and to an increase in the probability of getting a job, but there is also an important dynamic relationship with past flows of emigrants. The migratory phenomena analyzed are influenced very little by changes in policies governing entry to the labor market; instead, family reunification policies, which influence the effect of the migratory chain, seem to be important.

The lesson learned through these empirical tests indicates that to manage immigration, countries should, in the short term, control the domestic demand for foreign labor and the policy of family reunification and should favor labor-intensive foreign aid projects, which, however, will reduce migratory pressure only in the long term.

The theme that has attracted most attention in the debate regarding the south European countries, is certainly the effect of immigration on the destination country, and it is dealt with in Chapter 3. It is arranged in five strands, which are dealt with in the first part of the chapter, where the theoretical models and empirical evidence for Europe are presented critically. The second part of the chapter is dedicated to the question of competition in the labor markets of the southern European countries, and some new empirical results are presented.

The analysis of the effect of immigration on the destination country begins by considering the impact of foreign workers on the labor market (the first strand). The effect can be *complementary* or *competitive*. It depends on various factors, including the way the labor market operates, the presence of trade unions, and the wage and employment aims proposed by the trade unions. Various models are presented critically and the implications for labor market equilibrium are highlighted. Two important differences emerge in the southern European case: The first refers to the competition produced by foreigners working in the informal sector, and the second, more specific, difference is the displacement of native internal mobility, namely natives unemployed in less-developed areas.

The second strand is wage assimilation, that is, whether foreigners, during their life cycles, can achieve wage profiles similar to those of comparable native workers. A survey of the theoretical approach and the problems of empirical estimates is followed by a discussion of the main U.S. and northern European findings, where the inability of many recent immigrants to achieve a similar wage pattern to that of natives can be traced to three main factors: They have less human capital, economic growth is decreasing, and many immigrants today are refugees. Southern Europeans were able to assimilate in the destination countries, and the little evidence available on immigrants working in the southern European countries shows that they are not discriminated against in terms of wages.

The third strand examines the effect of immigration on the growth in the destination country's per-capita income. This is closely linked to how much human capital the foreigner possesses compared with native workers. If foreigners have more than the national average, there is an increase in per-capita income; if they have less, there is a decrease. Some studies of the European case have found that the average human capital of an immigrant is lower than the national average, and that leads to slowed growth in per-capita income. However, especially when the demand for labor is linked to a shortage of native workers, employing foreigners with lower than average human capital favors an overall growth in production.

Less attention has been paid in the southern European countries to the fourth strand, the impact of immigration on social expenditure, probably because the phenomenon is new and there is not yet sufficient data available to carry out an adequate analysis. The theoretical approach is outlined, and the main U.S. and European findings are presented. In the American case, during the first migratory wave, foreigners made less use of welfare services than did similar natives. However, in the case of more recent flows, it seems that the situation is reversed; foreigners are aware of the benefits they can claim, and they settle where these benefits are most generous. In the European case there has been less research, but it seems that there are two contradictory models: a Swiss model, where foreigners contribute with positive transfers to the social expenditure of the native workers, and a German model, where foreigners are net users of social services.

The fifth and final strand concerns the impact of foreigners on the demographic structure of the population of the destination country and on the pension system. The importance of this strand is seen in that recent immigration into the southern European countries occurred in countries with a high rate of aging, and so immigrants are also considered positively for their overall generational contribution. The positive contributions made by foreigners to the structure of the population and to the pension system must not be confused with the probability both of reaching a stationary population and of reducing the pension deficit with flows of immigrants who, as this research shows, in the medium term would make the problem worse.

The second part of Chapter 3 develops in greater detail the theme of complementarity and competition between foreigners and natives in the southern European countries. A brief description of the findings regarding the United States, Canada, Australia, and northern Europe highlights two general rules,[4] which favor complementarity: a selective migratory policy and a flexible labor market. The absence of these two factors would suggest that there is competition between native workers and foreigners; however, empirical findings suggest that complementarity prevails, at least in regular labor markets. In contrast, evidence of competition emerges between the irregular and regular activities of foreigners in both Italy and Greece, however limited in absolute value. Results differ according to the model of analysis used: a micro test on individual data, which generally suggests complementarity, or an aggregate general computable equilibrium model, which is less optimistic. In the latter case, the aggregate economy is under control and its equilibrium conditions are the result of the labor market. A less optimistic view should prevail because many implicit effects of immigration, including the displacement of internal mobility, are missing in the empirical analysis.

[4] See Chapter 3.

The effect of emigration on the departure country is analyzed in Chapter 4. Destination countries are also involved in this issue. With the aim of reducing migratory pressure, these countries emphasize the negative effects of emigration on economic growth in the country of origin and have considered whether giving developmental aid can slow emigration.

There are two main lines of research on this question. The first considers the effect of emigration on the structure of the population and on total human capital and how this affects the growth of the country of origin. The second considers the effect of emigrants' remittances on savings, the distribution of income, and the growth of production in the country of origin.

Some studies show that emigrants are selected positively (they are willing to risk, they have entrepreneurial ability, and their qualifications may be higher than the national average). Therefore, their departure is a loss for the productive system in the area of origin, and this means that its rate of growth decreases. However, other theoretical and empirical studies come to the opposite conclusion: that there is an increase in average productivity as a result of a reduction in the labor force. Remittances, even when they are not directly invested in the productive sectors, can also have important multiplier effects on growth.

In addition to the findings of the theoretical models, this chapter presents empirical data regarding changes to the age and gender structure of the population caused by emigration of southern Europeans. Changes to the labor market and economic growth are also considered, together with evidence on the so-called brain drain. The empirical findings cover countries in the Mediterranean basin, and the effect of remittances on the balance of payments, income, and economic growth is considered analytically. Empirical evidence shows that some southern European countries and others in the Mediterranean find it difficult to replace exported workers with exported goods.

Chapter 5 considers how effective migratory policies are in managing migratory flows and provides a quite discouraging scenario. Migratory policy in its strictest sense is a blunt weapon. The German and French experience in the 1970s taught us that if entry for work is reduced, pressure on other channels of entry increases: family reunification, applications for political asylum, and illegal immigration. All these channels of entry are examined, and evidence is provided of how difficult it is to achieve specific objectives. The high cost and limited effectiveness of border controls, are highlighted, as are the economic effects, of an increase in the alternative channels of entry on the dynamics of the migratory phenomenon. The problems associated with regularization measures – especially those introduced in the southern European countries that experienced repeated regularizations (every three to four years) in the context of a large irregular economy – are also discussed at length. If it is difficult to control borders and manage the entry of foreigners into a country, it is even more difficult to reduce their presence. The policy of offering incentives to return home has been shown to be rather ineffective, and often it is difficult to carry out deportation without first making repatriation agreements with the countries of origin. Other policies that consider the sphere of citizenship are mentioned, and as such they define who is a foreigner and therefore who is subject to migration laws.

The importance of knowledge of the language as a prerequisite for economic integration is the only theme dealt with in the debate about a foreigner's integration. This theme is still in its initial stage in the southern European countries because the migratory phenomenon is new, but it will certainly receive much more attention from economic researchers in the next few years. The chapter concludes with a synopsis of the characteristics that can make migration laws more effective in the southern European case. However, the details will not be revealed here; the reader is invited to consider them later.

1

The Evolution of Migration in Southern European Countries

1.1 THE EVOLUTION OF MIGRATION

1.1.1 From Countries of Emigration to Countries of Immigration

Almost without its being noticed, the southern European countries have been turned from emigration countries into countries of immigration. This change was not sought, and in fact it was unexpected, as shown by the flurry of immigration legislation in the various countries, initially in Spain in 1985 and in Italy in 1986, later in 1992 in Greece, and in Portugal[1] in 1993. This was designed to revise the immigration laws and regularize situations that had built up during the period when the authorities were taken by surprise and had not yet passed specific provisions. The decline in emigration from Italy, Spain, Greece, and Portugal took place before the 1980s. In fact the decrease occurred before 1974, the year when economic recession in the main northern European receiving countries led them to introduce restrictive immigration policies for foreign workers (see Figure 1.1). However, between the end of the 1970s and the beginning of the 1980s, the balance between inflows (+) and outflows (−) changed from negative to positive for all the southern European countries: Italy, Spain, Greece, and Portugal

---

[1] In Italy the most important laws are 943/1986, 81/1988, 39/1990 (known as the Martelli law), and 40/1998, which reviewed all the regulations governing a foreigner's entry and residence in the country. In 2001 the law was revised, with a restrictive approach to immigration and legalization established by the end of 2002. In Spain the review of the laws began with 7/1985 and continued with 1119/1986. In August 2000, a new law was brought before Parliament (and approved in November) that tried to fight illegal immigration and began the third regularization operation. The Portuguese government began its review of the laws governing entry with 59/March 1993, and continued with 244/August 1998, which was amended in July 2001, introducing a further regularization provision. Greek laws governing the entry of foreigners began with 1975/1991 and two presidential decrees (358/1997 and 359/1997), which authorized the first regularization processes. A revision of the Immigration Act was started in 2001, and a second regularization is on the way.

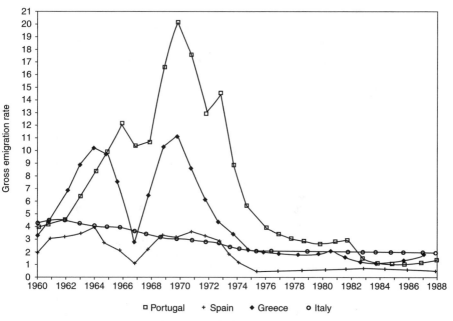

Figure 1.1. Total emigration rate

(see Table 1.1). In the case of Italy, especially, positive flows, counted in the thousands, first turned into tens of thousands and then hundreds of thousands. For short periods in Italy, Spain, and Portugal, seasonal emigration and bursts of limited emigration created a negative balance, but except for Portugal – where workers continued to leave, mostly to Switzerland – the phenomenon of emigration is extremely limited and stops completely in the 1990s.

The foreign population in the southern European countries increased rapidly in the 1980s, more than doubling (see Table 1.2). Although the southern European countries have very different immigration traditions and their non-EU immigration varies considerably, the recent increase in immigration into these countries mainly comprises people from Africa and Asia. However, the 1990s saw a flow of immigrants from eastern Europe.

The data in Table 1.3[2] clearly show the increasing importance of immigration from Africa and Asia, and its growth is highlighted by the legalizations passed in Italy and Spain in the early 1990s. The most numerous immigrants

---

[2] After 1977 the Greek National Statistical Service stopped collecting data regarding inflows and outflows, so no more recent data are available (Douglas 1993, quoted in Lianos, Sarris, and Katseli 1996).

Table 1.1. *Total net migration 1960–98 (+ inflows – outflows)*

Year	Greece	Italy	Portugal	Spain
1960	−30,500	−80,860	−55,528	−142,000
1961	−23,861	−130,848	−38,081	−82,664
1962	−48,200	−75,694	−73,853	−128,725
1963	−56,038	−77,966	−90,882	−102,144
1964	−47,500	−82,261	−133,494	−93,330
1965	−39,978	−61,350	−175,424	−50,200
1966	−4,800	−100,835	−181,744	−95,566
1967	−28,966	−91,275	−144,289	94,182
1968	−38,500	−102,566	−138,002	−24,865
1969	−66,847	−115,326	−208,839	−73,832
1970	−46,200	−107,276	−121,951	−50,479
1971	−15,501	−158,251	−121,549	55,192
1972	−600	16,591	−72,100	−68,000
1973	−42,500	14,097	−83,900	−67,000
1974	−19,300	9,779	174,400	−24,000
1975	58,500	22,424	347,000	14,000
1976	55,900	2,612	10,000	54,000
1977	22,004	4,624	19,747	67,137
1978	105,800	3,597	30,227	42,965
1979	41,571	−3,281	37,021	−36,622
1980	52,410	4,914	41,900	112,000
1981	2,408	−33,033	7,876	−30,913
1982	12,370	−45,195	−3,318	−33,000
1983	8,878	−35,512	−17,347	−19,323
1984	10,100	−29,993	−6,988	−25,000
1985	6,055	−20,405	−27,373	−12,115
1986	15,199	−14,282	−38,180	−26,288
1987	19,801	−3,880	−53,475	−28,251
1988	27,142	9,554	−50,195	−17,880
1989	53,852	16,324	−57,710	−13,989
1990	71,135	24,212	−60,068	−20,012
1991	87,246	4,163	−24,644	32,284
1992	48,878	181,986	− 9,587	20,224
1993	56,025	181,070	19,954	24,717
1994	27,320	153,364	10,314	24,023
1995	20,859	95,499	5,375	47,314
1996	21,558	149,745	10,246	45,490
1997	22,070	126,554	15,270	35,609
1998	22,500	113,804	15,244	32,320

Source: EUROSTAT 1995a, *Migration Statistics*; 1999, *Demographic Statistics*

Table 1.2. *Stock of foreign resident population, share of domestic population, and growth rate*

Year	Italy	%	Spain	%	Greece	%	Portugal	%
1970	143,834	0.29	147,700	0.39	n.a.	–	n.a.	–
1975	186,413	0.34	165,289	0.47	n.a.	–	n.a.	–
1980	298,746	0.53	181,544	0.49	n.a.	–	58,091	0.59
1985	423,004	0.74	241,971	0.63	233,500	2.21	79,574	0.78
1990	781,100	1.37	275,000	1.06	290,000	2.98	107,767	1.10
1993	987,400	1.76	430,362	1.20	295,841	3.00	121,500	1.23
1995	991,419	1.77	499,800	1.30	n.a.	–	168,300	1.70
1996	1,095,600	1.91	539,000	1.40	n.a.	–	172,900	1.74
1997	1,140,700	2.00	609,800	1.53	n.a.	–	175,300	1.77
1998	1,033,200	1.87	719,700	1.82	309,000	3.09	177,800	1.80
1999	1,250,000	2.20	801,329	2.00	n.a.	–	190,896	1.84
Growth Rate								
1970–75	0.30	–	0.12	–	n.a.	–	n.a.	–
1975–80	0.60	–	0.10	–	n.a.	–	n.a.	–
1980–85	0.42	–	0.35	–	n.a.	–	0.36	–
1985–90	0.85	–	0.71	–	0.24	–	0.36	–
1980–95	0.26	–	0.4	–	n.a.	–	0.1	–
1995–99	0.26	–	0.8	–	n.a.	–	0.6	–
1970–80	1.1	–	0.22	–	n.a.	–	n.a.	–
1980–90	1.61	–	0.58	–	0.20	–	0.86	–
1990–99	0.6	–	1.6	–	0.1	–	0.65	–

n.a. Not available

Source: SOPEMI, Eurostat, and the Ministry of Interior for Spain

in both Italy and Spain are Moroccans. In contrast, the most recent regularizations in Italy and Greece reveal that the importance of the flow of immigrants from eastern Europe, especially the Balkans, has increased rapidly, as shown in Chapter 5.

What has caused these changes? The first possible explanation is economic growth in the southern European countries, where per-capita income has increased faster than it has in the traditional receiving countries. This growth reduces the incentives for southern European workers to emigrate and makes the southern European countries attractive to non-EU workers. In addition, the restrictive immigration policies adopted by the northern European countries may have, on the one hand, encouraged the decrease in emigration from the southern European countries while, on the other hand, diverting some of the immigrant pressure toward this area.

Before interpreting the causes and consequences of migration, we should try to define the characteristics of emigration and immigration in the

Table 1.3. Foreign residents in southern Europe by area of origin (percentages)

Area of residence	Italy[a]				Greece				Spain[b]				Portugal			
	1981	1987	1993	1998	1981	1987	1993	1998	1981	1987	1993	1998	1981	1987	1993	1998
EU	39.1	38	17	13.7	76.4	57	32.5	–	60	57.1	32	41	26.6	26.8	26.9	27.2
Non-EU	60.8	62	83	96	23.5	43	66.1	–	40	42.9	67	59	73.3	73.2	73.1	72.8
Eastern Europe	–	–	–	22	–	–	–	–	–	–	–	–	–	–	–	–
Africa	7.5	16	31	28	2.7	5.7	10	–	2.7	5.5	18	24.9	44.6	42.5	41	46
Asia	1.3	16	17	18	–	–	19.5	–	4.4	7.9	8.6	8.4	2.2	2.8	4	4
Latin America	2.9	4.2	8.9	8	–	–	2.7	–	21.6	16.5	18.8	18	12.9	15	16	14.4
Other	49.1	25.8	26.1	19	20.8	37.3	10.8	–	21.3	13	21.6	7.7	13.6	12.9	12.1	8.4

[a] For Italy the 1981 and 1987 data refer only to Brazil, Argentina, Venezuela, and Chile.
[b] For Spain the 1981 data refer to 1983.

southern European countries so that we can identify any differences and similarities. We can then infer, from the way it evolves, a possible extension to immigration.

1.1.2 Trends in European Migration

There has been a long tradition of emigration from the southern European countries, mostly movements between continents, that goes back to the times of colonization. Then toward the end of the 1950s in Italy, Spain, and Greece and at the beginning of the 1960s in Portugal, this mainly transcontinental immigration was replaced by migration within Europe. The migratory flows from southern Europe were directed to France from Italy, Spain, and Portugal and to Germany from Greece. France quickly lost favor and by the end of the 1950s, Italian emigrants were going to Switzerland and Germany (see Figures 1.2 and 1.3).

The evolution of European migration is usually divided into three phases, with two more recent phases added to complete the picture. The initial phase extends from 1945 to the early 1960s. It is the period of settling down after the end of the war and the end of the period when the colonies were granted independence.

The second phase, from the end of the 1950s to 1973, is a period when emigrants left their own countries to find jobs. There was a big increase in emigration from the southern European countries toward northern Europe as well as from Turkey, Morocco, and Yugoslavia.

The third phase should have witnessed a decrease in migration due to economic recession and to social problems arising from immigration, problems that discouraged its growth. The flows from southern European countries did decrease, but in the receiving countries such flows were replaced by immigrants from other countries.

The additional two periods involved the European countries in different ways. One period was during the 1980s, when the southern European countries became areas of immigration from the nearby Mediterranean countries and Asia. The final period was after the fall of the Berlin Wall: from the end of the 1980s into the 1990s. This period is characterized by a rapid increase in the number of political refugees and a wave of emigration from the eastern European countries. At first this emigration was directed mainly to the northern European countries and to a lesser degree the southern European countries, but later in the 1990s these countries, too, became much sought-after havens.

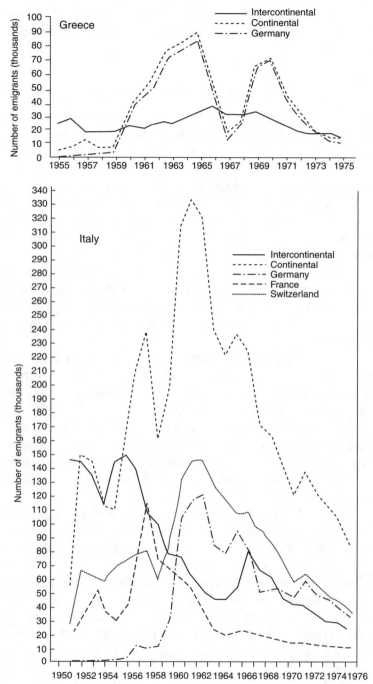

Figure 1.2. Italy and Greece: Destinations of emigrant flows. *Source:* UN, *Labour Supply and Migration in Europe* (1979)

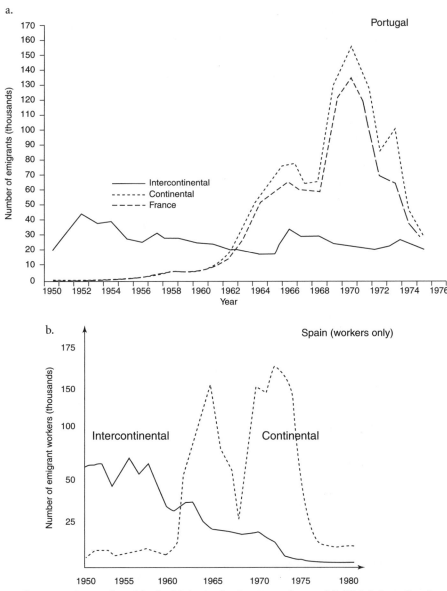

Figure 1.3. Portugal and Spain: Main destination areas. *Source:* (a): UN, *Labour Supply and Migration in Europe* (1979); (b) INE (1995)

Table 1.4. *Emigrants according to main destination 1950–75*

Country of origin	1950–59	1960–69	1970–75
ITALY			
TOTAL (thousands)	2,753.8	2,879.0	789.9
Intercontinental (%)	45	19	22
Continental	55	81	78
France	20	9	6
Germany	2	28	31
Switzerland	23	38	35
GREECE			
TOTAL (thousands)	143.8[a,b]	783.4[b]	270.1[b]
Intercontinental (%)	72	33	34
Continental	28	67	66
Germany	6	58	61
PORTUGAL[c]			
TOTAL (thousands)	350.0	785.6	675.0
Intercontinental (%)	94	32	20
Continental	6	68	80
France	6	60	57
Germany	–	–	15
Switzerland	–	–	5
SPAIN			
TOTAL	550.0	810[d]	473[d]
Intercontinental (%)	80–90	26	9
Continental	20	74	91
France	–	60	25
Germany	–	26	23
Switzerland	–	12	47

[a] Only 1955–59.

[b] A small number of emigrants whose final destination was not known have been excluded.

[c] The data have been revised to include clandestine immigration into France.

[d] Estimates are based on national statistics.

Source: Derived from UN, *Labour Supply and Migration in Europe* 1979, p. 87.

Size and Destination of Emigrant Flows

Emigration across the ocean peaked between 1900 and 1935 (with two short, more intense periods, 1910–13 and 1919–24) and resumed to a lesser degree after the Second World War from 1945 to 1960 (see Table 1.4).[3]

---

[3] To maintain uniformity in valuing the importance of destination I have used data mainly from the country of departure.

Table 1.5. *Emigration flows from southern Europe to the main destination countries, 1960–85*

Year	Total (absolute value)	France %	Germany %	Switzerland %
SPAIN				
1960	49,610	61	18	1
1965	80,916	45	25	10
1970	102,079	25	39	25
1975	22,645	17	1	72
1980	14,252	3	0	92
1985	17,382	4	0	75
ITALY				
1960	383,908	15.3	26.2	33.4
1965	282,643	7.1	32.1	36.5
1970	151,854	5.8	28.2	35.3
1975	92,666	6.5	30.5	32.8
1980	84,877	5.7	35.1	26.2
1984	66,737	6.1	35.7	36.4
PORTUGAL				
1960	35,159	18.3	1.7	0
1965	91,488	65.9	12.9	0
1970	183,205	74.0	12.3	0
1975	52,486	44.6	15.5	1.5
1980	25,173	19.4	13.7	7.5
1985	11,551	10.4	4.8	21.8
GREECE				
1960	47,768	0.1[a]	57.5	0
1965	117,167	1.7	66.8	0
1970	92,681	0.9	94.5	0
1975	20,330	3.9	89.5	3.0
1989	37,337	1.5	79.0	1.1

[a] Belgium replaces France for Greek outflows.

Source: OECD: various SOPEMI reports and, for Italy, national statistics

During the 1960s emigration within Europe gradually grew in importance, even though the size of the outflows was smaller (see Figure 1.1) and the number of people returning increased, producing a net positive flow (see Table 1.1). France and Belgium, which were the favored European destinations for Italian emigrants before the Second World War and at the end of the 1950s, were replaced by Switzerland and Germany (see Table 1.5). Spain had a similar migratory pattern even though it extended over a much longer period. France remained the most important destination for the Portuguese until the end of the 1970s, when France was replaced by Germany and

Switzerland. In contrast, Greek emigrants preferred Germany to all other countries.

The substitution of southern European immigration with emigrants from other countries is very evident in France, where Italians, Spanish, and Portuguese produced three successive waves (see Figure 1.4) but then were replaced by flows from nearby Maghreb. In Germany the contribution of Italian immigrants in the 1960s was integrated with increased immigration from Portugal and Greece in the 1970s. During this period, however, immigrants started to come from Turkey and Yugoslavia. These two countries continued to be the most important sources of immigration until the end of the 1980s, when immigration from the nearby eastern European countries began.

What caused this change in destination and this strong link between the receiving country and the country of departure? The direction of the migratory flows depends mainly on economic factors, and the change in direction of Italian immigration can be interpreted in these terms. It was no longer directed toward France, where wages were not much higher than in Italy, but toward better-paying jobs in Germany and Switzerland. According to data supplied by the Swedish Employers' Confederation, the wage differential in manufacturing between Italy and France was 16% in 1964 and fell to a negative value (−6%) in 1985, and the differential with Germany fell from 38% to 29% during the same period.

Other factors, such as colonial links, alliances, and cultural ties, affect the direction of migratory flows. These factors help to explain the flows between Greece and Germany and to a lesser extent to some other European countries. Note that although available data regarding emigration flows can be gathered in the departure country or in the receiving country, data regarding the stock of immigrants are available only in the country of emigration.[4]

Table 1.6 shows the stock of foreigners according to the southern European country of origin in the receiving countries: France, Germany, the Netherlands, Belgium, and Switzerland.[5] Table 1.6a shows the level of the foreign population. After allowance is made for Portuguese immigration to Switzerland, both the incidence of southern European immigration and its

---

[4] These two sources do not usually match because there is a tendency to underestimate emigration in the country of departure, which cannot register illegal emigration. There is also a certain overestimation in the receiving country, in that often immigrants who return home are not deducted.

[5] The data in Table 1.6 are limited to the early 1990s because information about residents in France is collected only at the time of a census and cannot be updated. However, the fact that only a limited period is considered does not invalidate our case.

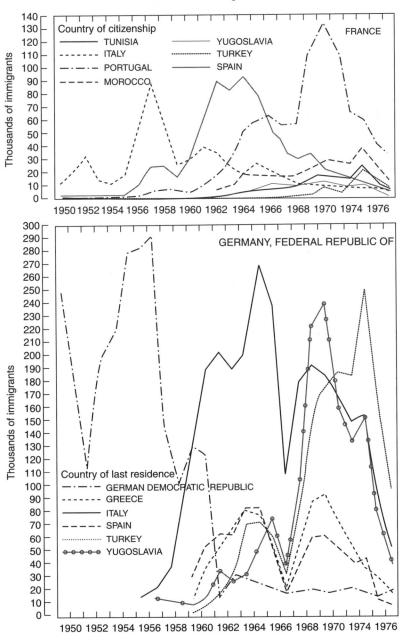

Figure 1.4. France and the Federal Republic of Germany: Origins of immigrant flows.
Source: UN (1979)

Table 1.6. Stock of foreign population and foreign workers resident by country of origin for the main receiving countries

a. Level (thousands)

Country of origin	France 1975	France 1982	France 1990	France 1999	Germany 1983	Germany 1988	Germany 1993	Germany 2000	The Netherlands 1983	The Netherlands 1988	The Netherlands 1993	The Netherlands 2000	Switzerland 1983	Switzerland 1988	Switzerland 1993	Switzerland 2000	Belgium 1983	Belgium 1988	Belgium 1993	Belgium 2000
Italy	462.9	340.3	252.8	201.7	565	508.7	563	619.1	20.9	16	17.5	18.2	404.8	382.3	367.7	321.6	270.5	241.0	216.0	195.6
Spain	497.5	327.2	216	161.8	108.6	96.9	113.4	129.4	21.6	17.4	16.8	17.3	104.2	114.0	105.9	83.8	56.0	52.6	49.9	43.4
Portugal	756.9	767.3	649.7	553.7	99.5	71.1	105.6	133.7	7.8	8	9.6	9.8	19.7	57.6	121.1	140.2	10.4	13.5	21.9	25.6
Greece	–	–	–	–	292.3	274.8	352	365.4	4	4.3	5.8	5.7	9	8.4	7.7	–	21.0	20.6	20.3	18.5
Algeria	710.7	805.1	614.2	477.5	5.2	5.1	23.1	–	–	0.6	0.8	–	–	–	–	–	–	10.1	10.4	7.7
Morocco	260	441.3	572.7	504.7	44.2	52.1	82.8	–	106.4	139.2	164.6	111.4	–	–	–	–	119.1	135.5	145.4	106.8
Tunisia	139.7	190.8	206.3	154.4	25.3	21.6	28.1	–	2.8	2.7	2.4	1.3	–	–	–	–	6.8	6.2	6.0	–
Yugoslavia	70.3	62.5	52.5	–	612.8	579.1	929.6	662.5	12.7	12.1	24.7	–	58.9	100.7	245.0	190.7	5.6	5.4	7.4	9.8
Turkey	50.9	122.3	197.7	208.0	1,552.3	1,523.7	1,918.4	1,998.5	155.3	176.5	202.6	100.8	48.5	56.8	75.6	79.5	70	79.5	88.3	56.2
TOTAL	3,442.4	3,714.2	3,596.6	3,263.2	4,534.9	4,489.1	6,878.1	7,296.8	552.4	623.7	779.8	667.8	925.6	1,006.5	1,260.3	1,384.4	890.9	868.8	920.6	861.7

b. Percentages

Country of origin	France 1975	France 1982	France 1990	France 1999	Germany 1983	Germany 1988	Germany 1993	Germany 2000	The Netherlands 1983	The Netherlands 1988	The Netherlands 1993	The Netherlands 2000	Switzerland 1983	Switzerland 1988	Switzerland 1993	Switzerland 2000	Belgium 1983	Belgium 1988	Belgium 1993	Belgium 2000
Italy	13.45	9.16	7.03	6.2	12.46	11.33	8.19	0.8	3.78	2.57	2.24	2.7	43.73	37.98	29.18	23.2	30.36	27.74	23.46	22.9
Spain	14.45	8.81	6.01	4.9	2.39	2.16	1.65	0.2	3.91	2.79	2.15	2.6	11.26	11.33	8.40	0.6	6.29	6.05	5.37	4.9
Portugal	21.99	20.66	18.06	16.9	2.19	1.58	1.54	0.2	1.41	1.28	1.23	1.5	2.13	5.72	9.61	10	1.17	1.55	2.38	2.7
Greece	0.00	0.00	0.00	–	6.45	6.12	5.12	0.5	0.72	0.69	0.74	0.8	0.97	0.83	0.61	–	2.36	2.37	2.21	1.8
Algeria	20.65	21.68	17.08	14.6	0.11	0.11	0.34	–	0.03	0.03	0.04	–	0.00	0.00	0.00	–	0.00	0.00	1.11	0.7
Morocco	7.55	11.88	15.92	15.5	0.97	1.16	1.20	–	19.26	22.32	21.11	16.7	0.00	0.00	0.00	–	13.37	15.60	15.79	12.4
Tunisia	4.06	5.14	5.74	4.7	0.56	0.48	0.41	–	0.51	0.43	0.31	0.1	0.00	0.00	0.00	–	0.76	0.71	0.65	–
Yugoslavia	2.04	1.68	1.46	–	13.51	12.90	13.52	0.9	2.30	1.94	3.17	–	6.36	10.00	19.44	13.8	0.63	0.62	0.80	1.1
Turkey	1.48	3.29	5.50	6.4	34.23	33.94	27.89	27.7	28.11	28.30	25.98	15.1	5.24	5.64	6.00	5.7	7.86	9.15	9.59	6.5

c. Workers (thousands)

Country of origin	France				Germany				The Netherlands				Switzerland				Belgium			
	1983	1988	1993	2001	1983	1988	1993	2000	1983	1988	1993	1998	1983	1988	1993	2000	1983	1988	1989	1999
Italy	138.5	104.2	98.3	72.2	273.4	211.6	234.8	392	–	–	–	–	230.9	232.3	228	177.4	63.8	58.1	60.6	98.8
Spain	143	114.4	81.9	58.3	79.2	69.4	61.7	64	9	8	8	9	65.8	73.4	67.9	50.1	16.2	14.3	14.5	23.1
Portugal	441	396.1	381.8	371	50.6	40.8	54.9	66	–	–	–	–	13.4	37.8	74.5	77	3.6	3.6	3.9	12.3
Greece	–	–	–	–	122.8	114.3	142	198	–	–	–	–	–	–	–	–	3.9	3.3	3.5	7.1
Algeria	292.2	268.8	237.4	233.6	–	–	–	–	26	23	30	27	–	–	–	–	1.6	1.7	1.9	3.4
Morocco	152	179.9	179.5	186	–	–	–	–	–	–	–	–	–	–	–	–	17	18.1	21.1	43.4
Tunisia	75.7	81.5	71	84.2	–	–	–	–	–	–	–	–	–	–	–	–	1.6	1.6	1.7	–
Yugoslavia	35.5	34.3	24.3	24.3	339.8	327	476.6	–	–	–	–	–	40.2	63.8	121.3	82.8	1.7	1.7	1.9	–
Turkey	31.3	60.8	73.5	81.7	652	638.5	766.6	1,290	36	33	44	24	24.6	29.3	37.2	33.7	10.8	9.5	11.4	26.6
TOTAL	1,574.8	1,557.0	1,541.5	1,617.6	1,983.5	1,910.6	2,575.9	3,546	174	176	219	235	529.8	607.8	725.8	717.3	190.6	179.4	196.4	386.2

d. Percentages of workers

Country of origin	France				Germany				The Netherlands				Switzerland				Belgium			
	1975	1982	1990	2001	1983	1988	1993	2000	1983	1988	1993	1998	1983	1988	1993	2000	1983	1988	1989	1999
Italy	8.79	6.69	6.38	4.5	13.78	11.08	9.12	11.1	–	–	–	–	43.58	38.22	31.41	24.7	33.47	32.39	30.86	25.6
Spain	9.08	7.35	5.31	3.6	3.99	3.63	2.40	1.8	5.17	4.54	3.65	3.8	12.42	12.08	9.36	7.0	8.50	7.97	7.38	6.0
Portugal	28.00	25.44	24.77	22.9	2.55	2.14	2.13	1.8	–	–	–	–	2.53	6.22	10.26	10.7	1.89	2.01	1.99	3.2
Greece	–	–	–	–	6.19	5.98	5.51	5.6	–	–	–	–	–	–	–	–	2.05	1.84	1.78	1.8
Algeria	18.55	17.26	15.40	14.4	–	–	–	–	14.94	13.07	13.69	11.5	–	–	–	–	0.84	0.95	0.97	0.8
Morocco	9.65	11.55	11.64	11.5	–	–	–	–	–	–	–	–	–	–	–	–	8.92	10.09	10.74	11.2
Tunisia	4.81	5.23	4.61	5.2	–	–	–	–	–	–	–	–	–	–	–	–	0.84	0.89	0.87	–
Yugoslavia	2.25	2.20	1.58	1.5	17.13	17.12	18.50	–	–	–	–	–	7.59	10.50	16.71	11.5	0.89	0.95	0.97	–
Turkey	1.99	3.90	4.77	5.0	32.87	33.42	29.76	34.4	20.68	18.75	20.09	10.2	4.64	4.82	5.13	4.7	5.67	5.30	5.80	6.9

Source: SOPEMI, OECD reports

Table 1.7. *Percentage of emigrants in the population and in the national labor force*

Country	1983	1988	1993
ITALY			
PE/POP	2.8	2.6	2.5
PE/PEL	4.2	3.7	3.6
LE/FL	3.0	2.5	2.7
LE/E	3.5	2.9	3.1
SPAIN			
PE/POP	1.6	1.6	1.3
PE/PEL	2.6	2.4	1.9
LE/FL	2.3	1.8	1.6
LE/E	2.8	2.4	1.9
PORTUGAL			
PE/POP	8.9	9.2	9.2
PE/PEL	13.9	14.1	13.7
LE/FL	11.2	10.4	10.8
LE/E	12.3	11.2	11.5
GREECE			
PE/POP	3.3	3.1	3.7
PE/PEL	5.1	4.6	5.5
LE/FL	3.3	3.0	3.5
LE/E	3.6	3.2	3.9

PE/POP Percentage of native population who emigrated in Europe
PE/PEL Percentage of native population of working age who emigrated in Europe
LE/FL Percentage of labor population who emigrated
LE/E Percentage of those employed who emigrated

absolute value were stable or decreased in the 1980s and 1990s. The total number of workers also followed the same trend (Table 1.6c), decreasing both in percentage terms and in absolute terms. Again, Portuguese workers are an exception in that the number going to Switzerland in the 1980s increased.

The share of foreign workers in the foreign population fluctuates more widely for the receiving country than for the country of origin. Although national differences are maintained, the percentages are higher in Germany, the Netherlands, and Switzerland than in France and Belgium, highlighting the fact that the attraction of work is stronger in those countries and that the economy is more able to select its foreign population.

The southern European countries had an outlet for part of their population and workers abroad. As shown in Table 1.7, in 1983–93 the percentage of the Italian, Spanish, and Greek populations abroad in Europe varied between 2 and 4%, with higher percentages for those of working age, 2–5%. Much higher percentages were recorded for Portugal, with 9% of the population and 13% of the working population. During the same period the percentage of the Italian, Spanish, and Greek labor forces working abroad was 3–4%. These levels did not vary very much in the 1980s, but there was a big decrease in the 1970s. For example, in 1974 the percentage of the labor force working abroad was 4.2% for Spain, 4.9% for Italy, 7.6% for Greece, and 16.4% for Portugal (Straubhaar 1988).[6]

Size and Origin of Immigrant Flows

The history of the four countries being considered differs greatly, depending on their colonial ties, their stage of economic development, and the role their immigrants played in the country of origin. The only comparable data available refer to the foreign resident population. The percentage of foreigners in the national population grew rapidly in the 1980s and reached a value of almost 3% in 1999 (see Table 1.2). Considering the pattern of the national population in the 1980s, the increase in the percentage of non-EU foreigners from Africa and Asia after the 1991 regularization measures is particularly evident. In Spain and Portugal the percentage of immigrants from Latin America also increased,[7] while the flows of immigrants from eastern Europe to Italy and Greece increased in the 1990s.

Differences in the types of the immigrant flows into the southern European countries are gradually disappearing. Greece and Spain have always attracted flows of immigrants from the rich countries, people who moved there at retirement; in 1981, 64.3% of the EU foreign residents in Spain did not work. The composition of such flows and the importance of the immigration of skilled workers from European countries have slowly changed in favor of people from developing countries and eastern European countries.

The migratory patterns of Portugal and Spain – and, to a limited degree, of Italy – also reflect these countries' ties with the old colonies, in that there are relatively large flows from Latin America for the former two and from Ethiopia and Eritrea for the latter. Portugal has also attracted nationals from

---

[6] The results reported by Staubhaar for 1985 (p. 58) are more or less halfway between those reported for 1983 and 1988.

[7] In the preceding section, data from the countries of departure have been used. This cannot be done in this case because the data from the countries of origin are not representative. For example, the number of Filipino emigrants who are in Italy is not relevant for the country of origin but is for the receiving country.

various African countries, mostly from the former colonies: Cape Verde, Mozambique, Bissau-Guinea, Burkina Faso, and Angola. Only recently have Moroccans begun to emigrate to Portugal.[8]

A high proportion of the immigrants in Greece come from descendants of old Greek communities in the former USSR (Pontus), Albania, Turkey, and Cyprus. However, only those from Pontus receive preferential treatment (54,000 were accepted in 1989, 25,500 in 1993, and 4,400 in 1999). Members of other Greek communities are not encouraged to return, and only recently have immigrants of Greek origin from Albania and Georgia been given special treatment and status.

Despite these factors, which affect the nationality of the stock of immigrants (see Table 1.8b), in the 1980s there were additional substantial migratory flows of immigrants from neighboring and distant developing countries. Italy saw immigration rise from the nearby Maghreb countries and especially from the Philippines. Because Italy has no tradition of immigration, these groups have quickly become a majority in the stock of immigrants; in 1993 the non-EU immigrants accounted for 83% of foreign residents, and by 1998 it had risen to 86%. In Spain the number of Moroccans has increased rapidly, and after three regularization procedures they make up the largest ethnic group, with 19% (1998) of the resident foreign population. In Greece the number of African and Asian immigrants has increased, and during the 1990s eastern European immigrants were more numerous than immigrants from many other communities, some of them coming from areas of Greek origin (Russia) and others from Albania and Yugoslavia (see Table 1.8a, b, c, d).

Unfortunately, the information about workers is not so complete. In Italy the number of residence permits granted to workers increased steadily. The number of permits issued rose from 384,675 in 1990 to 455,879 in 1991, 514,496 in 1992, 532,618 in 1993, and 614,604 in 1999 (Caritas 2001), and workers account for about 57% of the foreign resident population. The big increase between 1991 and 1992 can be explained by the end of the regularization procedures in 1992.

In Spain, too, the number of work permits increased rapidly with the regularization procedures, which caused an increase from 58,000 in 1988 to 69,100 in 1989, 85,400 in 1990, and 171,000 in 1991. Work permits decreased

---

[8] In the case of Portugal the data shown in Table 1.8 refer to resident permits and are derived from Eurostat. The data from the 1981 census show much higher values than those in the table. Foreign residents number 108,526, of whom 35,426 (32.6%) are from Europe, 47,836 (44.1%) from Africa, 23,098 (21%) from the United States, and 2,163 (2%) from Asia and Oceania, as reported in do Céu Esteves (1991).

Table 1.8. *Foreign residents in the southern European countries*

a. Italy	1981	1987	%	1993	%	1998[b]	%[a]
TOTAL EU	113,069	219,731	38.41	160,322	17.36	171,601	13.7
Germany	26,150	44,641	7.8	39,456	4.27	40,749	3.3
France	17,519	28,297	4.95	25,381	2.75	29,477	2.4
Italy	–	–	–	–	–	–	–
Netherlands	4,479	–	–	7,032	0.76	7,621	0.6
Belgium	3,294	–	–	4,636	0.5	5,187	0.4
Luxembourg	–	–	–	19	0.02	218	17.4
United Kingdom	21,149	32,749	5.72	28,391	3.07	27,016	2.2
Denmark	1,139	–	–	2,416	0.26	2,408	0.2
Ireland	1,370	–	–	2,531	0.27	3,351	0.3
Greece	24,129	31,424	5.49	16,243	1.76	13,350	1.1
Portugal	3,471	2,221	0.39	5,285	0.57	5,602	0.4
Spain	10,369	15,577	2.72	15,559	1.68	20,410	1.6
Austria	–	–	–	8,322	0.9	9,894	0.8
Finland	–	–	–	1,638	0.18	–	–
Sweden	–	–	–	3,242	0.35	4,126	0.3
Yugoslavia	11,942	19,018	3.32	44,531	4.82	48,848	3.9
Albania	–	–	–	28,541	3.09	91,537	7.3
Poland	3,743	14,005	2.45	21,194	2.29	28,199	2.3
Romania	–	–	–	16,394	1.77	37,114	3.0
Turkey	1,890	1,087	0.19	5,096	0.55	5,364	0.4
OTHER EUROPEAN COUNTRIES							
MIDDLE EAST	–	–	–	–	–	29,514	2.4
Jordan	3,537	16,501	2.88	3,861	0.42	–	–
Iran	1,266	16,581	2.9	11,127	1.2	7,901	0.6
Iraq	3,369	5,890	1.03	1,257	0.14	–	–
AFRICA	23,499	9,160	16.01	284,383	30.79	360,051	28.8
Egypt	3,080	11,016	1.93	23,497	2.54	27,664	2.2
Algeria	773	1,341	0.23	845	91.49	12,061	1.0
Morocco	829	15,705	2.75	95,581	10.35	145,843	11.7
Tunisia	1,488	11,950	2.09	50,351	5.45	47,261	3.8
Senegal	192	5,700	1.03	27,539	2.98	35,897	2.9
Somalia	1,300	3,400	0.62	14,916	1.61	8,941	0.7
Ethiopia	4,527	10,528	1.84	12,953	1.4	7,075	0.6
Cape Verde	–	4,924	0.86	5,399	0.58	4,922	0.4
Bissau Guinea	–	–	–	10	1.08	–	–
Monzambique	–	–	–	325	35.19	–	–
Angola	–	–	–	845	91.49	–	–
San Tome	–	–	–	30	3.25	–	–

(continued)

Table 1.8 *(continued)*

a. Italy	1981	1987	%	1993	%	1998[b]	%[a]
ASIA	41,660	90,752	15.86	158,021	17.11	241,232	19.3
Philippines	491	15,050	2.63	44,097	4.77	67,574	5.4
China	–	5,800	1.03	22,481	2.43	38,038	3.0
AMERICAS	–	–	–	148,680	16.1	164,040	4.7
United States	41,409	60,819	10.63	62,066	6.72	55,839	4.5
Canada	3,006	5,615	0.98	4,688	0.51	3,103	0.2
Latin America	–	–	–	81,926	8.87	105,098	8.4
Brazil	2,781	7,581	1.33	18,719	2.03	197,661	1.6
Argentina	3,843	7,018	1.23	14,854	1.61	–	–
Venezuela	572	6,574	1.15	5,282	0.57	–	–
Chile	1,721	–	–	4,638	0.5	–	–
Peru	–	–	–	–	–	26,832	2.1
TOTAL NON-EU	191,296	352,372	61.59	763,303	82.64	1,078,613	86.3
TOTAL	304,365	572,103	100	923,625	100	1,250,214	100

[a] In 1999, eastern European immigrants reached 21.4% of total foreigners.

b. Greece	1981	1987	%	1993	%
TOTAL EU	198,446	110,941	57.37	65,084	32.49
Germany	5,114	8,970	4.64	14,079	7.03
France	3,191	5,175	2.68	7,993	3.99
Italy	3,834	5,692	2.94	7,378	3.68
Netherlands	1,092	2,225	1.15	3,693	1.84
Belgium	51	1,018	0.53	1,667	0.83
Luxembourg	12	30	–	47	0.02
United Kingdom	7,915	13,280	6.87	20,705	10.34
Denmark	365	888	0.45	1,636	0.82
Ireland	188	426	0.22	709	0.35
Greece[a]	175,664	72,298	37.39	–	–
Portugal	153	245	0.13	411	0.21
Spain	399	694	0.36	1,034	0.52
Austria	–	–	–	1,858	0.93
Finland	–	–	–	1,155	0.58
Sweden	–	–	–	2,296	1.15
Yugoslavia	686	1,298	0.67	2,563	1.28
Albania	–	–	–	3,529	1.76
Poland	–	–	–	10,688	5.34
Romania	–	–	–	3,934	1.96
Turkey	–	3,036	1.57	3,586	1.79

b. Greece	1981	1987	%	1993	%
OTHER EUROPEAN COUNTRIES	–	–	8,410	18,146	9.38
MIDDLE EAST					
Jordan	–	–	–	2,173	1.08
Iran	–	–	–	3,543	1.77
Iraq	–	–	–	3,938	1.97
AFRICA	7,288	11,014	5.70	19,605	9.79
Egypt	–	–	–	9,671	4.83
Algeria	–	117	0.07	235	0.11
Morocco	–	219	0.11	360	0.18
Tunisia	–	262	0.15	388	0.19
Senegal	–	–	–	29	0.01
Somalia	–	–	–	84	0.04
Ethiopia	–	–	–	2,622	1.31
Cape Verde	–	–	–	32	0.01
Bissau Guinea	–	–	–	15	0.00
Mozambique	–	–	–	10	0.00
Angola	–	–	–	6	0.00
San Tome	–	–	–	–	–
ASIA	–	–	–	39,119	19.53
Philippines	–	–	–	9,423	4.70
China	–	–	–	441	0.22
AMERICAS	–	–	–	29,245	14.60
United States	13,229	18,989	9.82	22,001	10.98
Canada	1,070	1,314	0.68	1,884	0.94
Latin America	–	–	–	5,361	2.68
Brazil	–	–	–	646	0.32
Argentina	–	–	–	420	0.21
Venezuela	–	–	–	161	0.08
Chile	–	–	–	439	0.22
TOTAL NON-EU	61,414	82,444	42.63	135,253	67.51
TOTAL	259.86	193,385	100	200,337	100

[a] Foreigners of Greek origin who return for a period of time.
[b] Later Greece does not publish data on total stock of foreign population.

c. Spain	1981	1987	%	1993	%	1997	%	1998	%
TOTAL EU	120,438	194,628	57.1	128,364	32.65	254,134	41.67	295,301	41.0
Germany	23,609	39,596	11.62	30,493	7.76	49,890	8.18	55,901	7.8
France	15,349	23,677	6.95	22,644	5.76	34,308	5.63	38,301	5.3
Italy	9,718	13,070	3.83	13,581	3.45	22,638	3.71	25,801	3.6

(continued)

Table 1.8 *(continued)*

c. Spain	1981	1987	%	1993	%	1997	%	1998	%
Netherlands	8,350	13,821	4.05	10,499	2.67	14,467	2.37	13,808	1.9
Belgium	6,127	9,730	2.85	7,221	1.84	10,457	1.71	9,008	1.3
Luxembourg	–	–	–	111	0.03	191	0.00	–	–
United Kingdom	28,530	55,981	16.42	53,441	13.59	68,271	11.20	72,505	10.1
Denmark	3,491	5,451	1.6	3,984	1.01	5,134	0.84	–	–
Ireland	650	1,684	0.49	2,055	0.52	2,868	0.47	–	–
Greece	451	606	0.18	474	0.12	652	0.01	–	–
Portugal	24,150	31,012	9.1	28,631	7.28	38,229	6.27	40,701	5.7
Spain	–	–	–	–	–	–	–	–	–
Austria	1,492	2,136	0.65	1,469	0.37	2,847	0.47	–	–
Finland	1,128	3,077	0.97	1,944	0.49	3,568	0.59	–	–
Sweden	3,844	6,540	1.92	5,258	1.34	7,029	1.15	–	–
Yugoslavia	107	269	0.08	565	0.01	2,622	0.43	–	–
Albania	–	–	–	34	0	–	–	–	–
Poland	231	495	0.14	3,167	0.81	5,496	1.49	–	–
Romania	64	138	0.04	664	0.02	2,385	0.39	–	–
Turkey	168	240	0.07	297	0	370	0.01	–	–
OTHER EUROPEAN COUNTRIES	12,790	22,535	6.61	–	–	–	–	–	–
MIDDLE EAST									
Jordan	–	727	0.21	657	0.02	597	0.01	–	–
Iran	–	2,623	0.77	1,844	0.47	–	–	–	–
Iraq	–	–	–	365	0.01	–	–	–	–
AFRICA	5,400	18,945	5.56	71,298	18.14	142,816	23.42	179,501	24.9
Egypt	221	342	0.1	680	0.02	778	0.01	919	0.1
Algeria	–	–	–	2,864	0.73	–	–	7,043	1.0
Morocco	3,595	11,312	3.32	54,105	13.76	111,101	18.22	140,896	19.6
Tunisia	–	–	–	387	0.01	–	–	536	0.1
Senegal	–	–	–	3,191	0.81	–	–	–	–
Somalia	–	–	–	5	0	–	–	–	–
Ethiopia	–	–	–	20	0	–	–	–	–
Cape Verde	–	–	–	1,939	0.49	–	–	–	–
Bissau Guinea	–	–	–	321	0.01	–	–	–	–
Mozambique	–	–	–	47	0	–	–	–	–
Angola	–	–	–	369	0.01	–	–	–	–
San Tome	–	–	–	35	0	–	–	–	–
ASIA	13,555	27,125	7.96	33,596	8.55	49,111	8.05	60,701	8.4
Philippines	4,046	8,311	2.44	8,004	2.04	11,357	1.86	13,202	1.8
China	758	3	0.96	6,783	1.73	15,754	2.58	19,801	2.8
AMERICAS	–	–	–	96,844	22.72	126,961	20.82	–	–
United States	10,680	16,010	4.7	14,199	3.61	13,345	2.19	15,099	2.1
Canada	1,020	1,490	0.44	1,077	0.27	1,232	0.20	–	–

c. Spain	1981	1987	%	1993	%	1997	%	1998	%
Latin America	43,390	56,250	16.5	77,782	18.83	–	–	–	–
Brazil	620	1,378	0.43	3,758	0.96	6,283	1.03	–	–
Argentina	7,634	13,845	4.05	21,571	5.49	17,188	2.82	16,501	2.3
Venezuela	6,910	7,857	2.35	7,086	1.8	6,188	1.01	–	–
Chile	3,852	6,094	1.84	5,933	1.51	5,594	0.92	–	–
Peru	–	–	–	–	–	21,233	3.48	23,901	3.3
TOTAL NON-EU	80,473	146,254	42.9	264,737	67.35	355,679	58.33	424,301	59.07
TOTAL	200,911	340,882	100	393,101	100	609,813	100	719,601	100

d. Portugal	1981	1988	%	1993	%	1998	%
TOTAL EU	18,114	25,296	26.78	33,601	27.65	48,201	27.1
Germany	2,552	4,133	4.38	5,404	4.45	8,801	4.9
France	2,069	2,803	2.97	3,674	3.02	5,801	3.3
Italy	975	1,060	1.12	1,353	1.11	2,401	1.4
Netherlands	893	1,546	1.64	2,011	1.65	3,301	1.9
Belgium	499	910	0.96	1,118	0.92	–	–
Luxembourg	–	26	–	36	0.3	–	–
United Kingdom	3,692	7,115	7.53	9,284	7.64	12,701	7.1
Denmark	211	348	0.36	499	0.41	–	–
Ireland	105	199	0.21	244	0.2	–	–
Greece	–	51	0.05	65	0.05	–	–
Portugal	–	–	–	–	–	–	–
Spain	7,110	7,105	7.52	7,734	6.36	10,201	5.7
Austria	–	229	0.24	302	0.25	–	–
Finland	–	138	0.13	245	0.2	–	–
Sweden	–	536	0.57	722	0.59	–	–
Yugoslavia	–	52	0.05	80	0.06	–	–
Albania	–	–	–	3	0	–	–
Poland	–	73	0.07	155	0.13	–	–
Romania	–	16	0.01	52	0.04	–	–
Turkey	–	22	0.02	43	0.03	–	–
OTHER EUROPEAN COUNTRIES	1,810	3,530	3.74	–	–	–	–
MIDDLE EAST							
Jordan	–	13	0.01	50	0.04	–	–
Iran	–	460	0.48	515	0.42	–	–
Iraq	–	97	0.1	152	0.12	–	–
AFRICA	28,900	40,112	42.47	52,037	42.82	82,717	46.5
Egypt	–	16	0.01	39	0.03	52	0.0
Algeria	–	24	0.02	40	0.03	80	0.0
Morocco	–	47	0.05	100	0.08	297	0.2
Tunisia	–	13	0.01	20	0.01	26	0.0

(continued)

Table 1.8 (continued)

d. Portugal	1981	1988	%	1993	%	1998	%
Senegal	–	26	0.02	64	0.05	–	–
Somalia	–	–	–	–	–	–	–
Ethiopia	–	3	0	4	0	–	–
Cape Verde	–	26,953	28.54	31,127	25.62	40,101	22.6
Bissau Guinea	–	3,021	3.2	5,808	4.78	12,901	7.3
Mozambique	–	2,762	2.92	3,574	2.94	4,401	2.5
Angola	–	4,434	4.69	6,601	5.43	16,501	9.3
San Tome	–	1,730	1.83	2,519	2.07	4,401	2.5
ASIA	–	2,645	2.8	4,767	3.92	7,193	4.0
Philippines	–	54	0.04	104	0.08	–	–
China	–	1,002	1.06	1,489	1.23	2,501	1.4
AMERICAS	–	–	–	29,391	24.19	35,847	5.9
United States	4,983	6,184	6.55	7,321	6.02	8,101	4.6
Canada	1,726	2,266	2.4	2,109	1.74	–	–
Latin America	–	14,168	15	19,961	16.43	25,274	14.2
Brazil	–	9,333	9.88	14,048	11.56	19,901	11.2
Argentina	–	246	0.26	331	0.27	–	–
Venezuela	–	4,828	5.11	4,911	4.04	3,501	2.0
Chile	–	67	0.07	103	0.08	–	–
TOTAL NON-EU	50,039	69,156	73.22	87,912	72.35	129,600	72.9
TOTAL	68,150	94,452	100	121,513	100	177,801	100

Source: Eurostat Demographic Statistics for Spain and Portugal (1981, 1987); Ministry of Interior for Italy 1981 and 1987; Eurostat Migration Statistics for Greece, Spain, Portugal, and Italy 1993; National Sources for 1998.

to 139,400 in 1992 and 115,400 in 1993 because they were renewed during the economic recession. However, later the economic growth increased the number of work permits issued in 1999 to 175,600. Workers represented only 25% of the foreign population because, as has been said, in Spain a high percentage of the immigrants go there to retire. The percentage increases to 52.3% in the case of non-EU citizens and to 70% for specific communities, such as the Philippines and Morocco.

In Greece work permits numbered about 28,000 between 1980 and 1992. At the end of 1993 they increased to about 30,000, but in the first quarter of 1994 only 25,000 new permits were issued, suggesting rapid growth in the stock of workers. Therefore, the percentage of workers holding permits appears to be very small, only 15%; but again an explanation is found in the high incidence of retirement migration and a high level of clandestine activities. In the last year after the conclusion of the first legalization, 147,800 green card holders were added to the labor market.

In Portugal foreigners holding work permits numbered about 43,000 in 1988 and represented about 46% of the foreign population. In 1999 they reached 91,600 and remained at the same share.

Legal foreign workers represent a very limited share of the labor force in the receiving country. In Greece, they represent about 0.9% of those employed and 0.78% of the entire labor force, increasing rapidly with regularization to about 2%. In Spain the percentage increases to 1.4% of those employed and 1.1% of the labor force, and in Portugal the percentages are 2% and 1.8%, respectively. The highest figures are those for Italy, where legal foreign workers represent 2.8% of those employed and 2.7% of the labor force. These percentages are very small when compared with the percentages in the northern European countries. The foreign labor force makes up about 7–9% of the entire labor force in France, Germany, and Belgium, with a peak of 17% in Switzerland.

Similarities and Differences between Emigration and Immigration in the Southern European Countries

The most evident similarity between past outflows and present inflows lies in the kind of activities and jobs that immigrants do. Just as Italians, Spanish, Portuguese, and, in part, Greek immigrants were mainly unskilled workers who did unskilled jobs, so today most of the immigrants into these countries do low-skilled jobs. One difference, however, between current immigration and the immigration that took place in the 1960s and 1970s is that then the emigrants left to find work mainly in the industrial sector, whereas today's immigrants are employed mainly in services, agriculture, and building, and only a small number are employed in industrial activities.

Experience in France and Germany illustrates the former point. Table 1.9 shows that most workers in Germany and France were manual and unskilled workers. The 1970s has been chosen because later the share of foreign workers from southern Europe decreased substantially, and generalizations are no longer significant. Immigrants from the southern European countries in France accounted for 51% of total immigration in 1974, whereas in 1987 the percentage decreased to 41%. In Germany in the same period the percentage decreased from 36.3% to 23.4%. There was a similar trend

Table 1.9a. *Distribution of workers in Germany by skills (1977)*

Skill level	Total (%)	Germans (%)	Foreigners (%)
Unskilled	36.1	33.3	52.0
Semiskilled	25.8	27.3	33.5
Skilled	35.1	39.4	14.5
TOTAL	100	100	100

Table 1.9b. *Distribution of workers in France by socioprofessional status (1975)*

Status	Foreigners (%)	French (%)
Agricultural workers	4.4	1.72
White-collar workers	5.4	17.64
Skilled manual workers	22.9	16.24
Manual workers	49.0	20.94
Family workers	6.9	5.71
Other	11.4	32.75
TOTAL	100.0	100.0

Table 1. 9c. *Inflows of workers in France and Germany by nationality and skill (1973)*

Nationality	France		Germany	
	Total Inflows (thousands)	% skilled	Total Inflows (thousands)	% skilled
Spanish	12.9	35	27.3	10
Greeks	0.3	67	4.98	15.5
Italians	5.4	44	3.3	19
Portuguese	64.3	20	28.3	33
Turks	5.7	33	101.3	30
Yugoslavians	7.2	26	67.2	36
Moroccans	20.7	16	–	–
Tunisians	10.0	37	2.7[a]	33

[a] 1971

Source: Grammenos 1982

in all the other European countries; in Switzerland the decrease was from 66.5% to 57%, in Belgium from 48% to 33%, and in the Netherlands from 27.7% to 12%. Table 1.9c shows that apart from the Greeks in France, the percentage of skilled workers in the labor force according to nationality varied between 10% and 44% in the two cases examined. There is the same

Table 1.10. *Skill level of jobs held by foreigners in Spain (1992)*

Country of origin	High (%)	Middle (%)	Low (%)
Total foreigners	18.6	18.5	61.7
Asia	5.0	20.5	71.5
Africa	2.7	12.7	84.0
Latin America	26.4	17.8	54.8
European Union	32.5	25.7	40.4

Derived from Collectivo IOE (1995), p. 3.

trend for regular workers who are employed in Italy, Spain, Greece, and Portugal.

In Italy, aggregate data on the employment of foreigners can be used because 72% of the foreigners who immigrated in the 1980s came from developing countries. The data of those registered with the employment office as unemployed and those who entered employment show that in the north 81% are unskilled workers and in the south, 92%. In northern Italy the percentage of white-collar workers reaches 5%. In Spain the data show a similar pattern, with most new immigrants doing unskilled work (see Table 1.10). At least 70% of the Africans and Asians do unskilled work. The same trend was revealed for Greece in the research done by Lianos et al. (1996). It is the same for Portugal, where recent immigration has been made up of unskilled workers; work permits for unskilled workers account for 51% of the total, and in 1988 this percentage had reached 82.3% for Africans (do Céu Esteves 1991). In 1995, 52.6% of foreign workers did low-skilled work and 49% were factory workers, a percentage that rose to 79% for Africans (Baganha 1998).

When we consider the sector classification of immigrants employed in Germany and France in the 1970s, we see that most immigrants (73–76% in Germany and 63–65% in France) were employed in the industrial sector, especially in manufacturing and building (see Table 1.11). The services, commerce, and transport sectors employ no more than 25% of the immigrant workers, with their share of the specific workforce never exceeding 8%.

The picture changes for today's immigration into the southern European countries. Employment in the services sector has become more important than in industry or agriculture. In Italy 44% of foreign workers are employed in services (with 15% doing domestic work and 16% in catering), 36% in industry, and 20% in agriculture (Caritas 2000). In Spain 56% are employed in services, 6.5% in industry, 8.7% in building, and 18% in agriculture

Table 1.11. Occupation of foreigners by sector of activity

Germany

Sector	1972	1976	% Foreigners within sector	1981	1987
Agriculture	0.9	0.1	9.6	0.8	0.9
Mining	3.3	–	–	–	0.2
Industry	76.7	73.8	–	–	–
Manufacturing	42.8	62.6	13.6	58	53
Construction	17.8	11.2	12.6	11	9
Other	16.1	–	–	17.1	16.3
Trade	5.9	6.1	4.0	12.2	7.1
Transport and Telecom.	–	2.9	7.4	3.8	3.9
Banking	13.3	0.2	.07	2.5	0.8
Services	–	14.5	5.3	11.3	17
TOTAL	100	100	–	100	100

France

Sector	1972	1976	% Foreigners within sector	1981	1987
Agriculture	8.7	5.7	4.1	4	2.3
Industry	63.1	65.1	–	63.3	53.8
Intermediate goods	–	14.2	12.4	–	–
Capital goods	–	12.6	9.1	–	–
Consumer goods	–	8.6	8.1	–	–
Other	2.7	3.3	5.6	12	14.1
Construction	30.1	26.8	21.2	23	20.2
Trade	8.6	6.6	3.8	14	15.3
Transport	–	2.3	2.9	27	3.0
Services	17.0	19.7	4.0	21.0	25.3
Banks	–	–	–	4.7	6.3
Other	–	–	–	17.3	19
TOTAL	100	100	–	100	100

Source: For the 1970s, SOPEMI from reports OECD; for 1981, 1985, 1987, Eurostat

(Ministero de Asuntos Sociales 1999). In the case of Asians, 93% are employed in the services industry (Ministero de Asuntos Sociales 1999).

In Greece, 7% of legal foreign employment is in agriculture, 6% in building, 70% in services, and 12% in industry.[9] Data regarding work permits issued in Portugal in 1999 showed that most job opportunities were in tradable (21%) and nontradable services (29.97%), with industry providing jobs for only 16%; agriculture, 21.22%; and the building sector, 1.1% (SOPEMI 2000). Again considering one ethnic group, the Africans, we see that the building sector increases in importance, providing jobs for about 14% of those employed (Baganha 1998).[10]

Another difference between the emigration flows and the immigration flows in the southern European countries is the size of the firms in which foreigners get work. The difference in the first place is based on different productive structures and the historical period. The size of firms in the sectors of domestic service, commerce, and catering is typically small. But firms that employ foreign workers in the industrial sector in the southern European countries are also small or medium-sized. For example, in Italy in 1996, 70% of foreign workers were employed in small firms, those that hire fewer than 50 employees. Local surveys[11] reveal that large firms do not employ foreign labor for three reasons: (1) economic recessions affect large firms more than small ones, (2) reorganization of production has reduced the demand for unskilled labor, and (3) where there is a strong trade union the cost of negotiation is higher.

In agriculture, the survey carried out by Lianos et al. (1996) in northern Greece found that most regular employees were employed by larger firms and medium-sized firms tended to employ more irregular workers. However, as is well known, large firms in agriculture are relatively small.

Three other aspects should be considered: the foreigner's age, gender, and level of education. When these aspects are considered the general impression is that the flows of emigration and immigration are substantially similar.

Emigration from the southern European countries was primarily male. In fact, the data show that no more than 80 women per 100 men migrated within continental Europe (see Table 1.12).

---

[9] See NSSG (1995), p. 9.

[10] The picture of foreign employment in Portugal, supplied by do Céu Esteves (1991), highlights higher participation in the building industry (30%) and less in agriculture (3.22%). These data confirm Baganha's findings, which showed that immigrants had entered agriculture only to a limited extent and that Portuguese nationals continued to work in this sector.

[11] For example, research in the provinces of Bergamo and Brescia (Beretta 1995) shows that 91% of the foreign workers are employed by small local firms with between one and nine employees.

Table 1.12. *Number of female emigrants per 100 men 1960–74*

Country of origin	Nature of destination	1960–64	1965–69	1970–74
Greece		59	82	79
Italy	Total	–	41	49
	Intercontinental	–	86	82
	Continental	–	39	42
Portugal		61	76	66
Spain	Continental	–	29	15

Derived from UN, *Labour Supply and Migration in Europe* 1979, p. 104.

Table 1.13. *Age distribution of migratory flows*

	All ages (%)	< 15 (%)	15–24 (%)	25–34 (%)
GREECE				
1960–64	100	6	34	43
1965–69	100	12	31	34
1970–74	100	16	30	28
ITALY				
TOTAL				
1965–69	100	11	29	29
1970–74	100	13	22	27
INTERCONTINENTAL				
1965–69	100	23	29	20
1970–74	100	19	23	21
CONTINENTAL				
1965–69	100	7	29	32
1970–74	100	12	21	29
PORTUGAL				
1960–64	100	23	27	25
1965–69	100	28	18	29
1970–74	100	27	20	31
SPAIN				
1965–69	100	1	31	39
1970–74	100	–	32	35

Derived from UN, *Labour Supply and Migration* 1979, p. 104.

The 25–34 age cohort, which covers 29 to 43% of the emigrants from Spain, Italy, Portugal, and Greece, was the most important age cohort for European continental emigration (see Table 1.13). The percentage of females in the 15–24 cohort is much higher because, as is well known, women emigrate at an earlier age than men. For example, for Portugal and Greece in 1970–74 there were, respectively, 113 and 107 women for every 100 men in the 15–24 cohort. However, the ratio varies according to destination. For example, in 1970 it was higher in Belgium, Sweden, and Switzerland (about 70 women for every 100 men) than in France, Germany, and the Netherlands (29–46 women for every 100 men) because family reunification was more frequent in the former group of countries.

Little information is available about the level of education. The low level of education of the emigrants in the 1960s can be explained in part by the limited school attendance at that time and by the fact that most emigrants were semiskilled workers. Historical surveys provide fragmentary information, that nevertheless leads to a homogeneous picture of low educational levels. The pattern of intercontinental migration is different; more-educated emigrants went to South America, and people with less schooling went to North America.

The pattern of immigration is similar in all the southern European countries. *Male immigration predominates*, with a lower percentage of females for some nationalities than others – for example, North Africans. In Italy, for example, the average distribution of regular immigration is 117 men for every 100 women, a number that increases to 196 men for every 100 women for irregular immigrants. The ratios are very different for North Africans legally resident in Italy; there are 404 men for every 100 women, and the ratio rises to 1,074 men for every 100 women for irregular workers. In contrast there is a prevalence of women in the Asian community.[12] More recently, the flows of immigrants from eastern Europe, where males predominate among the Albanian immigrants and women among Polish and Rumanian immigrants, have not changed the basic trend, and the percentage of males is still higher – 55% in 1999.

Male immigrants predominate in Greece, where they account for 65% (130 for every 100 women) of regular workers. The percentage varies between 60% and 68% for irregular workers. The ratio of men to women for permanent workers is lower than for temporary workers, where in northern Greece, for example, it reaches an average of 89%, with a maximum of 97% (Lianos et al. 1996). The regularization process causes the male component to increase because 70% of all the applicants are men, the most important group being Albanian immigrants, who are mainly men.

---

[12] In census terminology *resident* (*rooted*) is used to refer to foreigners who are legally resident in the country even when they are not registered at the Registrar's office, and *nonresident* (*nonrooted*) refers to those immigrants whose residence permit has expired or who entered the country clandestinely.

Male immigration prevails in Spain, too (52% in 1997). The percentage is decreasing (in 1993, 60% of the foreign population were males), but there are many variations between nationalities. Women predominate among the Latin Americans (63% in 1997, 58% in 1993), especially from the Dominican Republic and Colombia, as they do among Asians. European immigrants are more or less equally divided between the sexes, whereas men are more numerous among African immigrants – 68% in 1998, the percentage having fallen from 73.8% in 1993 (SOPEMI 1999). Looking at employed foreigners, the share of men is higher at 60% in 1998, but again it has decreased from 72% in 1993 (SOPEMI 2000). In Portugal males also prevail, with 58% in 1998 (SOPEMI 2000), with only slight differences between the various nationalities.

When *average age is considered, trends are similar,* with the flow of immigrants being made up mainly of young people. In Italy the 1991 census data show that 50.4% of the regular residents are concentrated in the 15–34 age band, with the highest percentage being registered for North Africans (62.4%); when non-regular residents are considered, the average percentage in the 15–34 age band is even higher (63%) and rises to 76% for Africans. In 1998, 65.2% of foreigners are in the 19–40 age group. This figure has decreased from 71.1% in 1993, in favor of the 40–60 cohort, thus confirming that migration has more or less stabilized and that the immigrant population is getting older (Caritas 2000).

In Spain the most important age cohort for the average foreigner is 30–34, and it is the same for Europeans, Asians, and Americans, whereas the most important age cohort for Africans is the 25–29 band. There are two important cohorts for Moroccans – one from 20 to 24 and the other from 25 to 29 – and they account for 12% and 13% of total immigrants, respectively (Census for 1991, INE 1993).

The average age of immigrants in Greece varies widely according to ethnic group. Immigrants from the Philippines, Egypt, Albania, and from other countries that do not have Greek communities are mainly young people in the 20–29 cohort, whereas the average age is higher for immigrants of Greek origin. Regularization data for 1998 confirm that the 20–29 cohort is the most important, accounting for 44% of the regularization applications, followed by the 30–44 cohort with 38%. However, only when the initial (white card) permits have been changed for permanent (green card) permits will it be possible to measure the impact of age on the number of legally resident foreigners.

It is the same in Portugal, where the flow of immigrants is made up of young people 15–34 years old (SOPEMI 1995, p. 115). In 1988, the 14–25 and 26–45 cohorts accounted for 74% of all immigration and for 87% of immigrants of African origin (do Céu Esteves 1991).

It is very difficult to assess the level of education of foreigners. If the data are based on personal statements there is the problem of overestimation, but if the information is derived from data at the labor office there is the problem of failing to recognize qualifications. There is also the tendency of immigrants to understate their qualifications to improve their chances of getting a manual job.

Census data in Italy reveal that illiteracy is limited (6.5%), with a high percentage of the population having received elementary schooling, or eight years (68.8%). Higher levels of education are found among the Americans and Europeans. The data show that 60% of the irregular residents have completed eight years of study and so have some kind of basic education. Data regarding education levels gathered when foreigners register for a job is contradictory in that 80% declare they have no school qualifications at all, and 14% have only a high school certificate. This can only indicate a lack of formal education and difficulties in getting levels of basic education recognized.

In the case of Spain the data supplied by the General Executive of INE show that in 1993 2% of the immigrants did not have any qualifications, 49% had attended elementary school, 18% had attended high school, and 25% had attended a university. The survey also shows that, in general, immigrants from the developing countries had received elementary schooling, whereas Europeans had attended a university.

The data available for Greece should be interpreted circumspectly. In 1991, 30% of the regular workers had received elementary education, 28% had attended high school, 30% were high school graduates, and 12% had attained a higher level. Because the data have not been separated into ethnic groups, it should be noted that a relatively high percentage of immigrants into Greece (42%) are skilled Europeans and Americans. This trend seems to be confirmed by the data regarding the regularization measures taken in 1998, where immigrants generally seem to have received an elementary or high school education, and only 2% of those who benefited from the measure were illiterate, 37% had attended elementary school, 49% had gone to high school, and 9% had received a higher education than what the Greeks had had (SOPEMI 2000). But, as stated earlier, such results should be treated with extreme care because educational degrees differ greatly between countries.

In Portugal the 1991 census data show that 47% of the foreigners do not have any school qualifications. The percentage for Africans rises to 52% having no qualifications whatsoever and 41% having elementary education.

The picture changes for the European immigrants, among whom a higher education level is common.

Information gathered from the European Labour Force Survey frequently provides a different scenario, namely that immigrants are more educated than natives. This dataset, as we have already said, is not yet able to cover the new immigration flows. For new immigration countries, it provides a distorted picture because it overemphasizes the characteristics of old inflows. These immigrants are already settled and are frequently of different quality and from different areas of origin than the more recent ones.

Another characteristic of the waves of immigration into the southern European countries today is the high level of illegal entry and non-regular employment. This high level is due to two parallel phenomena. First, a relatively large proportion of income and employment in the countries involved is non-regular, estimated at 10% of national income and about 25% of the working population. Second, the laws that have been passed to accommodate the evolution of the phenomenon have encouraged ex-post and spontaneous (irregular) growth of immigration.

For this reason Spain, Portugal, and Italy introduced repeated measures to regularize the presence of immigrants more or less at the same time, something that allowed 20–25% of the non-regular foreign workers to be regularized. The Greek government, too, passed its first regularization law in 1998.

The figures for the many measures cannot be added together to calculate the stock of immigrants because the characteristics of the measures were different, and frequently there were repeated regularizations by the same persons. In Italy, for example, street traders were not mentioned in the first measure. They benefited from the law by declaring themselves as unemployed, but in the second measure they were regularized as street traders.

The number of regularized immigrants compared to the number of regular workers may seem high, but it appears to be lower than what was expected, because at the time irregular foreign residents were estimated to be two to three times the number of legal immigrants. ISTAT (1999) estimates that the contribution of irregular foreign workers is equal to 3.8% of the total of regular labor, whereas the foreign labor force in the country is estimated at 5.8%.

In 1992 the Greek Ministry of Public Security estimated that the total number of foreigners in the country was about 500,000, of whom 220,000 had a regular resident permit and 280,000 were in the country illegally. This represented about 2.8% of the national population (Lianos, Sarris, and Katseli 1996). In 1992 the Greek Workers' Federation also tried to estimate the number of irregular residents according to nationality and found that Albanians were the most numerous group of irregular residents.

Egyptians	55,000	of whom	35,000 were illegal
Poles	50,000	of whom	5,000 were illegal
Filipinos	16,000	of whom	few were illegal
Albanians	160,000	of whom	140,000 were illegal
Total	271,000	of whom	181,000 were illegal

The results of the 1998 regularization measure (as shown in Chapter 5) show that these estimates were not far off and that the Albanian community was easily the largest non-regular group.

In Spain, the estimated number of irregular workers in 1991 was about 300,000, of whom only a small number took advantage of the regularization measures. The regularization measures were introduced to reduce the presence of irregular foreigners in Spain, and when the period was over the IOSS (Inspectorate for Employment and Social Security) launched a campaign against illegal employment of both natives and foreigners. The number of inspections and checks was increased, and this action reduced the number of cases of illegal employment being taken to the courts. Unfortunately, the results were not what had been hoped, and the Spanish government, like the Italian government, turned to further amnesties.

1.2 APPROACHES TO THE ANALYSIS OF MIGRATORY PHENOMENA

Migration is a social phenomenon and its study involves many branches of the social sciences. This introductory section offers a broad review of the research in this field and then concentrates on the economic approach.

1.2.1 The Demographic Approach

The discipline of demography has a long-standing role in analyzing migration. Traditional demographics once covered labor economic issues, and demographic data have always included migrants.

Immigrants, in fact, are a part of the population and from a demographic point of view are compared and can be compared to births. The situation is changing, but until few years ago, Eurostat included information on immigrants under the heading "demographic statistics" and only recently introduced a series of migration statistics.[13] This was because the net rate of immigration (net of those returning home and emigrants), together with the birth rate and death rate, is the indicator of the flows that cause the stock of population to grow or contract.

By analyzing the evolution of the population cohorts, net of deaths, it is possible to calculate departures and entries from the national population and thereby measure the regional, national, and international mobility of the population. A "strong" demographic interpretation of the migratory phenomenon, which is criticized by demographers themselves (for example, Livi-Bacci et al. 1990 and Gesano 1995), explains migration as a "siphon" phenomenon in which a relative excess of population in one area causes the movement of a part of the population to another area. Such an interpretation is implicitly based on the hypothesis of a uniform distribution of resources that creates incentives for the redistribution of the population at a territorial level. If the cause of migration in this model is exclusively demographic, then the effect is exclusively demographic, too – that is, a reequilibrium of the population.

A "weak" demographic interpretation, in contrast, emphasizes the importance of the demographic factor in the interpretation of migration and emphasizes the importance of fertility rates to explain the rise and subsequent fall of emigration from Italy in the 1960s (Hatton and Williamson 1994; Tapinos 1994). This approach attempts to relate fertility to cultural, social, and economic factors, which determine the evolution of the decision to migrate.

1.2.2 Sociological and Psychological Approaches

Sociological studies have gone deeper into the dynamics of the migratory phenomenon. However, it is difficult to apply the findings at a national level, because they generally refer to local field studies and are usually limited to one ethnic group. These studies examine such questions as the reasons people migrate, the planning that is involved, the importance of migratory networks, the kind of life that foreigners lead in the receiving country, access to social services, integration, and conflicts that migration creates. In the same way, the effect of immigration on national attitudes is studied.[14]

---

[13] The migration series no longer exists.

[14] See, for example, research done by Calvanese and Pugliese (1983, 1988), Barsotti (1988), Melotti (1988), and, at an international level, Portes (1978).

These studies are important because there are numerous flows that cannot be explained by economic factors but can be more easily traced to sociological theories. These are the role of the nation state, the attraction that the center exerts on the periphery, and cultural colonization, to mention the most important. As well as increasing general knowledge of the phenomenon, such studies offer clues to its future evolution and to policy prescriptions.

Individual and social psychology has many topics in common with sociology. It is mainly concerned with problems such as being separated from the country of origin and integration into the receiving country. The difficulties faced by immigrants often lead to deviant behavior, lawlessness, and conflicts with the local community, or an aggressive reaction from the natives toward foreigners. Similarly, anthropological studies analyze the behavior of the foreign communities in the areas of departure and arrival to show which behavioral habits change and which do not change.

1.2.3 The Economic Approach

The economic approach is wide-ranging and involves studies that belong to heterogeneous disciplines. Each discipline analyzes migration within its own area of reference. Growth theory considers migration a factor that favors or hinders the growth of the country of departure. In international economics migration is considered a factor of production that can move so as to achieve an equilibrium of relative prices of factors and goods. In contrast, economic geography considers migration a problem of reallocating resources within the territory, and labor economics analyzes the economic causes of mobility and the way it affects salaries and wages and the levels of employment of the natives. Public finance focuses attention on the effects on public expenditure of the immigration of adults whose characteristics are different from the natives'.

This incomplete list can highlight only some of the many facets of migration and the difficulties of an exhaustive approach. Having accepted such a limitation we have grouped the economic studies under two main headings: partial equilibrium or microeconomic studies, and aggregate studies.

Three main topics are developed in the first group: the decision to migrate, the effects of migration on the country of origin, and the effects on the receiving country. Each topic is developed both on a theoretical level and on an empirical level.

The *decision to migrate* – in its first version (Sjaastad 1962) and in many subsequent ones – was considered an investment in human capital. Namely, the migration decision results from an individual utility maximization upon a positive wage differential and higher probability of getting a job in the destination area. Other versions introduce into the decision-making process elements such as the characteristics of the country of origin and whether the immigrant is a member of a family group. In this way other variables are inserted that encourage or discourage the decision to migrate or influence the length of the stay in the country (Djajic 1989; Stark 1991).

The effects on the economic system of the receiving country have been widely researched. Using both theoretical and empirical models, such studies investigate the impact of immigrants, representing varying quantities of human capital, on the growth of the productive system. They consider whether the relationship between immigrants and natives is competitive or complementary and analyze the economic integration of foreigners. Further research analyzes the effect of immigration on the structure of the population and its contribution to the pension system.

Even though they are equally important, much less research has been done on the effects of emigration on the economic system of the country of origin. This is because good data are lacking. An analysis of the effect of migration on the economic growth of the country of departure considers, on the one hand, the traditional links between economic growth, population growth, and human capital and, on the other hand, the financial contribution of emigrants' *remittances* (money sent to family members in the country of origin) to domestic economic growth, which traditionally is referred to as capital growth. Two aspects should be emphasized: not only the loss of workers – that is, the loss of human capital, which can be vital for economic development in the country of departure – but also the probable enrichment of the stock of human capital when the emigrant returns home.

Emigrants' remittances home also have important effects on the distribution of income, on the standard of living of the families who receive them, on national consumption, and on prices. The outcome is uncertain and depends on the period and the level of development of the country of departure (Tapinos 1994).

The *macroeconomic,* or *aggregate,* approach concentrates mainly on two aspects. Migration is analyzed either in a closed economy and attention is focused on economic growth, or in an open economy when its effect on international trade is paramount.

An example of the first kind of model is A. W. Lewis's seminal paper (1954), in which migration occurs from backward sectors with low productivity and low subsistence wages into modern sectors with high productivity, high wages, and full employment, thereby setting off an equilibrium mechanism that, with the added hypothesis of fixed technology and reinvesting profits, favors a country's economic development. The Harris-Todaro model (1970) reached the opposite conclusion. This model introduced unemployment in the receiving area, and made the decision to migrate depend on expected wages, which were given as a weighted average of the probability of getting a job in the receiving area (represented by the unemployment rate). In fact the creation of additional jobs in the receiving area, instead of reducing unemployment, stimulates it and so increases the stock of individuals looking for a job. The migratory flows in this case amplify the existing macroeconomic imbalances.[15]

In models of international trade, if two countries – which have identical omothetic preferences and identical technology with constant returns to scale and in which firms operate in conditions of perfect competition – are endowed with a different mix of the factors of production (Ohlin 1933), trade or factor mobility will lead to equal relative prices. Migration arises in the presence of different relative earnings in the two areas and ends when this difference is eliminated. Trade is a perfect alternative to the movement of productive factors because it produces the same effect.[16]

If, however, the original endowments of productive factors are the same but the technology used in the two countries is different, the mobility of factors of production can be complementary to trade in goods (Markusen 1983). The mobility of productive factors can be hindered, or there can be "specific factors" of production, which are not mobile, and so a relative price equilibrium cannot be reached.[17]

The advantage of aggregate studies such as the models of Lewis (1954) and of Harris-Todaro (1970) and the models of international trade is that it is possible to consider the interrelationship with other markets, such as the markets for goods and for capital. Furthermore, these models analyze both the causes of migration and its effects on both the receiving country and the country of departure. However, the conclusions of these models are based on highly specific and in some cases very simple hypotheses regarding the functioning of the economic system. This approach – which, without wanting to underestimate the contribution of the other disciplines, seems particularly interesting – has not received the same attention.

---

[15] Galor Oded (1986) examines the implications of applying the Golden Rule to the migration phenomenon in a dynamic analysis of general economic equilibrium.

[16] For a survey of this question see Daveri and Venturini (1993); Razin and Sadka (1992); and Faini and Venturini (1993).

[17] See, for example, Albert and Vosgerau (1989).

There are many reasons why relatively little attention has been given to questions of migration. Firstly, on the one hand the simplicity of the hypotheses regarding the behavior of individuals, the way in which migration takes place automatically, and its effects (on economic growth or the convergence of relative prices) does not seem to be confirmed by the evolution of migration or by the complex economic conditions in the country of departure and in the receiving country; on the other hand, it is difficult to draw general conclusions from highly complex hypotheses. In addition, the researchers who have developed aggregate models of growth and international trade were not particularly interested in migration but in growth and trade, whose variations are affected much more by financial, technological, and political changes than by the mobility of labor – and, above all, because the migratory phenomenon adjusts much more slowly than economic and financial variables and it is much more difficult to manage than those phenomena.

1.2.4 Juridical and Institutional Approaches

The law is a very relevant area in the study of migration. Moving from one country to another, and becoming subject to two different institutional systems, is a question of international law.

The topics that have received most attention are the right to enter a country, the right to family reunion, and the protection of a citizen's rights during a stay abroad. Then there is the right to work, which also comes under the jurisdiction of international law. In fact, national laws are applied to foreigners only when they can be considered to be similar to natives – that is, after a period during which they enjoy rights as foreigners temporarily resident in the country.[18]

The institutional approach focuses on how national laws governing flows of foreign population affect the size and quality of the immigrants. Such a topic is particularly relevant where the laws regarding the access of foreigners is the responsibility of the Ministry of the Interior, which defines the rules and grants visas and resident permits. It does not respond to the exclusive needs of the labor market or to social expenditure.

In addition to juridical and technical studies of the most suitable procedures to make legislation more efficient,[19] there is a wide range of economic studies of the efficiency of such measures and their economic cost. There are

---

[18] A comparative analysis of this topic can be found in Nascimbene (1988) and Callovi (1988).

[19] See, for example, Urbani and Granaglia (1991) and Nascimbene (1988).

three kinds of study: research on policies that aim at regulating the supply of immigrant workers, policies that encourage immigrants to return home, and policies that regularize the presence of those who are already in the country.

The first group analyzes ways to select the labor supply according to certain "desirable" requisites. These policies depend partly on the demand for labor by firms and partly on structural supply factors such as age, gender, nationality, and family ties, which are considered to be important variables if there is going to be integration in the receiving country.[20] This group includes studies of the efficiency of policies of raising barriers to entry introduced in some European countries in the 1970s. Their effect was reduced by people applying for family reunification and requests for political asylum, which were a legal way of surmounting the barriers to entry for work.[21]

The second group – policies to encourage immigrants to return home with the aim of reducing unemployment among foreign immigrants – have been implemented in France and Germany, but they were not very successful. A limited number of workers took up the offer, and generally these policies were accompanied by an increase in the number of new immigrants and family reunification, which weakened, their effect.

Clandestine immigration is a spontaneous response to a foreigner's wish to emigrate. It is a way of getting around the restrictive norms governing access to a country. Amnesties or regularization procedures, the third types, are introduced to rectify such cases before a more restrictive law is introduced or before existing laws are applied more rigorously.

Regularization can be individual or collective. The latter is more frequently adopted when there is a high level of irregular immigration and the measures that have been adopted have had mixed success. In fact although they manage to rectify the presence of some irregular immigrants, the announced measures attract new waves of immigrants and the number of irregular immigrants does not change.

[20] See Atchinson (1988), Samuel (1988), and Bean, Vernez, and Keely (1989).
[21] See Venturini (1988), Tribalat (1988), and Marie (1994).

2

The Choice to Migrate

This chapter considers the choice to migrate. We chose an approach of individual (or family) choice, ignoring the structural explanations, which suggest that individuals move only because of deep social change. However, it is acknowledged that the historical-sociological context in which the choice to migrate is made is extremely relevant, and so such factors are incorporated into a model of individual choice.

The aim of this chapter is to carry out empirical tests on the choice made by immigrants from Spain, Greece, Italy, and Portugal to northern European countries in the postwar period. We compare the explicative power of three approaches – economic, gravitational, and sociological – to analyze the choice to emigrate.

The economic approach draws on the theory of human capital and its development. Individuals decide to invest in migration if it implies a better return on their human capital, net of economic and psychological costs.

In contrast, the gravitational pull approach emphasizes territorial factors, in that it is derived from regional economics. Movement from one area to another is interpreted as in the physical sciences – that is, forces attract each other but are hindered by the inertia of distance.

The sociological approach to the individual choice to emigrate emphasizes the relevance of certain factors, such as social organization, especially the networks of knowledge and family links that can be found in the migratory chain.

The decision to consider these three approaches recalls a lively debate in which economists, although neither denying nor ignoring the importance of information networks, often use variables that can be considered proxies of the migratory chain in their empirical tests. Their content is not specified, however, so one of the aims of this empirical test is to specify the economic and sociological content of such variables.

Furthermore, in the past few years there has been a return to gravitational models in order to interpret the movement of individuals and production factors between areas. Hamilton and Winter (1992), for example, use a gravitational model when they interpret the flows of imports and exports that might be generated between the EU countries and the eastern European countries. Similarly Gowa and Mansfield (1993) use this type of model to interpret international trade, grafting onto it a variable of systems of alliances. In a critical overview of aggregate economic approaches to the study of the migratory phenomenon, demographer M. Termote (1996) asserts that gravitational models offer greater insight into the territorial dynamics of migratory phenomena.

It would be interesting and certainly relevant to conduct an empirical analysis of the current migratory choice of emigrants toward southern European countries from Maghreb, the Philippines, Albania, and Yugoslavia. Unfortunately, such an analysis would need data from the departure country, and at the moment such information is limited and not completely reliable. In addition, information about the level of employment and unemployment is not available in these countries, and such information is indispensable in an empirical analysis. Even when the data on total inflows of immigration into the receiving country are used, the recent and frequent regularizations make it impossible to have a historical series that is sufficiently long and reliable.

This chapter introduces a survey of the economic models, starting with the traditional human capital theory and continuing with the most recent and the most interesting specifications of the choice to migrate. This review has the twofold aim of emphasizing how much effort economists have made to find realistic explanations and how these efforts are an attempt to overcome, at least at a theoretical level, the interpretative limits of using only wage differentials, and not territorial or sociological factors, as the engine of migration.

The first part of this chapter reviews various economic interpretations of the choice to migrate, and then it defines an empirical model that can be used to conduct empirical tests. This is followed by an analysis of the gravitational model and the sociological model. Data describing the trend and the evolution of emigration flows from southern European countries to northern Europe are presented later, together with separate estimates of the three models and combinations of them. The conclusions include comments on the implications that can be drawn from the current migratory phenomenon in the southern European countries.

2.1 AN OVERVIEW OF THE ECONOMIC MODELS

The models of migratory choice begin with models in which the choice to migrate is the result of a maximization process based on labor market variables. Then some causal models whose relations go beyond the labour market are examined. Later some papers are presented not only because of their intrinsic value in the definition of the migratory process but also because they overcome some of the limits of the neo-classical approach such as perfect rationality, perfect information, and homogeneous agents.

2.1.1 The Human Capital Model

In the human capital theory, migratory choice is considered an *investment* by an individual (Sjaastad 1962) who wants to maximize his or her income and therefore finds it advantageous to emigrate because of an income differential, net of the monetary and psychological costs of the transfer. The choice is an intertemporal one in which the future flows of income that can be earned in the area of origin (o) and the area of destination (d) are compared, migration can be permanent or temporary, and employment is immediate.

$$M = f(Wd - Wo) \qquad (1)$$

Where $f > 0$, $M = 1,0$, and $M = 1$ if $Wd > Wo$ and $M = 0$ if $Wd < Wo$.

$$Wd = \int_0^t Y d_e^{-rt} dt - C \qquad (2)$$

$$Wo = \int_0^t Y o e^{-rt} dt \qquad (3)$$

Where M indicates the individual's decision to migrate, positive or zero, Wi $i = d, o$ represents the flow of future incomes discounted for the present, r is the discount rate, Yi is the income in the two areas, and C is the cost of migration.

This formulation of the choice to migrate suggests that the larger the differential is, the more probable the choice to migrate will be, and the longer will be the period during which the benefits can be enjoyed – that is, the younger the immigrant is, the higher the expected income will be and the more probable will be the choice to migrate. Later specific studies on migration have tried to analyze the choice to migrate closely, introducing elements that integrate or substitute income differences as the central element in the choice.

2.1.2 Expected Income Model

In the seminal study by Todaro (1969), workers find themselves exposed
to the risk of being unemployed in the destination area, and therefore their
migratory choice is made comparing the income earned in the area of departure with the expected income in the receiving area.[1] In Todaro's study, the
probability of finding work is linked to the rate of unemployment. Therefore,
the expected income in the receiving area (*Ewd*) depends on the probability
(P_1) of getting a job at wage *Yd* and the probability ($1-P_1$) of receiving
unemployment payments *Ydu* (which could be equal to zero), as shown in
equation (4). In the departure country the expected wage (*Ewo*) is given
by the probability P_2 of getting a job at wage *Yo* (equation (5)), generally
considered to be equal to 1.

$$E\,Wd = \int_0^t [P_1 Yd + (1 - P_1)Ydu]e^{-rt}\,dt \qquad (4)$$

$$E\,Wo = \int_0^t P_2 Yoe^{-rt}\,dt \qquad (5)$$

If it is possible to enter the receiving country illegally, the valuation of the
expected wage in the receiving country should be extended, with the introduction of the possibility of not being deported (equal to 1 in the case of legal
immigrants, and with a value of less than 1 in the case of illegal immigrants).

The analytical differences in the models have important implications for
economic policy. In the first case, the optimum policy to reduce the rate of
migration would be to reduce the difference in income between the departure
area and the receiving area. In the second case, an increase in the level of
employment would increase the probability of the emigrant's getting a job
in the area of potential emigration and so increase the flow of immigrants.
However, only a limited number of immigrants will manage to get a job,
and the rest will join the ranks of the unemployed, again influencing the
expected wage. In this second model it is not the equal wage level but the
equal expected wage that slows migration.

Summing up the models presented thus far:[2]

- Central to this version of the neoclassical model of the choice to migrate is
  the dynamics of the labor market: Wage and employment levels determine
  the dynamics of the expected return to migration.

---

[1] In Todaro's 1969 version, there is only the first part of equation (4); unemployment benefits are
not considered. $Ydu = 0$, and $P_2 = 1$.

[2] See Massey et al. (1993).

- Migration will be more probable among individuals whose human capital guarantees them a higher income and a higher probability of getting a job abroad.
- The probability of migration will also be higher if the individual's characteristics and the social and technological conditions reduce the costs of moving and so increase net return.
- At an aggregate level, migration flows are the sum of different individual choices that depend exclusively on the trend of the labor market.
- A policy to slow migration can intervene exclusively on expected wages; that is, wages earned, the probability of getting a job, and the probability of being deported. They also include long-term policies in the departure country. These can increase production and therefore employment and wages, thereby increasing expected wages so that wage differentials are reduced and migration is discouraged.

2.1.3 Risk Propensity and Risk Aversion

A difference between expected wages in the receiving country and certain income in the departure country can, however, be sufficient to decrease migration in the case of individuals averse to risk. Empirical literature tends to suggest a positive relationship between individuals who emigrate and their propensity to risk. The more the worker is willing to risk – that is, has a convex utility curve with respect to wealth – the more probable it is that the worker will emigrate even if the difference in income is limited (Langley 1974; Hart 1975).[3]

An interesting development of the introduction of risk into the utility function is put forward by Oded Stark (1991; Stark and Katz 1986). The coordinates of the choice to migrate were changed radically, and for this reason the authors called the theory "The New Economics of Labour Migration."[4] In this case it is not the individual but the family that decides on the migration issue in order to diversify the portfolio of sources of income

---

[3] Langley (1974) in his theoretical work introduces a utility function with aversion to risk ($U = a - ce^{-bD}$, where b identifies the aversion to risk and a, b, and c are parameters, $c, b > 0$ and $a \geq 0$, and D represents the net return of migration in the period considered), which, however, is not estimated in empirical work. Hart (1975) does not elaborate a model with aversion to risk; he limits himself to emphasizing its relevance.

[4] The New Economics of Labour Migration covers the theme in which the choice is familiar and is made with the idea of diversifying one's portfolio. In addition, there are two other interpretations: asymmetric information and relative deprivation. The article that summarizes these three themes and has the title later given to this theory is Stark and Bloom (1985).

and insure against the risks of poor agricultural income.[5] Therefore, it is not the propensity to take risks that favors the choice to migrate, but risk aversion, which, joined to a particular return function of wealth (for example, very high for low levels of income), enables the family to enjoy the fruits of modernizing agricultural production. Something that would otherwise not be possible. Stark shows that the concavity of the utility function (aversion to risk) is neither a necessary nor a sufficient condition for the convexity of the admissible set; that is, the average value is always preferred to an extreme value.

Given a sum of wealth A held by an individual, he or she will be indifferent to emigration if the utility obtained from wealth A and from its return R is equal to the expected utility of emigration, which has a probability q of guaranteeing employment at wage W, and a probability $(1-q)$, in the case of unemployment, of consuming part C of the person's initial wealth (see equation (6)).

$$U A[1 + R(A)] = qU(A + W)[1 + R(A + W)] \\ + (1 - q)U(A - C)[1 + R(A - C)] \qquad (6)$$

For every given A, an isoutility curve can be drawn, where C is a function of $C = G(W)$ and its slope $W = C = 0$ is

$$\frac{dC}{dW} \propto \frac{q}{1 - q} \qquad (7)$$

$$\frac{d^2C}{dW^2} = \frac{q}{(1 - q)^2} \left[\frac{U''(.)}{U'(.)} + \frac{2R' + AR''}{(1 + R + AR')^2} \right] (1 + R + AR') \qquad (8)$$

and whose second derivative can be positive or negative because its sign depends on the degree of Arrow-Prat aversion to risk (without the negative sign), and the rate of return (R'), which, if very high, can result in the derivative having a positive sign; therefore it can be concave with an admissible nonconvex set. If R' is sufficiently large, the potential emigrant worker overcomes his or her aversion to risk, even if it implies accepting an *unfair game* and a nonconvex admissible set. The important implication of this analysis is that in this case income is not a homogeneous good, as assumed

[5] In a very interesting study, Daveri and Faini (1999) analyze the family's choice to spread risk by sending its members to different countries. Assuming that the correlation between income in various countries is not zero, concave family mobility costs and idiosyncratic preferences of destination theoretically explain and check empirically two contradictions of the phenomenon in the Italian case: spatial agglomeration and territorial spread.

in neoclassical theory, but the source of income is important because it is linked to different risks.

An indirect estimate of mobility as insurance against the risk of agricultural income has been made by Rosenzweig and Stark (1989; republished Stark 1991). This study used longitudinal data on about six Indian villages in a semiarid area of the tropics carried out by the International Corps Research Institute from 1975 to 1985.

Therefore the most relevant implications of this approach in defining the causes of the choice to migrate are:

- The family and not the individual is the decisional unit, and it tries to maximize future income by minimizing the risk for present income.
- Therefore, the fact that there is a difference in expected income is no longer a necessary condition for mobility given that the family is interested in spreading risks.
- The family is involved in both local work and migration, and therefore the higher local growth does not necessarily mean that pressure to migrate will be reduced.
- The implications for economic policy are clearly different in this case, where the decrease in the migratory flow passes through more agricultural finance and wider insurance against its risks – that is, market intervention outside the labor market.
- Insurance intervention in the labor market in the departure country, such as unemployment payments, influences the family's need for protection.
- However, in these models even though the choice to migrate is made within the family, no family decisional process has been elaborated; instead, the family operates as an individual.

2.1.4 Relative Deprivation Model

Stark, who developed a theoretical model with Levhari (1998) and an empirical version with E. J. Taylor (1991), identifies *relative deprivation* as a reason for migration. It is assumed that it is not the level of income in absolute terms that pushes an individual to emigrate but the level compared with the number of individuals who have a higher income. This approach assumes that the utility of wealth is not constant in society. Individuals emigrate so that they can improve their (and their families') relative position in the departure country. It is therefore not the income differential that causes migration. Rather it can take place even when there are not any average income differences.

If $F(y)$ represents the cumulated income distribution and $h[1 - F(y)]$ represents the perceived unhappiness of the family whose income is y, the relative deprivation $RD(y)$ can be expressed in equation (9).

$$RD(y) = \int_{y}^{ymax} h[1 - F(y)]dz \qquad (9)$$

In the simplest version, where n = 1, it is equivalent to equation (10).

$$RD(Y) = [1 - F(y)]E(z - y|z > y) \qquad (10)$$

That is, the relative deprivation is the product of two terms: the members of the family who have an income higher than y and the average difference of income between the richest families and income y.

Stark and Taylor (1989; republished Stark 1991) carried out an empirical test using individual data taken from a survey of two Mexican villages with migration to the United States. The importance of relative deprivation in determining the choice to emigrate was revealed.

This approach questions several points:

- Whether the utility of wealth is constant for an individual depending on the economic environment. Even if the expected income from migration remains unchanged, a change in the distribution of income can encourage a family to send a member abroad in order to improve the family's relative position. Therefore, it is a change in the income of the other elements in the area of reference that represents an incentive to migrate.
- Whether the policies that are aimed at limiting migration must influence the distribution of income and make its distribution more egalitarian.
- Whether government policy and the economic shocks that influence the distribution of income will influence migration independently, irrespective of their effect on average income, in as much as it is relative wealth and not absolute wealth that determines migration.

It is necessary to emphasize that in the models, the choice to emigrate is analyzed using a neoclassical model even though some non-neoclassical components – such as the nonhomogeneous utility of income and the utility of income that varies depending on external conditions – have been added. In such models individuals have perfect information, are able to maximize returns, and are homogeneous – that is, they can have different characteristics initially but cannot differ in their decisional processes.

Future studies will consider not only the specific assumptions regarding what determines the choice to migrate (which is of particular interest in this review) but also the following:

- The heterogeneity of individuals, as in the work of Faini and Venturini (1993, 1994a, 1994b) – with the use of a Pareto distribution of "probability" and "possibility" of emigrating – and the work of Domenicich and McFadden (1975) on the use of random utility functions
- Uncertainty concerning the convergence of wage differentials, as introduced in the work of Burda (1993), and asymmetric information in the work of Katz and Stark
- Procedures of choice different from maximization, as examined in section 2.1.9.

2.1.5 Differences in the Utility of Consumption

Another type of theoretical work uses a utility function of an individual who attributes *greater utility to consumption* in the departure country with respect to consumption in the receiving country. Djajic and Milbourne (1988) and Hill (1987) use this assumption to explain the length of migration. Dustmann (1994) uses it in his theoretical model to interpret *remigration*: the decision to remain in the receiving country.

Such an assumption is used by Faini and Venturini (1994a) to explain the particular role played by wages (or income) in the departure country in the choice to migrate. The authors represent the utility of the potential emigrant as a function made up of two elements: consumption and a localization factor, which leads the worker to prefer to remain in the departure country – for example, with the family:

$$[U(Wi, fi)]$$

where W identifies the wage, f is the localization factor, and i is the area of destination (d) and the area of origin (o). It is reasonable to assume that wages in the area of destination are higher than wages in the area of departure, so we have $W_d > W_o$ and $f_o > f_d$. Migration will take place if the wage differential is large enough to compensate the worker for the loss of utility due to localization being less attractive.

Migration will take place if $U(Wd, fd) > U(Wo, fo)$. Later, the authors develop the analysis taking a first-order expansion of $U(Wd, fd)$ around

$U(Wo, fo)$ in which the condition of migration becomes

$$\frac{1-d}{d} \geq \frac{f_o - f_d}{W_d - W_o} \left(\frac{W_o}{f_o}\right)^{(1+\rho)} \tag{11}$$

The right side of equation (11) is only the marginal rate of substitution between the real wage and the localization factor; on the left side, ρ represents the distributive parameter of the CES function, associated with f, and $(1/1 + \rho)$, the elasticity of substitution between W and f.

The important implication of equation (11) is that, as expected, the probability of migration $[(1-d)/d]$ will be much greater, the higher the income differentials $(Wd - Wo)$ are and the less unpleasant it is to be a long way from home $(fo - fd)$. But, above all, an increase in wages in the departure country (Wo) – even if accompanied by a similar increase in wages in the receiving country (Wd) so as to maintain the wage differential constant $(Wd - Wo)$ – would make the migration less likely.

The result is quite logical. Because the good, "localization," is a normal good, when income increases in the departure country, the potential emigrant will try to consume more of it; this is an example of the traditional *income effect*. Migration, when wages are increasing, will be less likely because of the reduction in the difference in wages and because of the income effect.

The authors also argue that workers are not homogeneous, and therefore it is reasonable to imagine that the probability of emigrating ($[(1-d)/d]$ will have a Pareto distribution in the population. Defining g (the left side of (11)), z (the right side), and Xo (the lower limit of the distribution of g), we get (12).

$$\frac{M}{P} = X_o^\theta Z^{-\theta} X_1^\varepsilon C^{-\varepsilon} \tag{12}$$

It is also reasonable to assume that migration is conditioned not only by the probability of wanting to emigrate but also by the possibility of achieving it. If a potential emigrant wants to emigrate, he or she must have an initial endowment of resources in human capital (A) higher than a minimum threshold (C). The authors assume that the possibility of emigrating is distributed in the population according to a completely independent Pareto distribution, and therefore the probability that those who want to emigrate will have the resources necessary to achieve it will be given by the intersection of the two sets. The lower limit (X_1) of distribution A has been associated with a positive, but decreasing, function to wage in the country of origin ($X_1 = W_o e^{(a+bW_o)}$, $a > 0$, $b < 0$).

Therefore, it follows that the number of emigrants M as a share of the population P will be equal to 12, where θ and ε are the parameters of the Pareto distribution of the willingness to emigrate and the possibility of actually emigrating, respectively. Substituting in (12) and inserting logarithms we get expression (13).

$$Ln(M/P) = \theta LnX_o + \theta Ln(W_d/W_o) - \theta pLnWo + \theta Ln(f_o - f_d)$$
$$+ \theta(1 + \rho)Lnf_o + \varepsilon aLnW_o + \varepsilon b(LnWo)^2 - \varepsilon LnC \quad (13)$$

From equation (13) the following working conclusions are drawn:

- The higher the differential between the country of origin and the receiving country, the higher the migration.
- The wage effect of the country of origin a priori will be ambiguous. On the one hand, if $\varepsilon a > \theta\rho$ the increase in income in the departure country has a positive effect because it implies that a restriction on emigration has been relaxed, in that more people can now consider the opportunity of leaving the country; on the other hand, if $\theta\rho > \varepsilon a$ the effect of the increase in wages is negative because, as shown earlier, the wage increase slows migration and favors consumption of the localization good in the departure country (the income effect).
- The square of the wages logarithm has the expected negative sign ($b < 0$). The authors have carried out an empirical test on European emigration after the war and have found that the coefficient of the per-capita income logarithm has a positive sign, although it is negative for the square.

The implications to be drawn from this model are very different from those already examined.

a. The income differential is a necessary condition for migration. However, its dynamics for a given differential are determined by the trend of wages in the country of origin.
b. At low levels of per-capita income, an increase in income has a positive effect on migration because it reduces the restraint of insufficient human capital resources. Only at a later stage of development – for medium or high levels of per-capita income in the country of origin – does the growth of income slow migration and produce an income effect.
c. The implications for economic policy are reversed because policies aimed at reducing income differentials between areas of departure and areas of destination, if pursued when the difference are very high (as in very poor countries), have only the effect of reducing the potential emigrant's

human capital restraint and so encourage a larger number of individuals to emigrate and enter the foreign labor market. Furthermore, the more egalitarian growth policies are, the larger will be the number of individuals who can enter the foreign labor market. This result contradicts the conclusions of the previous model of relative deprivation.

2.1.6 Random Utility Model

Another microeconomic model that considers an individual's heterogeneity is that of *random utility*, developed by Domenicich and McFadden (1975) in their analysis of urban transport. The utility function, which individuals maximize in a traditional way, is made up of a component that reflects the representative individual's behavior and a second factor that reflects an individual's unobserved idiosyncrasies.

$$U_{kin} = V_{in} + \varepsilon_{kn} \tag{14}$$

Where U_{kin} represents the expected utility of the individual k who lives in i and who wants to emigrate to n, which forms the set of possible destinations in which there is i. V_{in} is the nonrandom element that reflects an individual's preferences, and ε_{kn} is a random variable that reflects differences in preferences due to individual idiosyncrasies.

In the case of random utility, although the error term, ε, is usually introduced into the empirical version of the models, here the error term is introduced explicitly. Thus, if we make assumptions about the distribution of the stochastic element, it is possible to get a series of models of discrete choice – namely, the probability that the individual k emigrates from i to n.

The advantage of this approach is that it explicitly models the individual's error and considers a discrete choice, the best known models of which are the logit and the probit. As suggested by Domenicich and McFadden (1975, p. 69), if it is assumed that the error has a Weibull distribution – double exponential – an extremely simple version of probability (P_{kij}) is obtained in which the individual k who lives in i chooses destination j from a possible set n (which includes i).

$$P_{kij} = \frac{e^{V_{ij}}}{\sum_{j=1}^{n} e^{V_{in}}} \tag{15}$$

This model not only inserts an individual's heterogeneity into the choice to emigrate and models this choice in a discrete way, but also it has the advantage of inserting different possible destinations into the choice. In this way, the analysis is no longer limited to bilateral mobility. The possibility of using such a model empirically is conditioned, however, on the availability of appropriate individual data.

2.1.7 The Option to Migrate Model

Burda (1993), in contrast, tries to link the choice to migrate to the research done by Dixit (1992) on the *option value*. The models of option value can be extended to the choice to migrate as long as there is (a) a fixed cost, which, in a certain way, cannot be recovered, (b) an uncertainty that is revealed over time and that cannot be insured against, (c) the possibility of waiting and postponing the decision without paying any penalties.

As Dixit and others have shown, the return on projects in this context must exceed the *Mashallian trigger*, that is, the ex ante return has a present value of zero. This assumes that the worker has an infinite future horizon and has the possibility of earning the wage Wo in the departure country and Wd in the receiving country, where $Wd > Wo$. It is also assumed that the differential $Dt = (Wd - Wo)/Wd$ follows the trend in equation (16), that is, it is reduced to the rate n minus time changes v_t.

$$\Delta D_t = -n + v_t \text{ for } Wd > Wo; \quad \text{or } \Delta D_t = 0;$$
$$\text{with } E v_t = 0; \quad E v_t^2 = \sigma^2 \tag{16}$$

In a finite time horizon, wages in the departure country will converge on wages in the receiving country at the expected rate n. Ignoring savings and assuming that the worker's utility is logarithmic at wage level $U(.) = logW = w$, the differential becomes the wage log difference $D_t = W_{dt} - W_{ot}$, which approximates the instantaneous differential of utility. Furthermore, assuming that the cost of migration is to be a fixed share of utility in the departure country, f, and in conditions of certainty (that is to say, $v_t = 0$ for $t \geq 0$) the worker emigrates if equation (17) is true.

$$\frac{D_t}{d + n} > f; \quad \text{where } d \text{ is the time discount rate} \tag{17}$$

Therefore, if the terms of drift n (the expected rate of wage convergence) increases or if fixed costs (f) increase, then the critical value of differential $\hat{D} = (d + n) f$ (the Marshallian trigger value) increases, namely raises the value beyond which migration increases utility.

Uncertainty shifts the distribution of the differential and allows waiting to increase an individual's utility. This is because if a negative shock takes

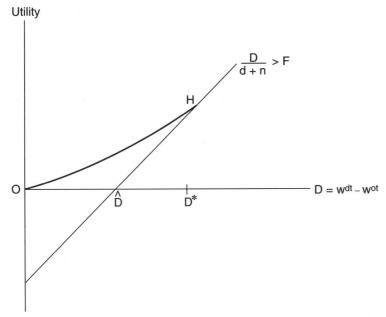

Figure 2.1. The decision to migrate and the optimal option value. *Source*: Burda (1993), p. 10.

place, the potential migrant does not necessarily incur fixed costs; while if there is a positive shock, the decision to migrate can still be undertaken.

The wage differential on which migration occurs is D^*, higher than $\hat{D}$ (the Marshallian trigger). The option value is shown in Figure 2.1 by the difference between OH and the value of the case of certainty, and it depends negatively on the discount rate d and positively on the rate of wage convergence n as well as on the variance vt (s_v^2). The greater the uncertainty, the greater will be the probability of improving the results of the decisional process. Using a binomial logistic function and a sample of 3,710 individuals, the authors estimate the willingness to emigrate to West Germany or West Berlin.

2.1.8 The Asymmetric Information Model

Another model of the choice to emigrate, developed by E. Katz with Oded Stark (Stark 1984; Katz and Stark 1986; Stark 1991), introduces into the choice to emigrate *asymmetric information* from agents, which can cause migratory flows in the opposite direction of those expected considering the

wage differentials. This assumes that for a given job workers' wages depend –
in a linear and positive way – on their level of skill (£) and assumes that in
the receiving country the wage paid is higher ($Wd(£) > Wo(£)$) than that
in the departure country. Because the worker tends to prefer the departure
country, a discount factor must be applied (k positive and lower than 1) to
the wage in the receiving country; therefore, the choice to emigrate will be
decided by comparing $kWd(£)$ and $Wo(£)$.

The author assumes further that the wages are a linear function of skill
so that

$$Wd(£) = ro + r£ \qquad Wo(£) = po + p£ \qquad ro, po, r, p > 0 \qquad (18)$$

If skill £ is defined in the closed interval [0,1], it can be assumed that workers
are spread uniformly within the interval [0,1]. Because it is impossible for
an employer to value an individual's productivity, the firm offers the worker
an average wage $Wd(£^*)$ relative to the interval being considered [0,£].

Considering the situation in which $kWd(0) > Wo(0)$ – that is, in the case
of symmetric information – it is advantageous for unskilled workers to emigrate. An individual's choice can be represented graphically. In Figure 2.2a
and b the solid line indicates the distribution of wages in the departure
country and the receiving country, where there is symmetric information;
the dashed line traces the case of asymmetric information. In case b, even
though asymmetric information induces the employers to offer a wage lower
than a worker's actual productivity, it does not reduce the incentive to emigrate for all levels of skill, and the migratory choice is not changed. In case
a, where the two wages intersect at skill level $£_1$, the choice to emigrate is
distorted and skilled workers are discouraged from emigrating. Thus, both
the number and the quality of migrants is reduced.

Therefore, also in this case

reducing differentials and adopting policies aimed at reducing the
pressure to migrate through economic growth are not necessarily
efficient.

On a related topic, even though he uses a purely empirical approach,
T. Hatton (2001) traces the dimension and the composition (skilled versus
unskilled) of the migration flows to the wage differential between origin
and destination countries but above all to the relative wage dispersion. If
for a given wage differential wage dispersion is relatively wider in destination countries, more skilled immigrants will arrive; but if wage dispersion

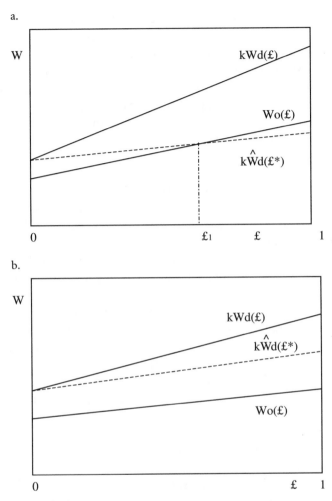

Figure 2.2. Migratory choice under symmetric and asymmetric information. £ = skill distributed between 0 and 1; Wo(£) = wage in the origin country; Wd(£) = wage in destination country discounted by a factor k. The dashed line represents wage payments at the destination under asymmetric information. *Source:* Stark 1991, p. 175

is relatively wider in origin countries, more unskilled immigrants will move.

2.1.9 A Non-Maximization Migration Choice Model

The models presented in this study describe migration as being the result of a choice of maximization. However, some researchers argue that foreigners are not in a position to choose because the little information available to them is very complex, offering a great many alternatives. This objection can be countered both factually and theoretically.

The facts show that there is a large amount of information available to foreigners. Often, they already have a contract for a potential job or a very clear idea of what their earnings will be because they have relatives abroad or because there are channels that coordinate the migratory flows. This situation is confirmed by Böhning (1984) and by Stalker (1994).

On the other hand, it might seem unlikely that individuals are aware of all the available possibilities and that they can choose from such a wide range of possibilities. It is more reasonable to assume that individuals adopt a different decisional procedure, building subsets of alternatives and deciding whether the return is sufficient. Thus, they can be considered to be *satisfying*, and not *maximizing*, agents.

This distinction, however, is semantic because an individual who is satis-fying can be seen as an individual who is maximizing returns but is subject to high constraints due to the cost of gathering information. Stark's model with asymmetric information (1991) points out the erroneous consequences and inefficiency of the procedure of choice but takes information errors for granted. The procedure of making a choice is represented ex post following a maximization process without uncertainty.

Drawing on Wolpert (1966) and Speare (1974), the choice to migrate can also be interpreted as a response to *stress*. A tolerance threshold can be imagined that is made up, for example, of a certain difference between expectations, aspirations, and reality; above this threshold an individual decides to actively look for information in order to emigrate. The concept of stress was used by Speare (1974) and redefined as *dissatisfaction* in his analysis of the mobility of Rhode Island residents, interviewing 1,081 individuals in 1969. The variations in time and place regarding the links between the observed variables and their satisfaction make it impossible to extend the observed relationships to other cases.

Amrhein and MacKinnon (1985) incorporated the concept of stress in an economic context, but their approach raises further problems. They assumed that the population is divided into "movers" and "stayers." The effective number of movers who emigrate is a function of the difference in perceptions that emigrants have of their actual job and a possible job in another region. Assuming that the expected value of an alternative job is the average of jobs that a similar worker can get in other regions, it is assumed that an emigrant can calculate such a value without making a mistake. However, some individuals will be risk averse, so some will move only if the differentials are very high, whereas others will move whenever the differentials are positive, as in the case, for example, of people who are unemployed.

The exact calculation of the sum of emigrants is based on the concept of stress. The level of stress (β_i^{kl}) for an individual i who lives in k and is thinking of emigrating to l can be calculated in the following way, where a_{ij}^k represents the nonwage benefits that the individual type i derives from work type j in the region k, and s_{ij}^k represents the wage that the individual type i earns in work j in the region k. The sum represents the whole benefit for the individual i of the job j in k, and this is compared with the average wage of a possible job that individuals of type i do in l, and it is obtained by dividing the wage bill by W_i^l for the number of individuals of type i in region l.

$$\beta_i^{kl} = \frac{\left[\sum_{j=1}^{N}\left(a_{ij}^l + s_{ij}^l\right) / W_i^l\right] - \left(a_{ij}^k + s_{ij}^k\right)}{\left(a_{ij}^k + s_{ij}^k\right)} \tag{19}$$

The percentage of individuals of type i who emigrate from k to l (P_i^{kl}), given a saturation level a at which all movers would emigrate, will be equal to 1 if the level of stress is equal to or higher than a, and will be less than 1 if the stress level is positive and less than a.

In this model the percentage of movers and stayers in the population is specified exogenously, and the saturation level can be higher or lower depending on how much the population is averse to risk. Amrhein and MacKinnon continue their analysis with a simulation of ten cases in which the stationary state or chaotic results are quickly reached.

However interesting and different this version of a choice is from the traditional maximization model, it does not offer a fruitful line of analysis. Because many terms are based on exogenous data and perfect information as well as on the ability of the individual to compare different incomes in both the departure area and the receiving area, it is no more illuminating than previous models. Also, Burda's study (1993) can offer an interpretation of the choice to emigrate based on stress. Recalling the previous discussion, the models with options of waiting imply that migration can respond to information that leaves the observed variables constant; therefore, migration as a response to stress can mean that the waiting option value is reduced when new information is received.

2.2 COMMENTS ON AN EMPIRICAL VERSION
OF THE ECONOMIC MODEL

The survey in section 2.1 highlights some of the efforts economists have made in their attempts to offer an interpretation of the choice to migrate that goes beyond the traditional process of maximizing one's own utility and the potential emigrant's simple calculation of income differentials between two areas in order to decide whether to invest in migration. As this partial overview shows, the effort has been substantial and extremely varied. Some of these studies have concentrated on specifying alternative causes of the choice to migrate, whereas others have concentrated on defining different decisional processes.

The implications of these works in terms of economic policy are often contradictory. For example, Faini and Venturini (1993, 1994a) find that a policy of egalitarian growth (in countries with low per-capita income) encourages migration, whereas an interpretation in terms of relative deprivation (Stark and Levhari 1988) suggests that such a policy would discourage it. Only empirical tests can settle these contradictions.

Together, these models try to present the choice to migrate in a broader picture of the income differentials and so question the belief that growth policies reduce migratory pressure. It is very difficult, however, to test these models. To test the assumptions empirically, it is necessary to carry out individual interviews or ad hoc surveys; data should be collected, or at least individual panels of data consulted.

Stark's model, which assumes relative deprivation or family choice under conditions of uncertain agricultural income, is an example in which it is necessary to gather details about the distribution of income and the expected trend of agricultural income. But the latter case shows how basically the differential in expected income is at the center of the choice to migrate and how the significance of this variable at an empirical level does not necessarily lead to a traditional model such as Todaro's. Some of these models describe a different decisional and economic context and suggest that expected income differentials are due to different causes, thus implying different economic policies.

For example, Katz and Stark suggest that the cause of expected income differentials is the impossibility of insuring against uncertain agricultural income. Therefore, the implications for economic policy do not favor a reduction only of income differentials but also of the expected income, which depends on easing and insuring credit.

Not all models can be so easily adapted to a version of expected income differentials, and other ways of interpreting the facts – such as asymmetric information or relative deprivation – cannot be traced in the information available about the flows of emigration from the southern European countries.

Unfortunately, individual data do not exist in the southern European countries; there is only aggregate data about the gross flows of emigration.[6] Because only this source of information is available, it is necessary to renounce possible tests that take into account the composition of the family and background in the area of departure. For this reason, only average or aggregate variables are used.

It is necessary to emphasize again that it is not the economic approach that is limited to examining the expected income differential as a function of the choice to emigrate. But it is the empirical version which is constrained by what data is available.

The theoretical reference that is used in this study is the well-known Todaro model (1969). In this model, migration (*Mod*) from the area of origin *o* to the area of destination *d* will take place only if the expected income differential is positive. Such a theoretical reference was used by T. Straubhaar (1988) in his estimates of emigration from the southern European countries, by Molle and van Mourik (1987) in their analysis of migration inside Europe, and by Hatton (1995) in his estimate of English emigration in the nineteenth century, as well as by other authors.

The empirical model can be found in section 2.1.2 of the previous review.[7]

2.3 THE GRAVITATIONAL APPROACH TO MIGRATION

The gravitational approach was first used to analyze mobility between two areas by Ravenstein in 1885. He elaborated a model in which mobility is the

---

[6] The most appropriate data that can be used to test the choice to emigrate is information about gross flows of people leaving the departure country. Gross flows are preferred to net flows, which are a better proxy of the success of the migratory process.

[7] The empirical version is derived as follows:

1. $Mij/Pi = (Yj\ Uj)/(Yi\ Ui)$ where $M/P > 0$ if $YjUj/YiUi > 1$
2. $Ln(M/P) = Ln(Yj/Yi) + Ln((LF{-}N)/LF)j - Ln((FL - N)/FL)i$
3. $Ln(M/P) = Ln(Yj/Yi) - N/FLj + N/FLi$
4. $Ln(M/P) = Ln(Yj/Yi) + U/LFj - U/LFi$

Where M, FL, and P mean, respectively, emigration flows, labor force, and population, N and U mean employed and unemployed workers, and i and j mean origin and destination countries.

result of two forces of attraction consisting of the population in the receiving country and in the departure country and a decelerating force represented by distance.

This approach differs from later models because it uses aggregates and is very often atemporal. The model has its own physical logic; the larger the number of individuals in the area $i(Pi)$ and the higher the number of individuals in the area $j(Pj)$, then the greater the flow of individuals who move from i to $j(Mij)$. This flow will be decreased by the distance between i and $j(Dij)$ and increased by factors of attraction (A) in j or expulsion (B) in i. This model has been applied mostly to internal migration; see, for example, Munz and Rabino (1988) in the case of Italy, or Salt and Clout (1976) in the EU area. It has been used less to analyze international migration.[8] It has been rediscovered[9] by Hamilton and Winter (1992)[10] and by other researchers in other disciplines.

Empirical versions of the gravitational approach to migration do not have a definite standard form, but it is generally represented as [a,b].[11]

$$\text{(a) } Mij/(PiPj) = Bi\,Aj\,f(Dij) \qquad \text{(b) } Mij = Pi\,Pj\,Bi\,Aj\exp(Dij) \qquad (20)$$

where Mij represents the net flow of immigrants from i to j; as previously mentioned, Pi,j is the population in i and j; Aj and Bi represent the factors of attraction and expulsion; and D is the distance between i and j.

The version proposed here (21) enables the results of this estimate to be compared with those of other models. It uses the rate of emigration (Mij/Pi) as a dependent variable and uses the respective rates of activity $(Fli/Pi$ and $FLj/Pj)$ as factors of attraction and the distance.[12]

$$Mij/Pi = Fli/Pi\,FLj/Pj\,Dij \qquad (21)$$

In this formulation the populations of the departure country and the receiving country lose their characteristic as factors of attraction (with an expected positive sign). Instead, in this interpretation of migration, the labor force assumes that role. In this formulation there are no specific factors of attraction or expulsion other than the rate of activity because (21) identifies

---

[8] Bianchi (1993) should be consulted here.

[9] Linnemann (1966) was the first to use the gravitational model to interpret the flows of exports.

[10] See also Wang and Winters (1991).

[11] This version of the gravitational model was dealt with by Gordon and Vickerman (1982).

[12] The gravitational model both in the case of migratory flows and in the flows of exports and imports is generally estimated in levels; there are, however, also cases (as in Linnemenn) in which the rate of exports over GNP is estimated.

a "basic" formulation of the gravitational model, which can be expanded by
adding variables to subsequent models.

2.4 THE SOCIOLOGICAL APPROACH TO THE
MIGRATORY CHAIN

The sociological interpretation of the choice to migrate incorporates processes of transition in society (Sassen 1988) and cannot be compared with
economic or traditional regional approaches. One element, however, that
is often found in such interpretations is the importance of the migratory
chain as a determinant in the choice to emigrate (Massey et al. 1993). It
is therefore a useful interpretative factor of the growth of migration when
wage differentials decline.

The *migratory chain* approach does not claim that economic variables
are irrelevant but rather that they are not sufficient – or, in some cases,
necessary – to interpret the decision to migrate. Migration from i to j will
take place if there are economic conditions (Zij) that favor it, and it will be
conditioned by the presence of relatives, friends, and acquaintances ($Cmij$).
These people represent channels of information and economic and moral
support as well as a lifestyle model for migrants.

The model can be represented in algebraic form as shown next, where f
and g represent two functions of an emigrant's interaction with the migratory chain and his or her reaction to economic factors.

$$Mij = f(Cmij)g(Zij) \qquad (22)$$

The most relevant problem in such an approach is to identify an adequate
proxy for the migratory chain. Gould (1979, 1980a, 1980b) proposes and uses
a lagged dependent variable as a proxy for the migratory chain. However, this
variable creates problems because it is used to build a short-term, dynamic
model. Therefore, it is not a specific variable for sociological models.

There are other reasons why lagged dependent variables are not chosen
as proxies for the migratory chain. One reason is that the concept that
must be approximated is not only what is remembered of the phenomenon,
and sums of a number of lags (with or without the first) could be better
indicators.

Another possible indicator could be the stock of foreigners in the receiving country. This kind of variable was used by Hatton and Williamson
(1994), but there are many objections. For example, why should the Italian
immigrants of twenty years ago influence recent immigration? They could

originate from different communities and therefore not have any contacts or links with the recent migrants.

2.5 THE EVOLUTION OF MIGRATORY FLOWS

Emigration to northern European countries from southern Europe – Portugal, Spain, Italy, and Greece – after the Second World War is the subject of our analysis. As was emphasized in the Introduction, this emigration can offer indications about the dynamics of the current flows of immigrants to the southern European countries. Unfortunately, there are not enough data to conduct an empirical analysis on the same scale.

Although emigration from southern European countries presents similar patterns, national differences exist. Emigration across the Atlantic Ocean had a common raison d'être for the four countries, with flows mostly to South and North America. The large wave of migration took place between the end of the nineteenth century and the beginning of the twentieth, before the United States introduced a quota system in the 1920s. Emigration across the Atlantic recovered during the two wars, but after the Second World War, despite a decrease in the cost of crossing the ocean, it became less important than migration to the northern European countries.

These flows were mostly for economic reasons, even though some migration from Spain and Greece was also for political reasons. The most consistent flows of emigrants from Greece, Spain, Italy, and Portugal to the northern European countries took place in the 1960s and the first half of the 1970s, when economic recession hit the northern European countries and restrictive emigration policies were introduced. Later there was a resumption of migration from Italy to Germany and from Portugal to Switzerland, but at much lower levels than before (see Figures 2.3, 2.4, 2.5, and 2.6). Available data, which refer to overall annual flows from the departure country to the main receiving country, come mainly from OECD sources and the central statistical offices in the departure countries.

In the case of Greece we can draw on an unbalanced panel made up of flows to the Netherlands (from 1963 to 1988), to Germany (from 1960 to 1988), to Switzerland (from 1974 to 1988), and to Sweden (from 1960 to 1981). For Spain, we have a balanced panel made up of flows to the Netherlands (from 1960 to 1988), to Germany (from 1960 to 1988), to France (from 1960 to 1988), to Switzerland (from 1960 to 1988), and to Belgium (from 1961 to 1988).

In the case of Portugal, we use an unbalanced panel with flows to France (1960), Germany (1960 to 1989), the Netherlands (1965 to 1991),

a.

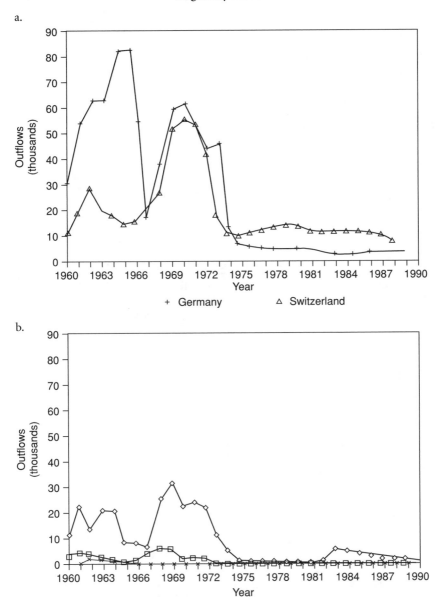

Figure 2.3. Gross emigration flows from Spain to the northern European countries.

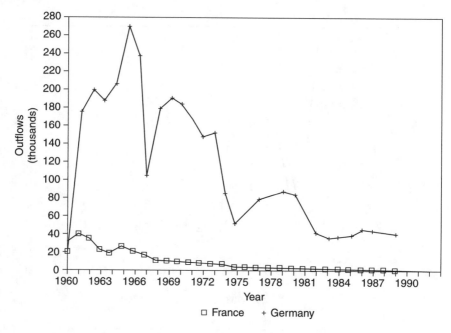

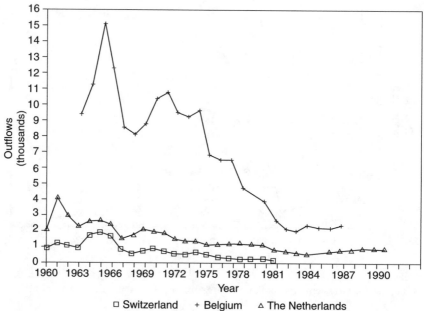

Figure 2.4. Gross flows of emigrants from Italy to the northern European countries.

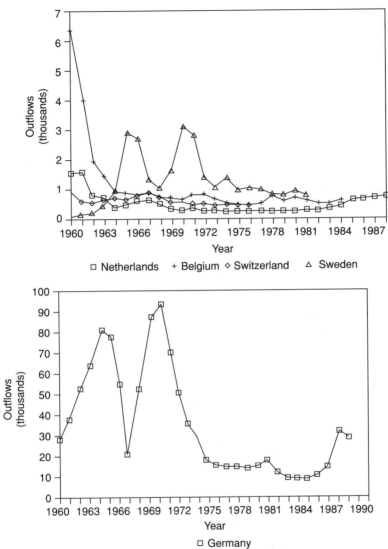

Figure 2.5. Gross emigration flows from Greece to the northern European countries.

Switzerland (1974 to 1990), and Belgium (1977 to 1987). In the case of Italy the available data are unbalanced, with flows to France and Germany (1960 to 1989), to Switzerland (1960 to 1981), to the Netherlands (1960 to 1991), and to Belgium (1963 to 1987). Other data, such as population, labor force, employment, and unemployment, are from OECD sources and were checked against national figures.

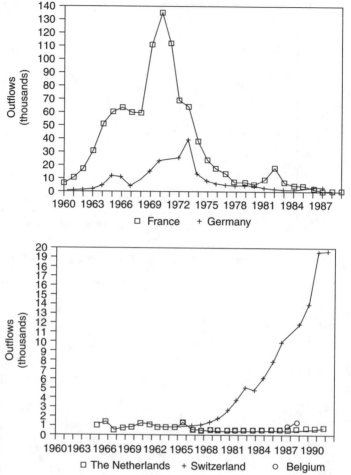

Figure 2.6. Gross emigration flows from Portugal to the northern European countries.

Distance refers to the number of kilometers between the departure area and the area of destination. For example, for Italy, where emigration was mostly from the south, the distances used were measured from a series of southern towns to the destination area.

Per-capita income was chosen instead of wages as a variable because, on the one hand, it was difficult to identify a wage level appropriate to all immigrants and, on the other hand, because studies emphasize that living standards in the destination area are an important factor in attracting immigrants. T. Straubhaar (1988) used this variable in his analysis of emigration to Germany and France from the Mediterranean countries. Choosing a real variable that provides an international comparison of purchasing power does not allow the monetary illusion to be tested; but it does not seem to be a very relevant phenomenon. However, the data we use came from Summers and Heston (1988).

The source of data regarding the stock of foreigners (or population born abroad) was derived from OECD or the emigration country's statistics, but unfortunately they cover a relatively short period. It should be noted that series were not examined for the degree of integration because in many cases the number of observations was so small as to make an empirical examination worthless. There generally seems to be a stationary trend with converging fluctuations that tend toward an equilibrium.

2.6 EMPIRICAL TESTS

The lack of empirical tests that can be used as points of reference for each single model (except for the economic model) and for the countries considered means that it is necessary to use an unusual procedure. We first tested each single model – gravitational, economic, and sociological – and than we tried to reconcile them.

The traditional procedure of passing from the general to the specific, even when it was done ex post, gave so many overparametrizations of the model that it was impossible to choose a useful line of statistical or economic research. Thus, we used the OLS technique of making estimates, with fixed effects and correction of the eterochedastic correlation in the coefficient estimates. Using the kind of panel available with five or six destinations and about twenty-eight observations for each destination, estimates are not appropriate in first differences but are appropriate in levels. For a high number of temporal observations, the estimated coefficients tend to be similar to the actual ones (see Urga 1992 and Nickell 1981).

2.6.1 The Gravitational Model

As emphasized earlier, the version of the gravitational model considered here is subject to empirical tests and refers to the basic structure of the model. To the equation (21) we can add further variables of attraction to the area of destination and of expulsion to the area of departure. However, the more variables that are added to the basic model, the more spurious it becomes and the more difficult it is to distinguish one from another.

As shown in Table 2.1, the migratory flows that seem to adapt better to such an interpretation are those for Spain, which show the highest Rsq (0.62).

Table 2.1. *Gravitational model*

Country	C	LFo	LFd	LDod	LDodSq	Rsq	n	F	Chow	T.Et.	LM
1 Portugal	7,105**	−10**	6.1**	−1,861**	121**	0.54	96	29**	6	10	69
	(4.8)	(−4.4)	(4.5)	(−4.8)	(4.8)						
1 Spain	6,336**	45**	22**	−1,716**	117**	0.62	144	61**	9	0.8	103
	(9.4)	(8)	(12)	(−9)	(−9.3)						
1 Greece	86**	4.2	2.7**	−10**	–	0.25	117	13**	5	26	99
	(5.3)	(1.5)	(2.3)	(−5)							
1 Italy	30**	0.5	0.18	−4**	–	0.37	166	33**	6	16	150
	(7.8)	(0.2)	(0.2)	(−12)							

C = constant,
Dependent variable: Emigration rate logarithm,
LFo = activity rate log of origin country, LFd = activity rate log of departure country,
LDod = distance from departure-destination country log, LDodSq = distance squared,
T.Et. = eteroschedasticity test of squared fitted values, Chow = test of constant parameters,
F = test of coefficients other than zero, LM = test of autocorrelation of residuals,
n = number of observations; t statistic of the corresponding variable in parentheses, ** 99% significant,
* 95% significant.

In an earlier work on Spain, Bianchi (1993) also got Rsq levels of around 50%. The chosen specification considers the log variable of distance (*LDod*), its square value (*LDodsq*), and the variable of attraction, which is made up of the logarithm of the activity rate in the country of origin (*LFo*) and the destination country (*LFd*). All the variables are significant, with the expected sign indicating that the effect of distance decreases as the distance between the country of origin and the destination increases, as is to be expected, and that the two poles of attraction are well represented by variations in the labor force. If economic variables, such as per-capita income, are included as factors of attraction and expulsion, the overall results are not improved. The economic variables are not significant even though they have the expected signs. The gravity variables – the coefficients and the significance – remain more or less unchanged.

In Portugal, too, the data seems to fit well to such a specification. All the variables are significant, and the distance and its square have the expected signs; the former is negative, and the latter is positive. However, the two "mass" variables – the rate of activity in the departure country and that in the destination country – are both significant; but the destination one is positive and the departure one is negative. The structure of the gravitational model is such as to expect positive signs for both variables, and a negative sign for the activity rate in the departure country suggests that these variables play an improper role as expulsion and attraction factors. If a dummy is inserted for the years 1960–73, it is significant and positive; the activity rate in the departure country has a positive sign, but it is not significant. This shows that the gravitational specification adopted does not correctly allow for the evolution of the migratory phenomenon in Portugal.[13] Such a specification would have been preferred if the 1960–73 dummy also allowed for the structural change of outward flows in the other empirical versions of Portuguese migration, but it does not.

Inserting the economic variables of attraction and repulsion as per-capita income in the destination and departure countries does not improve the results. The two variables are not significant, and both have positive signs without the signs for the gravitational variables being changed.

In the case of Greece, the very small Rsq shows that this interpretation does not clearly reflect the variations in the migratory phenomenon; the rates of activity in the destination and departure countries have the expected positive signs, but only the former is significant. The distance variable is significant and has the expected negative sign, but its square is not significant; in fact when it is introduced, the linear variable also becomes insignificant. This result is surprising because Greece is far from all the destination countries, and it would be logical to expect distance to exert a smaller effect once an emigrant is in continental Europe. However, this result probably can be explained by the fact that the migratory flow from Greece is concentrated in Germany, which is also the nearest country.

In this case, introducing economic variables of attraction and repulsion improves the regression Rsq, but the results are not as expected. Income in the departure and destination countries is significant, but the signs are the opposite of what was expected: positive for Greece and negative for the destination countries. The mass variable given by the activity rate in the country of origin is again not significant, but the sign changes. The signs for distance and activity rate in the destination country are significant and are as expected. Overall, therefore, the economic gravitational model does not offer acceptable results.

If the gravitational approach offers very little insight into the Greek case, it offers even less when applied to Italian emigration. Italian emigrants went initially east to France and then to Belgium, later to Germany, and finally

---

[13] This version would be preferred if the 1960–73 dummy had been introduced when the the other models of the phenomenon were specified.

	C	Lfo	LFd	LDod	LdodSq	D73	Rsq	F	n
1Po	6908	1.29	6.1	−1807	118	1.4	0.55	25	96
	(4.8)	(0.2)	(4.5)	(−4.8)	(4.8)	(1.9)			

to Switzerland only because it was outside the EU. The model performed poorly. In addition, Italian emigration has an older tradition than that of the other Mediterranean countries. In the period 1960 to 1973, flows into France decreased, and those into Germany and Switzerland increased – without, however, there being any clear geographic pattern. If the square of the distance is inserted, the variable changes sign and makes the mass variables significant, too, offering a contradictory interpretation of the phenomenon. In other words, this highlights the fact that the most important destinations are those farthest away. This is probable because such destinations offer better chances of getting an income. Similarly, if Sweden is excluded from the destination countries, the distance variable takes on a positive and significant sign, showing that distance does not allow for economic and cultural distance. Inserting a time dummy for the 1980s makes the coefficients more significant in this case, but not significant enough. Inserting an interactive dummy for the 1980s for the economic variables does not provide a better result, even though it reduces the significance of the dummy for the years 1980–88.

The variables of the basic gravitational model improve if we insert income in the departure and destination countries and their square. The activity rates in the two countries take on the role of proxies of the labor market as the coefficient of the activity rate in the departure country is negative and in the destination country is positive.[14]

The gravitational model, excluding Spain, is not really appropriate for analyzing mobility – or, more specifically, international mobility – in cases where historical and linguistic relationships are more important than geographic distance, and where immigration regulations and directly contracted labor mobility play an important role. This is also true for periods such as the 1970s, when some countries adopted restrictive immigration policies.

However, the biggest problem with this specification and estimate is that the mis-specification is revealed by the high correlation of residuals (*LM*), and corrections have been tried in two directions. The first, already described, is to insert economic variables, which can complete the model by supplying factors of attraction and expulsion; but this, as already stated, does not improve the results. A second correction is to insert lags into the explicative variables (of the basic model); but again in this case there are not

[14]

C	LLFI	LLFD	LYI	LYIsq	LYD	LYDsq	LDI	Rsq	F	n
91	−17	13	−106	6.8	160	−9.6	9	0.68	52	66
(−1)	(2.8)	(12)	(−2.4)	(2.5)	(8.2)	(−8.8)	(−23)			

any substantial improvements: The Rsqs increase slightly, and for Greece and Italy they are not more than 40%. The lagged variables are not often significant, as in the case of Portugal. Sometimes, they are the only ones that are significant, as is the case for Spain. On other occasions they have the opposite sign irrespective of whether the nonlagged variables are significant, as in the case of Greece and Italy. But above all, the residuals are still highly correlated.

2.6.2 The Economic Model (Human Capital)

The statistical tests are improved immediately when we pass from the gravitational model to the economic one. This is especially true for Rsq (excluding Portugal, where the same value is obtained), but this is due not so much to the economic variables as to the improved specification with fixed national effects. The distance variable in the gravitational model, which excludes the use of a fixed effects model, does not allow for such differences.

The specifications use the log of purchasing power per-capita income differential (*LDIF*) and a proxy for the labor market in the departure country (*Uo, Eo*) and in the destination country (*Ud, Ed*), where the level of unemployment and the rate of increase in employment are used, with the best specification being given for each country.

As mentioned earlier, we use the per-capita income variable instead of wages because, on the one hand, it is difficult to identify a typical wage level for all immigrants, and, on the other hand, many studies highlight how the standard of living in the destination area is the magnet for emigration. This choice was also made by T. Straubhaar (1988) in his analysis of the role of emigration to Germany and France from the Mediterranean countries. The choice of an actual variable of purchasing power parity, which can be compared internationally, does not allow researchers to test whether there is a monetary illusion effect. P. T. Pereira (1994), however, in his study of Portuguese emigration over the same period, was not able to find such an effect.

The results (Table 2.2) reveal the good performance of the labor market variables and per-capita wage differentials for all the countries considered, with two exceptions. In Portugal, the proxy variable for the domestic labor market trend – the rate of growth of employment – is not significant, and in Greece the proxy – the level of unemployment – is significant but does not have the expected sign.[15]

---

[15] Straubhaar (1988) had already found that the labor market variables for Greek emigration to Germany were not very significant.

Table 2.2. *Economic model of human capital*

	C	LDIF	Eo	Ed						Do	Db	Dg	Dsv	Rsq	n	F	Chow	TEt	LM
2Po	−1.8	2.2	.6	9.9						−3.1**		−1.2**	−2**	.54	96	19**	2.5	9	73
	(−1.3)	(1.8)	(.13)	(1.9)						(−5)		(−3.4)	(−3)	(−10)					
	C	LDIF	Uo	Ud						Do	Db	Dg	Dsv	Rsq	n	F			
2Sp	−1.3	3.2*	.05*	−.06*						−3.6**	−4.9**	0.3	−2.4**	.85	139	115**	6	13	77
	(−1.7)	(2.2)	(2)	(−9)						(−8)	(−10)	(.9)	(−3)						
	C	LDIF	Uo	Ed						Do	Db	Du	Dsv	Rsq	n	F			
2Gr	−.2	2	−.07**	6**						−4.2**	−3.3**	−3.7*	−4.2**	.86	117	105**	1.4	5.7	62
	(−.3)	(2.4)	(−3.6)	(2.3)						(−24)	(−16)	(−16)	(−22)						
	C	LDIF	LDIF80	Eo	Eo80	Ed	Ed80	D80	Df	Do	Db	Du	Dsv	Rsq	n	F			
2It	−.18	2.9**	−2.8**	−12**	10	11**	−10**	−.09	−.10	−4.2**	−2.7**	−5.4**	−1.9**	.96	166	343*	9	2.5	43
	(−.9)	(3.8)	(−3.3)	(−3.5)	(.7)	(3.9)	(−3)	(−.7)	(−.9)	(−47)	(−19)	(−49)	(−5.8)						

C = constant.
Dependent variable: Emigration rate logarithm.
LDIF = per-capita income differential log receiving country over country of origin, Eo, Ed = level of increase in employment in the receiving country and the country of origin, Uo, Ud = level of unemployment in receiving country and country of origin.
Do = dummy for Netherlands, Db = Belgium, Dsv = Switzerland, Df = France, Dg = Germans for Spain and Portugal, Du = Sweden for Greece and Italy.
The constant for Italy and Greece is Germany; for Spain and Portugal, France.
Statistics: Rsq, n = number of observations, F = test of coefficients other than zero, t statistic under the corresponding variable. TEt = heteroschedasticity test of squared fitted values; Chow = test of parameter constants, LM = test of autocorrelation residuals, ** significant at 99% and * significant at 95%.

From the beginning, we saw that different specifications were needed for Italy. The country was in a more advanced stage of emigration, and the interactive dummies turned out to be efficient, managing to neutralize the significance of the 1980s dummy.

The elasticity of the emigration rate related to the wage differential appears to be very similar in the four cases. It varies between 2 and 3%, and this means that if the per-capita income differential grows by 1%, there will be a 2–3% increase in the emigration rate. The coefficient for the growth rate of employment is greater than for the rate of unemployment, but this difference can be explained by the different units used for measuring the labor market variables. If employment in the destination country increases by 1%, the resulting increase in the emigration rate varies from 9% in Portugal to 6% in Greece to 11% in Italy; if the employment rate increases by 1%, emigration from Spain decreases by 0.06%.

The constant is not always significant, and it identifies France as the most important destination country for Spain and Portugal, and Germany for Greece and Italy. The dummies for other destinations are significant in most cases, and they can be identified as Do, the Netherlands; Db, Belgium; Dsv, Switzerland; Df, France; Dg, Germany for Spain and Portugal; and Du, Sweden for Greece and Italy. Statistical tests reveal the problems already mentioned: slight heteroschedasticity and auto-correlation of residuals.

To correct some of the uncertain specifications, definitions have been changed, and time dummies and lagged variables have been introduced. The specification, which uses the logarithm of the per-capita income in the departure country (*LYo*) and in the destination country (*LYd*) as the two variables instead of the differentials, gives worse results in all four cases. In the case of Portugal, the two variables are never significant; for Spain and Greece, wages in the departure country are not significant, whereas wages in the destination country are always significant but their sign is the opposite of what is expected.[16] In the Italian case, only the definition with interactive dummies for the 1980s gives results that conform to what the model predicts.

The introduction of a time variable dummy for the post-1974 period makes the results worse. The time dummies that identify a period during which there was a restrictive migratory policy are not often significant or are strongly interrelated with the variables for income or the labor market

---

[16] Straubhaar (1988) reveals that per-capita incomes in the destination and departure countries are not significant and that the differentials are significant. It is different for emigration from Italy and Greece, where the per-capita income for the departure country is significant but for the destination country it is not significant.

in the destination country. The reason is quite simply that when restrictive migratory policies are introduced at the beginning of an economic recession, the economic indicators in the destination country will have already identified a change in conditions.

Introducing interactive dummies for income variables for Spain, Greece, and Portugal does not improve the results.[17] The significance of the 1980s dummy in the Italian case shows how the economic model of migratory flows can be made significant. Interactive dummies have been inserted both for income differentials and for variable proxies for the growth of the labor market. The size of the coefficients of the income differentials shows that in the 1980s such an attraction factor has lost weight, as has also happened for the growth rate of employment in the destination country (Ed), whereas the growth rate in the departure country (Eo) kept its interpretative value in the 1980s. In the Italian case the level of unemployment did not prove to be a good proxy of the tensions in the labor market, probably because high unemployment is often limited to the least mobile workers.[18]

It is necessary, however, to acknowledge that in the Italian case, introducing dummies into the economic model improves the results. But it indicates that it is inadequate to interpret the dynamics of the migratory phenomenon, and extraeconomic elements are needed to understand what happens.

Finally, lagged economic variables were inserted, but they did not turn out to be significant in Italy or Spain. No variable is significant in Portugal, and in the case of Greece only the rate of growth of employment in the destination country is significant, but in all other cases there is still autocorrelation of residuals.

2.6.3 The Migratory Chain Model

As stated earlier, the empirical version of the model of the migratory chain considers the economic variables – which, however, are not considered sufficient – as well as a proxy variable of the migratory chain.

---

[17] In his study of Portugal, Pereira (1994) uses, for the country of origin and the destination country, two real income variables that are weighted for the probability of finding a job and interaction dummies for the post-1974 period. His findings show contradictory signs for the wage variables (weighted for the probability of finding a job). Wages in the area of origin are not significant until 1974 and then become significant, indicating a wealth effect, in which the higher wage allows individuals to finance migration. In the case of wages in the destination country (weighted for the probability of finding a job), the variable multiplied by the post-1974 dummy is not significant, and the coefficient is unique and positive. The specification also contains other expected wage variables for three periods and for the stock of immigrants.

[18] Introducing an interactive dummy for the 1980s does not improve the results of the gravitational model for Italy.

It is not easy to find a suitable proxy for the concept of a migratory chain. Previous debate suggests two lines of approach. One is to use *lagged dependent variables* (one or more years, or other combinations) and the *stock of foreigners* of the same nationality legally resident in the destination country. The following tests were carried out to settle some of these doubts.

The possibility of building a variable proxy of the migratory chain using lagged dependent variables was examined. A study of the lags concluded that in the case of Spain and Italy, only the dependent variable lagged one year is significant, and in Greece only the first and second lags are significant. In Portugal the second lag is often significant, but when it is significant, it has a negative sign.

This result means that a composite variable that excludes the first lag – so as to avoid being similar to traditional dynamic models – and adds various lags after the first lag gains more significance as fewer lags are added (the Rsq statistic and t increase). A similar result is obtained when lags are added to the lagged dependent variable only once. Such a result is to be expected because insignificant components are added to the variable.

Given the difficulty of building a migratory chain variable that does not contain the lagged dependent variable at least once, we attempted to identify to what degree the lagged dependent variable makes up a proxy of the lagged economic model or, instead, to what degree it is a proxy for the memory of the migratory phenomenon and therefore factors such as the migratory chain or others are not modeled.

Two models have been compared: a static economic model with a lagged dependent variable (1), and an economic model with lags (2). X represents all the economic variables that were used for the various countries in the specifications described earlier in Table 2.2.

1. $$(M/POP)t = \alpha_1 C + \beta_1 Xt + \gamma_1 (M/POP)_{t-1} + \epsilon_1$$

2. $$(M/POP)t = \alpha_2 C + \beta_2 Xt + \gamma_2 X_{t-1} + \epsilon_2$$

The J test used to compare "nonnested" models gives the expected results: Model 1 is preferred to model 2. The coefficient of fitted variables from model 2 (Fit2) inserted into model 1 turns out to be not significant, whereas the fitted variable from model 1 (Fit1) inserted into model 2 is always highly significant.

J test nonnested models	Portugal	Spain	Greece	Italy
t statistics of Fit2 in model 1	−0.3	1.7	0.36	0.6
t statistics of Fit1 in model 2	18	13	11.7	14.7

Such a result was to be expected because it was obvious that the lagged dependent variable was better and because coefficients of the lagged economic variables were not very significant. In the Portuguese case, the estimates for model 2 do not reveal any significant variables. In the Spanish case, the lagged variables were never significant and sometimes had the opposite sign of what was expected. It was the same for Italy, whereas for Greece only the lagged variable for the labor market in the departure country was significant.

The importance that should be given to the lagged dependent variable is crucial if the models are to be distinguished, and it appears that in the case being considered it can be stripped of its economic content and, there being no other specification, it can be used to interpret the migratory chain.

In addition, model 1 has been compared with the lagged gravitational model (3), where z identifies the variable in the base model. The J test suggests that model 1 is better and that the lagged dependent variable does not even represent a dynamic version of the gravity model.

3. $$(M/POP)t = \alpha_{3C} + \beta_3 Z_t + \gamma_3 Z_{t-1} + \epsilon_3$$

J test nonnested models	Portugal	Spain	Greece	Italy
t statistics of Fit3 in model 1	1.6	0.54	−1.6	−1.3

Now let's consider the *stock* variable. We have chosen the stock of foreigners (the foreign population) of the same nationality and not, for example, only workers. This is because the size of a community of origin in the destination country is a factor that can attract immigrants. It is a source of information, and it reduces the costs of making the choice to emigrate. Pereira (1994) used such a variable in his study of Portuguese emigration, and Antolin (1992) included it in his specification for Spanish emigrants returning home.

The stock variable is not simply a sum of entry flows because it is affected by the outward flows of immigrants returning home, moving to another country, acquiring the citizenship of the country in which they reside, and so on. There is less information available regarding the stock of resident foreigners than for other variables. There are 64 observations for Spain and Italy, 60 for Greece, and 45 for Portugal, compared with 114, 166, 117, and 96 for the other variables. Data about the stock of Spaniards in Belgium, Greeks in Sweden, and Italians and Portuguese in France are not available, so Germany replaced France as the constant.

The introduction of a variable representing the migratory chain (*MC*) into the economic model is anything but automatic because such a variable allows for autonomous dynamic factors, which can render redundant variables that were previously important or even indispensable to model the dynamism of migration.

The empirical test of the migratory chain model offers two specifications for each country of origin. The case of the lagged dependent variable will be examined first.

Lagged Dependent Variable

Introducing the lagged dependent variable improves the explicative powers of the economic model by causing the Rsqs to increase substantially. The coefficient of the lagged dependent variable is high, but except for the very high value (0.9) for Portugal, it settles at around 0.7.[19]

The income differential is significant in all the specifications. The variable for the rate of change of employment or the unemployment rate in the destination country is also significant. The proxy for the labor market in the departure country is not significant in the Greek case, and it is only slightly significant in Spain, Portugal, and Italy. In the Italian case an income dummy for the 1980s and an interactive income dummy for the 1980s have been introduced in order to get a satisfactory specification.

The introduction of a migratory chain variable changed the effects of the economic variables. If previously the elasticity of the income differential was very similar in the various countries, now it decreased to values near 1 in Italy, Greece, and Portugal. And in only one country, Spain, did it increase (to 4%).

The emigration rate is more responsive to changes in the labor market in the destination country in all versions. Where the coefficients can be compared, the coefficient is higher in Portugal and Greece, whereas in Italy and Spain the proxy variable for the labor market in the country of origin is not significant.

In the case of Portugal, both the constant (Germany) and the other fixed effects are not very significant. The constant in Greece is again Germany and is not significant, although the dummies for all the other destinations

---

[19] For the same period, P. Antolin (1992) analyzes Spanish emigration flows to Germany and France using a detailed specification in which he uses an index for house prices, the rate at which differentials change, the unemployment differential, disposable income differentials, the rate of change of unemployment in Germany and France, the level of interregional migration, and dependent variables lagged one period, which has a very low coefficient of 0.3.

are significant and are all negative. In Spain the constant is France, and it is significant, as is also the case for the dummies, which are all negative and significant (except for the one for Germany, which is not significant). In the case of Italy, the constant, Germany, is not significant, whereas all the others are significant and negative, except for France, which is positive and not very significant, indicating substantial differential effects. Inserting the 1960–74 dummy in the other cases does not improve the results and, in fact, the variables for the destination country are made worse.

A hypothesis that seems reasonable and must be tested empirically concerns the migratory phenomenon. Until 1974 it seemed to be driven by economic variables; then, after the economic recession, economic pressure to migrate decreased, and the migration phenomenon was driven by the migrant chain. A lagged dependent variable and its dummy were inserted into the specification, the dummy being the product of the variable itself with the value 0 until 1974 and 1 thereafter.

The introduction of this new dummy was expected to reduce the coefficient of the lagged dependent variable for the whole period, and to have a positive coefficient after 1974. The result was not what was expected in the cases of Spain and Portugal, for the dummy has a positive sign but is not significant. In the case of Greece it has a significant negative sign, and this suggests that the migratory chain plays a smaller role after 1974.

In the Italian case, a dummy for the 1980s was used, and it turned out to be positive and quite significant. In all cases the effect on the coefficient of the lagged dependent variable was very slight. It decreased in Greece (from 0.79 to 0.787), in Italy (from 0.75 to 0.73), and in Spain (from 0.77 to 0.68). In Portugal, where it was already very high, it increased (from 0.93 to 0.97), thus raising serious doubts about this interpretation.

The only country where the migratory chain explanation seems to be strengthened after the oil price increases is Italy, but it was so late in the migratory phase that it should be asked whether it reflects the phenomenon of family reunion more than the migration of workers.

Inserting the rate of lagged emigration also substantially improves the other economic specifications as we substitute per-capita income in the departure and destination countries for the differential. In the cases of Greece and Spain, income in the departure country, which previously was not significant and positive, and income in the destination country, which previously was negative and significant, are, instead, in this specification significant and have the expected signs. Among the labor market variables, the unemployment rate is not significant for Greece. In the case of Portugal, only the specification including the differentials is significant, both with and without the lagged dependent variables. In the Italian case, a dummy for the 1980s and an interactive term for income in the 1980s must be introduced into the specification with the two per-capita incomes, as was the case for the income differential case.

Above all, by including the lagged dependent variable, the statistical tests reveal the absence of autocorrelation and heteroschedasticity of residuals. The residuals remain not normal for Portugal and Italy. However, as is well known, the limited number of observations available does not justify the result being interpreted as relevant. The Chow test confirms that the coefficients are constant.

Stock of Foreign Population

Although the second specification of the migratory chain model is based on a lower number of observations, it performs better than the economic model alone. A square value was added to the stock variable, with the hypothesis that its effect decreases as the number of compatriots in the destination country increases and that there might be a level above which an increase in the number of compatriots can slow migration to that country.

Such a specification is more appropriate for the Portuguese[20] and Greek cases. In the Spanish case,[21] the square of the stock of foreigners is not significant, whereas for Italy no variable that represents the stock of foreigners is significant. The economic variables remain significant in all the specifications, except for the labor market proxy in the departure country, which is not significant in the cases of Portugal, Greece, and Italy. In the latter case, as before, interactive dummies were added for the 1980s. The version with the stock of foreign population in the destination country highlights the role played by the wage differential, which increases substantially in the cases of Portugal (7%) and Greece (5.2%); in Spain and Italy, the earlier values remain the same as in the earlier economic model.

Again in this specification of the migratory chain, the variable of the labor market in the destination country is more important than the corresponding variable in the departure country. It has a higher coefficient and is significant.

---

[20] Pereira (1994) also inserts the stock variable into the specification of emigration from Portugal. The multiplier dummy for the post-1974 variable is never significant, and the stock is significant only in the analysis of flows into France, contradicting the results shown in Table 2.3. This is probably because the author does not insert the square of the stock.

[21] Antolin (1992) introduces the stock variable only in the version of emigrants returning from Germany and France.

The fact that the coefficient of the stock is very small should not lead to a wrong conclusion about how important its effect is. The small size results from the high values that it assumes compared with the modest values of the emigration rates.

The introduction of the 1974 time dummy makes the results of the equation much worse. In the Spanish case it reduces the significance of the stock variable as well as alters the other income variables. And in Greece and Portugal, the significance of the destination variables is reduced.

Introducing stock variables into the other economic specifications, which include the two incomes of destination and origin, gives the same good results for Spain, Greece, and Italy. In fact, in the latter case, the stock variables are significant and have the expected signs for the level variable (positive) and for its square (negative). The income variables are accompanied by an interactive dummy for the 1980s. In the Portuguese case, only the specification with the differential is significant.

The high autocorrelation of the residuals in the specification for Portugal, Greece, and Italy raises many doubts. This indicates mis-specification but, above all, because the model with the lagged dependent variable performed well, it means that there is a lack of dynamics in this specification. It appears to be an extraeconomic and extragravity model but can be attributed to the migratory chain.

It is not possible to insert the lagged dependent variable into the model with the stock because different specifications of the migratory chain are being compared, but it is possible to try to insert a degree of economic dynamics into the specification with the stock.[22] Given the restricted number of observations for the stock of foreigners – in some cases only five observations are available – it has not been possible to insert more than one lag. The results, however, are not encouraging because the autocorrelation of the residuals is reduced, but not sufficiently in the cases of Greece and Portugal, where the lagged variables are not significant. The variable of the labor market in the destination country is an exception. The autocorrelation is reduced in Italy, where it was already low, but the stock variables are not significant and therefore the results cannot be attributed to such a model.

A specification was tried that included economic variables as well as the stock variable; its square lagged, but the results were similar. The reduction of the autocorrelation of the residuals by the insertion of lags leads to the conclusion that with a longer series, where more lags could be inserted,

---

[22] There is no gravitational approach in the literature that inserts the migratory chain explicitly. Because it is mainly a cross section, such a possibility was probably not considered.

better results would be obtained and they could be compared with the socioeconomic model, which includes a lagged dependent variable.

Comparing Two Specifications for the Departure Country

The limited amount of information available for the stock variable makes it difficult to compare various specifications for the same country of origin. Only in the case of Spain is the specification with the stock variable better than the one with the lagged dependent variable. In the Italian case, the lack of significance of the stock variables makes the former specification the only one worth considering.

The Spanish specification cannot easily be compared with the one used by Antolin (1992), even though it analyzes the same period, because it concentrates on Spanish emigration only to Germany and France. It also inserts variables, such as the level of interregional emigration and an index of house prices, which are not available for all countries. The employment differential and available income are two variables that are also in Antolin's study, and both have the expected signs.

Even if the lagged dependent variable is assigned to the migratory chain model, it is still a short-term, dynamic model in which the coefficients of the explicative variables are impact coefficients, in this case short-term elasticity. Long-term elasticity is obtained by dividing the coefficient by 1 minus the coefficient of the lagged dependent variable. A variation of 1% in the income differential in the short term produces an increase of 4.3% in the emigration rate, whereas in the long term, elasticity increases by about 14%. If the model with the stock identifies a long-term specification, the difference between the two elasticities would be very high – 14% compared with 3% – but the model with the stock incorporates a certain dynamic, even though it is less direct and clear-cut than that of the model with the lagged dependent variable. Thus, the comparison between the two specifications is not direct.

In the cases of the other countries, only the specification with the lagged dependent variable is acceptable. In the case of Greece, the two specifications show a not significant unemployment rate in the country of origin and a very high Rsq; but only in the first specification is there an absence of autocorrelation of residuals. In Greece and Italy, the long-term elasticity of the rate of emigration to variations in differentials is about 3%, returning to values similar to those of the static economic model (Table 2.3).

In the Portuguese case, the specification with the lagged dependent variable is much more significant than the one with the stock, and the level of employment in the country of origin has the expected sign and is more

Table 2.3. Migratory chain model

	C	LDIF	Eo	Ed	Lep(-1)	(other)	Do	Dg	Dsu	Dsv	Rsq	n	F	Chow	TEt	LM
3.1Po	-1.5 (1)	1.4** (3.6)	-3.2 (-1.8)	7.89** (3)	.93 (19)		-0.16 (-1)	-.07 (-0.5)		-0.15 (-1.4)	.94	92	239**	2.5	.34	.18
3.2Po	-10 (-3.3)	7.7* (2.6)	Eo 1.7 (.23)	Ed 8* (2.1)	Se .6e-4** (4)	Sesq -.28e-9* (-2)	Do .5 (.6)			Dsv -.5 (-1.1)	.63	45	11**	1.6	2.2	35
3.1Sp	-2.1 (-5)	4.3** (5.7)	Uo 0.02 (1.7)	Ud -0.16** (-2.9)	Les(-1) .7** (13)		Do -0.7** (-2.6)	Db -.7** (-1.8)	Dg -.05 (-0.4)	Dsv -1.8 (-4.7)	.94	139	283**	8	32	1
3.2Sp	-3.9 (-4)	3 (3.7)	Uo -.03 (-2)	Ud -0.17 (-1.9)	Se 0.11e-4* (2.4)		Do -5** (-7.6)	Dg -4.7** (-5)		Dsv -0.02 (-0.03)	.97	64	322**	7	20	2.3
3.1Gr	-.5 (2.3)	1** (2.9)	Uo -.5e-2 (-.4)	Ed 4.6* (2.7)	Leg(-1) .73** (13)		Do -1.1** (-4.7)	Db -.9** (-4.9)	Dsu -.9** (-4.7)	Dsv -1.2** (-4.2)	.97	112	553**	8	2.8	1.2
3.2Gr	-5.6 (-3)	5.2** (4.5)	Uo 0.02 (.7)	Ud -0.15** (-3.7)	Se 0.16e-4** (4.5)	Sesq -2e-10 (-3)	Do -.1 (-.1)	Db 0.8 (1.3)		Dsv -2.3** (-5)	.97	60	350**	8	.009	23
3.1It	0.7e-2 (.08)	0.9 (2)	Ldif80 -0.9 (-1.9)	Eo -3.7 (-1.6)	Ud -0.03 (-24)	Lei(-1) .76 (9.7); D80 .23 (1.6); Df 0.09 (1.6)	Do -0.9** (-2.9)	Db -0.5** (-3.6)	Dsu -1.3** (-3)	Dsv 0.67** (2.7)	.98	160	966**	8	1.4	2.9
3.2It	-.21 (-.05)	2.7 (2.7)	Ldif80 .42 (.59)	Eo -6.8 (-1.7)	Ud -.2 (-7)	Ud80 .08 (2); D80 -.02 (-.1); Sesq -0.45e-11 (-.4)	Do -3.3 (1.1)	Db -1.5 (-.5)	Dsu -5.3 (-28)	Dsv -3.2 (-13)	.97	64	250**	1.6	.31	11

C = constant,

Dependent variable: Emigration rate log

LDIF = per-capita income differential log in receiving country and country of origin; Eo, Ed = rate of increase of employment in country of origin and receiving country, Uo, Ud = level of unemployment in country of origin and receiving country, Lep(-1) = rate of lagged emigration in receiving country, Se = stock of foreign population in receiving country, Sesq its square.

Do = dummy for Netherlands, Db = Belgium, Dsv = Switzerland, Df = France, Dg = Germany for Spain and Portugal, Dsu = Sweden for Greece and Italy.

The constant for Italy and Greece is Germany; for Spain and Portugal, France.

Statistics: Rsq, n = number of observations, F = test for coefficients other than zero, and t bracketed statistic under the corresponding variable, TEt = heteroschedasticity test of squared fitted values; Chow = test of parameter constants, LM = test for autocorrelation residuals, ** significant at 99%, * significant at 95%.

significant. A direct comparison with the study carried out by Pereira (1994) is not possible. He introduced only the stock variable without its square, and it turns out to be significant only for migratory flows into France. The elasticity of the long-term income variables increases to about 14%, as in the case of Spain, but in this case the specification with the stock also gives very high values, even around 8%.

2.7 FINAL CONCLUSIONS AND IMPLICATIONS FOR THE FLOWS OF IMMIGRANTS TODAY

A comparison of the tests of the models reveals the weakness of the gravitational version, which, apart from the case of Spain, cannot take into account the dynamic of the migratory phenomenon in southern Europe. Such a weakness is not limited to the simple version of the model shown in Table 2.1; it is also found in both its combination with the economic and the socioeconomic models.

This weakness can be ascribed to the specification chosen – for example, the activity rate, which cannot take into account the physical idea of departure and destination mass. Furthermore, the traditional estimate of this model is achieved by using level variables and population standardization. These are adopted here to facilitate comparisons with the specifications of the other models, but they may be the cause of mis-specification.

The estimates adopted also differ from the traditional ones in the kind of data available. In fact, the cross section is dominated by the temporal dimension. The data used include five destinations and on average cover up to twenty-six years. In contrast, the empirical analysis that uses gravitational models generally presents a higher number of destinations but fewer annual observations.

Thus, the difficulty in reproducing previous results can be attributed to the length of the historical series and to strong time effects. The introduction of time dummies does not, however, improve the results of the basic variables in the gravitational model, which remain either nonsignificant or have the wrong sign.[23]

The economic interpretation shows in all simplicity that it can account for the migration dynamics of the south of Europe,[24] but it also reveals a degree

---

[23] The estimated gravitational model in version b – that is, in levels and with the variables of population on the right – presents a repeated negative sign for the population of the departure country even after temporal dummies have been introduced.

[24] J. Hunt (2000) used a simple interpretation based on an expected income differential to explain migration between East and West Germany.

of mis-specification that cannot be eliminated. The results also highlight that only the income differential can explain the high percentage of the flows between European countries and that the more complex interpretation described in the initial overview must in all the cases start from this empirical fact.

Various specifications were used, including the replacement of income differentials with the two incomes of the countries of destination and origin as well as various labor market variables. The specifications therefore show the best economic and statistical results.

The socioeconomic specification that adds the lagged dependent variable, as a migratory chain, to the economic specification described earlier provides better results. The kinds of proxies used to interpret the migratory chain can raise some doubts. The temptation to attribute all the significance of the migratory chain to the lagged emigration rate seems especially risky.

Furthermore, a comparison of the trends of the two proxies – stock and flows – seems to indicate that the two variables tend to go in the opposite direction. In fact, the stock variable also increases when flows of new immigrants decrease, even if the net flow is positive, whereas the rate of lagged emigration decreases and is affected by the downward or cyclical trend of immigration flows. It therefore tends to go in the opposite direction of the stock variable. The lagged emigration rate can also be seen as a proxy of a behavior that, as is well known, becomes habitual and repeated by other compatriots, at a lower psychological and economic cost. The underlying idea of a migratory chain is the idea of an active nucleus, which favors the exchange of information and helps migration, but it is not clear which of the two variables mentioned earlier accounts better for this concept. The results obtained, however, show that the socioeconomic explanation dominates the others presented earlier and the additional economic-gravitational version and the socioeconomic and gravitational model.

The variables of income differentials and of labor market changes in the departure or destination countries are significant and have the expected signs. The variable proxy of the migratory chain is also significant and has the expected sign, with the exception of the stock of Italian workers.

The results suggest that in the socioeconomic version there is a Todaro-like specification with the expected wage in the receiving country and the known wage in the departure country. It should be remembered that in the Todaro model the probability of getting a job in the departure area is equal to 1. Such a result was obtained by Straubhaar (1988) for the same countries even though the specifications used merged the components into a single variable.

Similar relationships were also found by Hatton and Williamson (1994) in their study of Italian emigration at the turn of the century, and by Hatton (1995) in his study of English emigration in the nineteenth century. Hatton gets better results by using separate variables than by using variables combined into a single index.

Institutional factors, such as the restrictive immigration policies introduced in 1974 in the northern European countries, do not seem to have had an autonomous effect on migration. The dummy introduced is not significant because the change in the trend is well identified in the receiving country by such variables as the product and the unemployment rate.

Eventually the policy of family reunion is more significant. It conditions the size of the migratory chain; in fact, it influences both the estimated stock of earlier emigrants and the lagged dependent variable, and it identifies a dynamic in the migratory phenomenon that is independent of labor market changes.

As was highlighted in section 2.6.2, the expected income differential does not necessarily have to be interpreted in its strictest sense. Instead, it can be seen as a development differential and can therefore have many causes, not least of which can be the lack of local employment. From this point of view, these results can be a tool for interpreting actual emigration to the southern European countries in which the per-capita income is three to five times as high as in the departure countries. Even though they often have a high level of unemployment, it is compared with countries where the level of employment is very low, but above all where detailed information about rural unemployment is not available.

Emigration seems to be inevitable in the medium term. It is not influenced by distance, which, as can be seen from the limited significance of such variables in the analysis of emigration from the southern European countries, is the same as a fixed effect. Instead, emigration is influenced by the migratory chain. This makes it difficult for destination countries to manage immigration by applying only economic priorities because there will be a positive flow even when expected income differentials decrease.

3

The Effects of Immigration on the
Receiving Country

This chapter concentrates on the welcome and unwelcome effects of immigration on the labor market and economy of the receiving country. We do not rehash the well-worn discussion of immigrant integration and assimilation, mentioning it only marginally in the wider context of the economic effects immigrants can have. We start with a survey of the main theoretical and empirical results derived from studies conducted in the United States and Europe, presenting, where available, results for the southern European countries. Special attention is given to the question of complementarity or substitution between groups of workers. Empirical evidence from the United States, Canada, Australia, and northern Europe is used to interpret the southern European cases and is compared to the limited research available for these countries. The aim is to assess the impact of illegal as well as legal immigrants on native wage and employment growth.

3.1 AN OVERVIEW OF MODELS BY MAIN THEMES

Four main lines of approach can be identified. The first analyzes the role played by foreigners in the labor market (complementarity or substitution), and the second studies how foreigners integrate into the structure of wages and jobs. The third examines the contribution of immigrants to economic growth in the receiving country, and the fourth tries to assess the impact immigrants have on social expenditure.

These four approaches are exclusively economic, and they should be integrated with analyses of the demographic consequences of immigration. Demographic changes affect an economic system deeply.

3.1.1 Complementarity or Competition

The first approach brings together studies that analyze the effect foreign workers have on the labor market through their impact on wages and on levels of native employment. The debate on this theme, which has an important influence on the kind of migratory policy a country tends to adopt, is characterized by conflicting and emotional stances. Supporters of competition argue as if there were a given number of jobs in an economy, and they assume that foreigners cannot create any growth in labor demand. In contrast, the supporters of complementarity assume that there is a clear segmentation between foreigners and natives and that no competition can arise. The impact of immigration can also be affected by changes in the business cycle, by periods of excess demand or excess supply, and by the contrasting effects of reduced wage growth and reduced inflation, the latter of which can be beneficial to natives, too.

The passionate discussion of hypothetical reactions of the labor market can go on forever, but economic theory is unequivocal on this point. Immigrant workers are defined as being *competitive,* or *substitutes,* when they have a negative effect on wages or native employment levels of both. They are defined as *complementary,* when the effect is positive.

Before we consider various models for representing the effect of immigrants on the labor market, it is important to specify the various categories to be considered at risk. The larger body of theoretical and empirical economic literature deals with competition or complementarity between natives and foreigners working regularly in the formal labor market with similar or different skill levels (cases A and B in Figure 3.1). The first model we will discuss illustrates how the labor market functions in the first case, assuming a standard neoclassical labor market without trade unions. The second case (Schmidt, Stilz, and Zimmermann 1994) explicitly models possible trade union behavior. Very little research deals explicitly with the competition between irregular foreign employment and regular native employment (case C in Figure 3.1). An exception is the Dell'Aringa and Neri study (1987) presented later. This issue deserves a lot of attention in the southern European countries, where irregular forms of work are more common than in other areas and where competition between natives and foreigners can also take place in the informal economy (case D in Figure 3.1), thus aggravating the poverty of already poor workers.[1] U.S. literature stresses the role played by

---

[1] The theoretical reference model for the analysis of case D is the traditional neoclassical model, presented later.

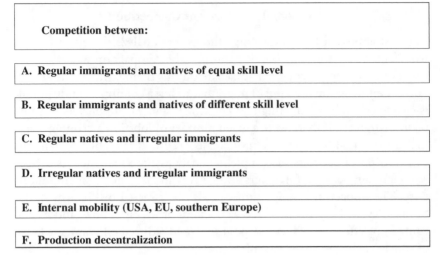

Figure 3.1. Competition or complementarity by categories

the internal mobility of natives as insurance against wage reduction induced by immigrants. In contrast, in Europe, and in particular in southern European countries, immigrants going into areas of high wages and high labor demand can displace the internal mobility of natives from low-wage and high-unemployment areas (case E in Figure 3.1) or can discourage the decentralization of production to high-unemployment areas in the country (case F in Figure 3.1), thus playing a competitive role. Very little research has been done on these last two issues relevant to the longer term, especially in Europe.

The most quoted model for analyzing the effect of immigrants on the native labor market is the neoclassicical model, where wages and employment are perfectly flexible. Its behavior is shown in Figure 3.2.

An increase in the supply of labor in a labor market that employs workers i, foreign labor being homogeneous, produces a decrease in the equilibrium wage only if the supply of labor is rigid (Figure 3.2b). If the supply of labor is elastic to wages, both wages and employment will decrease (Figure 3.2a). Native employment levels ONi decrease after immigration to ONi' because workers are discouraged from working by the decrease in real wages. There are similar results if the growth in supply is followed by or induces a demand shift of a smaller amount, so that the equilibrium variables are reduced (point A'' in Figure 3.2c and 3.2d).

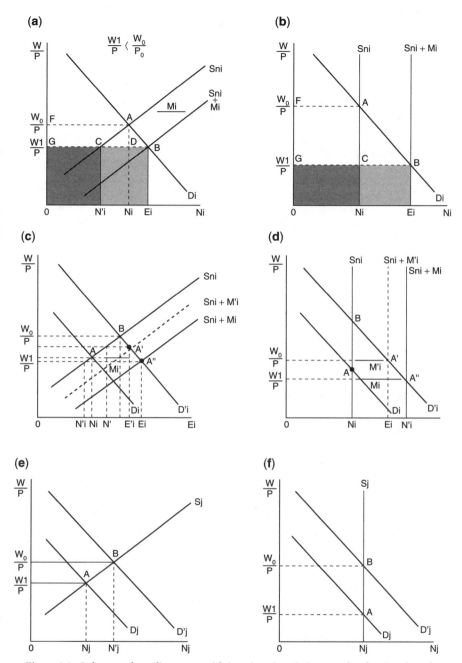

Figure 3.2. Labor market adjustment with immigration. Sni = supply of national workers of quality, i,Mi = number of immigrants of quality i, Di = Demand for labor of
quality i, W/P = real wage, W_0 > W1 monetary wage, Ni = native employment before
immigration, Ei, E'i = total employment after immigration, N'i, N''i = native emplyment
after immigration, Sj = supply of natives of quality j, different from i, OFANi − OGCN'i =
welfare loss by natives, section (a)

The more rigid the labor supply, the larger the decrease in wages and the smaller the decrease in employment; the more rigid the demand for labor, the greater the decrease in wages and the greater the number of workers displaced. However, if the demand[2] increases more than supply due to immigration, there is a complementary relationship, with an increase in both wages (point A′ in Figure 3.2d) and employment (point A′ in Figure 3.2c, which passes from ONi to Oni'; the increase is $NiNi'$).

Complementarity is found especially between the nonhomogeneous factors of production. For example, where the growth of Mi induces an increase in the demand of factor j, and depending on the characteristics of the supply, there will be an increase in both wages (Figure 3.2f) and employment (Figure 3.2 and $Nj' - Nj$).

Although this is a reasonable description of the workings of the market in the U.S. case, it is of little help in describing the European labor markets, where strong trade unions play a major role in wage determination and where both wage and employment flexibility are limited. Klaus Zimmermann in a series of theoretical studies – with Schmidt, Stilz (1994), and alone (1995), and with Bauer (1997)[3] – develops a working model of the labor market that assumes a monopolistic trade union; a labor supply made up of native skilled workers ($S°$) and unskilled workers ($N°$), the latter being homogeneous with the foreigners (M); and a quota of immigrants fixed by the government. The economic system produces only one good and is characterized by a production function for capital, skilled labor (S), and unskilled labour (L), with constant returns to scale. The output price is given, and the two factors of labor are q complementary, as in the standard case. The native workers offer a fixed amount of two kinds of labor. The immigrants (M) do not bring capital with them, and they do not influence the aggregate demand of the economy. A monopolistic trade union fixes wages (W^L) in the labor market for unskilled workers, and entrepreneurs determine the employment level; in the market for skilled workers (W^S), market forces determine the equilibrium wage.

The author suggests two cases: one where immigrants are perfect substitutes for unskilled workers (N), and a second where they can also replace

---

[2] The increase in demand either can be exogenous or can be induced by new employment.

[3] Bauer and Zimmermann in their study dated 1997 used a different specification of the trade union's utility function, which is expressed as a function of skilled and unskilled workers' wages. The results are, however, similar to those found in the neoclassical model. In the case of unskilled worker immigrants, the effect on wages and employment is negative. In contrast, in the case of skilled worker immigrants the effect on unskilled wages is uncertain, but for reasonable values of elasticity a negative sign prevails, whereas the effect on the employment of unskilled workers is positive.

skilled workers (S). In the first case, the employed unskilled native workers account for a share g of the total of unskilled workers: $N = gL$, where $g = N°/(N° + M°)$.

The trade union has an objective function in which there is the weighting δ for skilled workers' wages (W^S) and for employed unskilled workers' wages (W^L), and the weighting ϕ for unemployed unskilled workers $NU = (N° - gL)$ who receive unemployment benefits z.

$$MAX_{w^L} \Omega = \delta w^s \overline{S} + (w^L - z)gL + zN° + \frac{\phi}{2}(N° - gL)^2 \tag{1}$$

Where $\overline{S}$ and $N°$ indicate the values of skilled and unskilled native workers, respectively.

Profit maximization for the firm implies that wages are equal to the marginal productivity of labor, which in linear form is given by the following equation:

$$\overline{w^L} = a^L - b^L L + c\overline{S}; \quad w^s = a^s - b^s \overline{S} + cL, \quad dove \ a^2, a^L, b^s, b^L > 0 \tag{2}$$

Where the wage W^L is determined by the trade union and c identifies the degree of complementarity of the two factors.

From the first-order condition the following equation is obtained:

$$L - \frac{1}{b^L} W^L + \frac{1}{b^L} z - \frac{\phi}{b^L}(N° - gL) - \frac{\delta c \overline{S}}{g b^L} = 0 \tag{3}$$

From this it is found that the relationship between immigration and the changes in unskilled workers' wages is negative, and that pushes the unskilled labor market toward a competitive equilibrium. The link between increased immigration and unemployment is uncertain, and it depends on the degree of complementarity between the factors of production and the weights given by the trade union to the components of its utility function.

Because the link between unskilled workers' wages W^L and the number of immigrants M has the opposite sign of the link between W^L and g (the number of employed unskilled natives), the authors decided to investigate the latter relationship:

$$\frac{dw^L}{dg} = \frac{\frac{\delta}{g}c\overline{S} + \phi L}{2 + \phi \frac{1}{b^L}} > 0 \tag{4}$$

$$\frac{dNU}{dg} = \frac{\delta c \overline{S} - 2Lb^L}{2b^L} \approx 0 \tag{5}$$

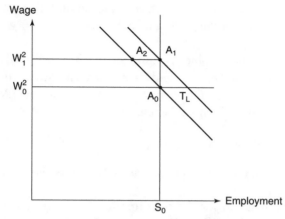

Figure 3.3a. Effect of unskilled immigration on the skilled labor market

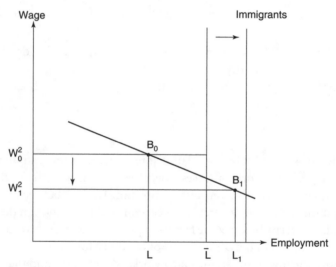

Figure 3.3b. Effect of unskilled immigration on the unskilled labor market

This result is shown graphically in Figure 3.3. The trade union has fixed a wage (W_0^L) for unskilled workers that is higher than the equilibrium level, resulting in a level of unemployment ($\overline{L} - L$). The entry of a number of unskilled immigrants (a quota fixed by the government) who compete with the natives forces the trade union to revise the market wage downward. This action brings the unskilled labor market to a more competitive equilibrium, with an increase in employment L_1, and this also has a positive effect on the

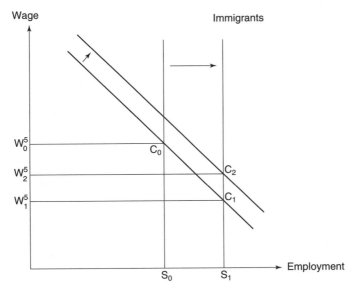

Figure 3.3c. Effect of skilled immigration on the skilled labor market

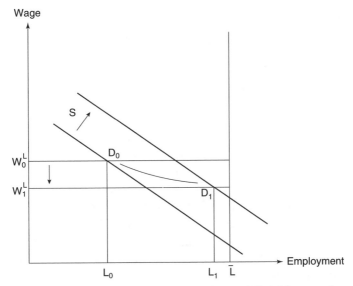

Figure 3.3d. Effect of skilled immigration on the unskilled labor market. *Source:* Zimmermann (1994)

employment of natives. Furthermore, given the complementarity between unskilled work, and skilled work, there will be an increase in skilled workers' wages.

The final effect on the employment and unemployment of unskilled natives can be positive or negative, depending on the weights that the trade unions assign to the components of the utility function. In the case described, the new equilibrium B_1 identifies the case of a decrease in native unemployment.

In the second case, when some of the immigrants are skilled workers (*SM*) who are similar to skilled native workers, skilled workers' wages will decrease because they are determined in a competitive market. It is uncertain how their presence will affect unskilled workers' wages because this depends on the weights that the trade unions give to skilled workers' wages and the number of unemployed natives. Instead, where there is complementarity between the two factors of production, the effect on the unemployment of unskilled workers is negative.

$$\frac{dw^L}{dSM} = \frac{c\left(g + \phi\frac{g^2}{b^L} - \delta\right)}{2g + d/b^L} \approx 0 \tag{6}$$

$$\frac{dNU}{dSM} = -\frac{gc}{b^L}\left[g + \frac{\phi}{b^L}(1 - g^2) + \delta\right] < 0 \tag{7}$$

Such a model is interesting because it explicitly introduces the role of the trade unions. The results depend crucially on certain hypotheses, such as the supply of labor being inelastic to wages. Because the number of immigrants is a quota established by the government, the trade unions are forced to reduce unskilled workers' wages more than would be necessary to absorb the same number of unemployed native workers.

Another interesting case, especially relevant to the southern European countries, is described in an article by Dell'Aringa and Neri (1987). Competition is expressed through the movement of capital from the official sector (*u*) to the informal sector (*i*). Because the substitution takes place through capital, this can be called *indirect competition*, or *indirect complementarity*.

The authors assume that there is only one good (*Q*) in the economic system, part of which is produced in the official sector (*u*) and the rest produced in the informal sector (*i*). Neither the firms nor the workers pay taxes, and therefore labor costs are lower. In sector *u*, capital (*Ku*) is used and skilled workers (*Lu*) are employed; in sector *i*, unskilled workers (*Li*), made up of native and immigrant workers, are used. The functions of production in the two sectors show constant returns to scale, but the returns in sector i are less efficient (the parameter c represents an efficiency parameter, which is inversely correlated to the risk of the informal firm that is identified).

$$Qu = Fu(Ku, Lu) \qquad Qi = Fi(Ki, Li) = cFu \quad (0 < c < 1) \qquad (8)$$

Wages in the official sector are fixed exogenously (w_u°) at such a level as to create an excess demand for labor in that sector. The firm maximizes profits when marginal productivity is equal to factor costs ($dFu/dLu = w_u^\circ$, $dFu/dKu = r$, $dFi/dLi = wi/c$, r cost of capital). In the case of wages in the official sector, factor costs are exogenous and in the informal sector are related to parameter c.

Adding the two conditions of full employment $K = Ku + Ki$ and $L = Lu + Li$, it is possible to identify the optimum combinations of capital and labor in the two sectors ($ku^* = Ku^*/Lu^*$ and $ki^* = Ki^*/Li^*$). There is a necessary and sufficient condition so that there is a positive solution for Lu^* and Li^* and that the following is true:

$$Ku^* > k > ki^*$$

That is, because the first is an increasing function of wages w_u° and the latter is an increasing function of c, it is necessary for wu^* to be sufficiently large and c sufficiently small. The previous condition can be rewritten substituting ku^* with the parameter m – which is function of wage w_u^* and of the parameters of the production function – and ki^* with tm, where t, which is less than 1, is a parameter whose value depends on c and on the parameters of the production function. The rewritten condition becomes $m > k > tm$.

At this point it is possible to calculate the equilibrium level of employment in the official sector Lu^* and in the informal sector Li^*. Employment in the official sector will therefore be equal to the following:

$$Lu^* = (K - tmL)/m(1 - t) \qquad (9)$$

It is now possible to find the derivative of the changes to the total labor force:

$$dLu^*/dL = -t/(1 - t) < o \qquad (10)$$

This means that an increase in immigration causes not only an increase in employment in the informal sector but also a decrease in employment in the official sector.

An increase in capital or a reduction in labor, ceteris paribus, makes it more convenient for firms to produce in the more efficient sector where the intensity of capital is greater. The opposite occurs if capital is reduced or if the number of workers willing to work in the informal sector increases.

As shown in these models, complementarity and substitution between workers can be caused by extremely different types and trends in the labor market. Not knowing a priori the behavior of the domestic labor market, the only way to settle the age-old dispute concerning the role played by immigrants is to empirically test the relationship between the factors of production.

In fact, most literature on this topic is concerned with empirical research. The direction of the empirical literature is two-pronged: Either a traditional production function is tested in order to compute the cross-factor elasticity, or, more frequently, the number or the share of foreign workers is included among the explicative variables that identify the causes of changes in the levels of employment and wages for natives using cross-area or cross-sector information.

The research began with the cases of the United States, Australia, and Canada (Abowd and Freeman 1991; Borjas 1990; Borjas and Freeman 1992), which attempted to test theoretical models using cities, metropolitan areas, or productive sectors as closed labor markets in which employment and wages were influenced by the share of foreign workers. A detailed description and analysis of the empirical results is presented in section 3.2. In the meantime, we simply mention that for various reasons complementarity dominates the relationship between foreigners and natives. In early research, Borjas (1990) found that in the United States the effect of immigration on native wages is positive or nil; it is negative and significant only for early immigrants, and this is because they are the ones who are replaced by new immigrants. Similar results were found for Canada and Australia. In Europe, less homogeneous results are found.

The only study with a primarily empirical approach, which we would like to introduce at this stage is the one carried out by Gang and Rivera-Batiz (1994). The authors overcame one of the limits of the traditional empirical studies, which ignore skill differentials in areas or sectors, by splitting the contribution made by workers into three components – labor, human capital, and experience – and using special data supplied in a survey made by Eurobarometro of the EU; it is assumed that the individual's wage i (Wi) is made up of his or her offer of physical labor (ru) plus a return for education (Edi) and experience (Exi).

$$W_1 = r\,u + r\,e\,Edi + r\,x\,Exi \qquad (11)$$

Where *re* and *rx* identify the return for education and experience in the
market. An individual without education and experience on the job will
earn only *ru*, whereas the other workers will receive a higher wage. The
rates of return are equal to the marginal productivity of each single factor,
given an aggregate production function ($Y = F(Le, Lx, Lo)$, where *Le*, *Lx*,
and *Lo* represent the supply of education, experience, and physical labor,
respectively). This function has the traditional neoclassical characteristics,
and therefore

$$r_u = \delta F / \delta L_u; \qquad r_e = \delta F / \delta L_e; \qquad r_x = \delta F / \delta L_x \qquad (12)$$

Dividing immigrants according to their human capital, it is possible to
measure the effect they have on the returns of each earning component and
their ultimate effect on the natives' earnings:

$$Ln(Wi) = bo + brEdi + bxExi + ui$$

The model includes two hypotheses: First, the factors of production are
assumed to be exogenous to each labor market, and therefore there is no
internal migration. Second, the factors of production other than labor –
capital, for example – are weakly separable from labor and so can be ignored.
Using the available data for European countries on wages, education, and
experience, the authors estimate the rates of return and get the price elasticity
of factor K with respect to a change in input J. If this price elasticity is
negative, it indicates substitutability between the two factors; if it is positive,
it indicates complementarity between them. They also get the price elasticity
of the factor with respect to its change.

$$\varepsilon_{kj} = \frac{dLnr_k}{dLnL_j} \qquad \varepsilon_{kk} = \frac{dLnr_k}{dLnL_k} \qquad (13)$$

The empirical results show that education is complementary to experience and to unskilled work, whereas unskilled work and experience are
substitutes. A 1% growth in unskilled labor in Europe leads to an increase in
the return to education of 0.10 and a decrease in the return to experience of
0.75. Choosing a sample of native workers with a combination of productive
inputs, it is possible to calculate the composite elasticity of complementarity
for different groups of immigrants who are supplied with different productive inputs. The results obtained show that complementarity is prevalent,
and there are few cases of substitutability – that is, negative cross elasticity –
and such cases are limited to those of native workers whose earnings are
based only on returns to experience.

3.1.2 Wage Assimilation

Another topic that is well researched and has been debated widely is the issue of *wage assimilation* for foreign immigrants in the receiving country. This issue is important because it is linked to the overall assessment of immigrants' success and their impact on social expenditure. The more successful immigrants are in the labor market, the larger their contribution to economic growth will be and the smaller will be their cost to the welfare system, making them a positive element in the receiving country.

In the case of the United States, the debate centers on the work of Barry Chiswick, George Borjas, R. LaLonde, and R. Topel, but there are many other relevant contributions.

The estimated equation uses as explanatory variables for the wages of workers (i): a vector of socioeconomic characteristics Xi, the worker's age as a proxy of experience Ai, a dummy Ii, which specifies whether the worker is an immigrant, and a variable yi, which indicates the number of years the worker has been resident in the destination country, which is of course 0 for natives.

$$\text{Log} Wi = Xia + b1Ai + b2Ai^2 + g^\circ Ii + g'yi + g''yi^2 + \epsilon i \qquad (14)$$

In his pioneering work (1978), Chiswick used a cross section drawn only from one census. He identified a negative coefficient for g° – which indicates the percentage difference between immigrants and natives at the time of arrival – and a positive coefficient for g' – which identifies the rate at which wages grow with respect to those of the natives – while a negative g'' shows an increase at a decreasing rate. The conclusion tended to support an "overassimilation" of immigrants, in that, in the short term they are able to catch up with and overtake corresponding natives. This result was not attributed to the lack of specific human capital in the receiving country at the time of arrival but rather to the fact that these people have a greater propensity to risk and possess more human capital, two factors that came to the fore over time.

Borjas (1985) reached a different conclusion. Using two censuses, he showed that the different wage structures of two cohorts can be missed in a single cross-section analysis, whereas a longitudinal analysis reveals a phenomenon of "underassimilation" (which can be attributed to the lower quality of the most recent cohorts) and therefore a higher g° and a lower g'. The different *quality* of cohorts at the time of immigration is imputed to various factors: changes in immigration policy to admit individuals with different characteristics, and different economic conditions in the destination country, which changes the national mix of the immigrants and thus causes changes in the productivity of the workers. The quality of cohorts can also depend on changes in the composition of the cohorts due to non-casual repatriation.

Finally, LaLonde and Topel (1992) report similar results to those of Borjas (underassimilation of foreigners and a lower g'), but they attribute this not to the lower quality of the cohorts but to worse economic conditions in the receiving country at the time when the foreigner entered the labor market, offering his or her labor at a lower entry wage (negative g^o) and having few career prospects (a lower wage pattern g'). The debate is ongoing, with new specifications and tests being introduced.

From an analytical point of view the problem is well known in labor literature. Building the pattern of wages in the life cycle using census data poses numerous problems of specification.

$$W_{it} = X_{it}\beta_t + \varepsilon it; \qquad \varepsilon_{it} = a_{it} + b_{it} + u_i \qquad (15)$$

The wage of an individual who belongs to the arrival cohort i in the year of the census $t(wit)$ is a function of a limited number of individual variables: Xit and the error ε. The latter is made up of three components: ait, the vintage factor, that is, the average value of human capital specific to the receiving country and accumulated by the cohort (i) on arrival; bit, the time factor, that is, changes in the labor market that have various effects on a foreign worker's human capital on arrival; and ui, the cohort factor, that is, the average value of the quality of the cohort, which is fixed for each given arrival cohort.

Using longitudinal data would simplify the problem because it would eliminate the error due to various qualities of cohorts. However, in the U.S. case and in many other panels, foreigners are undersampled or are not chosen in a random way. Thus, it has become the custom to build cohorts using census data, and this creates the problems of specification that we have mentioned.

With precise assumptions and specifications, it is possible to estimate the degree of assimilation of foreigners. In the studies by LaLonde and Topel, this does not reveal that the quality of the immigrants is getting worse but rather that the economic conditions are getting worse, causing the immigrants to have a lower wage pattern. More specifically, such an assimilation analysis suggests that the longer individuals live in the United States, the higher their wages will be and the closer their wage patterns will be to that of the natives who have the same characteristics. It is not possible to identify the different kinds of error in an analysis of only one year, but with two periods of reference the estimated error is as follows:

$$\varepsilon_{55,t} - \varepsilon_{65,t} = a_{55,t} - a_{65,t} + b_{55,t} - b_{65,t} + u_{55} - u_{65} \tag{16}$$

The estimate is correct if there is no time factor between the two cohorts ($E(b_{55,t} - b_{65,t}) = 0$) – a solution adopted in Borjas 1985 – and if there is no difference in terms of the average values of the quality of the worker ($E(u_{55} - u_{65}) = 0$) in the cohorts. If the quality of the worker decreases or if transitory changes reduce the new immigrant's wages, the assimilation of the foreigner will be over- or underestimated. LaLonde and Topel abandoned the use of cross-section estimates to create a quasi panel in order to follow the growth of wages of the immigrant cohorts from 1970 to 1980. It was indexed to a group of natives, and, using other simplifying assumptions, it was possible to specify the time component.[4]

The debate is not yet over. Daneshvary et al. (1992), for example, show how investment in knowledge and looking for work increases the wage that the worker manages to get and how it varies from one ethnic group to another. Chiswick (1991) shows how important the knowledge of written English is for wage assimilation. In the case of Canada, Baker and Benjamin (1994) come to the traditional conclusion that there are permanent differences between immigrant cohorts, and Bloom, Grenier, and Gunderson (1995) emphasize that the new immigration policy and the recession of the 1980s were the causes of the reduced assimilation of the most recent immigrants.

The debate in Europe is less heated because the studies are limited and extremely heterogeneous. Bevelander and Scott (1996) offer evidence that suggests that the case of Sweden can be interpreted in a similar way to that proposed by LaLonde and Topel. Using data from the 1970 and 1980 censuses and testing for the level of education, Bevelander and Scott show that the lower wage assimilation of foreigners – the inability of the more recent immigrants to reach 90–100% of the national wage within five years – can be attributed to the changed economic conditions in the receiving country.

Recent work by Rosholm, Scott, and Husted (2000) found in both Sweden and Denmark that from 1985 to 1995 the number of job opportunities for male immigrants decreased. However, these authors used a panel of administrative data showing that the worsening situation was independent of the different market trends in the two countries. Rather, it was caused

---

[4] For details see La Londe and Topel (1992), pp. 76–7.

by the structural changes taking place in the markets, where the demand was for workers with high interrelationship and communication abilities, something that placed immigrants at a disadvantage. In another study involving only Denmark and again using administrative data covering the same period and testing a random effect model on foreign wages, Neilson et al. (2001) found that a foreigner's job assimilation increases not with the number of years in the country but the number of years worked in the country, thus emphasizing that a worker increases human capital only when working.

The work of Penninx, Schoorl and van Praag (1994) highlights in the Dutch case two perverse effects that reduce a foreigner's ability to assimilate and to achieve wage integration after the mid-1970s. The slowdown in the national business cycle made it difficult to absorb new immigrants in general (a decrease in demand) and in particular the different kind of immigrant – not in terms of quality (meant as human capital) but in terms of being political refugees or family members joining their kin. This new kind of immigration transforms it from labor migration to residential migration. Again, Kee (1994), in the Dutch case, estimates that one of the causes of the lack of assimilation is that few immigrants continue their studies in the receiving country. Niesing, van Praag, and Veenman (1994) analyze the causes of the higher levels – two or three times as high – of unemployment among foreigners, who in 1988 represented 5.1% of the population. This high rate can be traced to three factors. The first factor, which explains half of the higher unemployment, is the different personal characteristics of the individuals; the second and the third factors, which share the remaining half, are the different individual patterns of supply and demand (discrimination).[5]

In a study of England, Chiswick (1980), using data taken from the General Household Survey of 1972, found little difference between the incomes of white foreigners and those of comparable white natives, whereas black foreigners earned 25% less than natives. The difference in wages increased with the number of years of education. The fact that most foreigners came from the Commonwealth meant that experience before emigration was more or less the same as in the receiving country.

The only controversial situation is the case of Germany. The empirical study carried out by Dustmann (1993) uses the individual data panel of

---

[5] The authors' estimates show that discrimination is much greater against Mediterranean immigrants than against immigrants from Antilles and Suriname. But if the latter lose their jobs, they have little chance of getting another one.

GSOEP and shows lower earnings for foreign workers during all their working life and traces this finding to the temporary nature of the migratory
flow. This conclusion is contradicted by an analysis of the same dataset by
Schmidt (1993), which shows that a foreign worker's earnings are equal to
a native worker's earnings after seventeen years. Pischke (1993) finds that
there is no difference in the rate at which incomes grow between foreigners
and natives in comparable jobs, even though foreigners never reach the same
wage level as natives.

The different findings depend on the reference group with which the
foreigners are compared. Because Dustmann uses all natives, white-collar
and blue-collar workers, the lack of convergence can be explained by the low
skills of the foreigners. However, the small number of recent immigrants in
the sample makes it difficult to study wage trends.

Mackay and White (1995) studied a theme, wage segregation, that is
dear to English researchers. The authors built a wage segregation index
for England in 1987. It revealed very little ethnic variability, but it varied
inversely to education, unemployment, and gender.

Granier and Marciano (1975) examined the case of France using data
from the 1968 census in a descriptive way. They reached static conclusions,
suggesting that the lower average wage for foreigners with a nuclear family is caused mainly by less investment in human capital, and this varies
substantially according to ethnic group.

For the southern European countries very little research exists on this
subject because the immigration phenomenon is recent. However, Venturini
and Villosio (1999; 2000; 2002a, b, c) studied the Italian case using an administrative dataset (INPS). Unfortunately, these data do not cover employment in the domestic services and in agriculture, but they represent about
70% of total regularly employed foreigners. The authors studied the dynamic of native–foreign wage differentials and turnover rates. In 1990–96
the average wage differential between natives and foreigners is 1.15 (log 0.13),
much lower than the gender wage differential, as usual.[6] The construction
of a specific variable – years of presence in the dataset (which proxies the
years of regular presence in the country) – improves the results and brings
the explained part due to the different characteristics of the two groups to
80%. It also contributes to a reduction of the wage differential over time. The
analysis by ethnic group shows that employers value potential productivity,
offering a wage premium (a negative wage differential) to foreigners who

---

[6] Using the same dataset Bonjour and Pacelli (1998) calculate a log gender differential of 0.225,
only 25% explained by the different characteristics of the labor force.

have average higher education and productivity (for example, Rumanians). These variables are missing in the dataset but are captured by the individual wage. In the same way, the turnover rate of foreigners decreases sharply after the second year of formal employment, stressing how regular foreign workers are economically integrated and how rapidly they assimilate into the wage and employment patterns of natives.[7] This positive result is probably induced by the evolution of the Italian immigration policy. Repeated amnesty provisions (legalizations) legalized only those workers who were already trained in the informal economy and in the culture of the destination country and thus found it easier to integrate.

From this brief survey of the main empirical results of wage and employment assimilation of foreigners, it is possible to conclude that assimilation depends on the average human capital of the group of immigrants, whether "group" refers to a cohort or to a country of origin. It also depends on the economic growth of the labor market in the destination area as well as on structural changes in the labor market, which can penalize the ability of the immigrants. Assimilation increases with actual work experience, not merely with longer residence in the receiving country or – in southern European labor markets where a black market is common – with informal employment.

3.1.3 Impact on Economic Growth

The third approach considers the impact of immigration on economic growth. The idea that the foreign labor force can represent the engine for economic growth is based on studies carried out in the 1950s and 1960s. It is sufficient to remember the famous work by A. W. Lewis (1954), where

---

[7] In the Italian case there are two very interesting local studies. The first one focuses on the gender differential among foreigners (Strozza, Gallo, and Grillo 2002), and the second on regular–irregular wage differentials (Baldacci, Inglese, and Strozza 1999). The first research uses a survey dataset that is much more informative than the administrative one used in the Venturini and Villosio work but is limited to foreigners. It includes important information, such as years of education, proficiency in the Italian language, and the number of relatives. Taking all this information into account, the log wage gender differential is 0.182 for Moroccans, 0.341 for former Yugoslavs, and 0.288 for Poles. It is higher than in the native–foreigners case shown before but is very similar to the native gender wage differential mentioned earlier. In addition, the different national employment behavior is reproduced in the male–female differential: In the former Yugoslav and Polish groups, the wage differential is caused mainly by differences in human capital; the unexplained part is about 10%, whereas, in the Moroccan case, the differential is totally unexplained.

The second research uses another dataset: the results of survey conducted in 1993–4 of foreign immigrants in two regions (Latium and Campania) with a much larger number of ethnic groups. Baldacci et al. (1999) estimate the legal–illegal wage differential, which results in log 0.246 for male and 0.192 for female immigrants in both cases, indicating lower earnings from illegal work.

migration from low-wage sectors to high-wage sectors not only brings relative wages into line but also favors the growth of output, through higher profits. C. Kindelberger (1967) interprets economic growth after the war as being the fruit of an infinite supply of immigrants in a situation of overemployment. V. Lutz (1961) also thinks economic growth derives from the transfer of productive resources from less productive sectors to more productive areas.

The problem has always been seen and analyzed in the context of links between population and economic growth and therefore the impact of population on the rate of accumulation and technological progress. The work quoted by Tapinos and de Rugy (1993) regarding the United States, Australia, and Canada[8] provides positive results, but they are of a limited number and are attributed exclusively to economies of scale and market expansion. The debate is often based on arguments that are difficult to test. For example, Simon (1989) argues that one of the many positive aspects of scattered migration is the positive impact of a multiethnic society on technological innovation.

The studies that analyze the impact of immigration on per-capita income adopt it as the only measure of the well-being of the native population. This does not necessarily imply a decrease in income for natives if foreigners' per-capita income is lower than that of natives.

In Europe before the mid-1970s, there was a consensus regarding the effect of immigration on economic growth in the receiving country (Garson and Tapinos 1981), but subsequent empirical studies have raised a number of doubts. The case of Switzerland, a country that has always exercised strict control over immigration, reveals that the output elasticity of the labor force is lower for foreigners (0.10) than for natives (0.46) (Butare and Favarger 1995). This means that foreigners have a positive impact on the growth of income but not on per-capita income.

To discuss clearly the impact of immigration, it is necessary to bear in mind the links that exist between the productive system and the level of human capital of foreign workers. Few studies manage to deal with these two aspects together. Solow's growth model is elaborated in a version proposed by Lucas (1988), which explicitly takes into account the growth of human capital and makes it possible to analyze the impact of immigration on the growth rate of the receiving country. The conclusions reached in the literature (Dolado, Goria, and Ichino 1994) converge in identifying a positive

---

[8] It has been impossible to trace the study of Mayer (1990), quoted by Tapinos and Rugy in their review (p. 165). See also the work of Swan et al. (1991) and Simon (1989).

effect on the growth of per-capita income in the receiving country if the foreigner's human capital is higher than the native's, and vice versa if it is lower.

The economy has a production function in which human capital is inserted explicitly,[9] where Y represents the level of output, H is human capital, and L is the total working population (natives plus net immigrants $L_o + M$), whose productivity increases at rate g.

$$Y = H^a (L e^{gt})^{1-a} \quad 0 < a < 1 \tag{17}$$

The total number of effective workers increases because the population, made up of natives and net immigrants, increases, and also because of the technological growth incorporated in that population.

Human capital in turn increases in relation to the share of output (s) invested, plus the share (b) of the existing stock of human capital introduced by each immigrant. Human capital is reduced by the rate of depreciation (d).

$$\dot{H} = sY - dH + bM\frac{H}{L} = sY - dH + mbH \quad \text{where} \quad m = M/L \tag{18}$$

$$y = h^a = \left(\frac{H}{L}\right)^a = \left(\frac{H_o + Mb\dfrac{H_o}{L_o}}{L_o + M}\right)^a \tag{19}$$

Using lowercase letters for the units of labor results in the following:

$$y = h^a; \; y = \frac{Y}{L_e^{gt}}; \; h = \frac{H}{L_e^{gt}} \tag{20}$$

Thus, the effect of net immigration will be positive or negative if b, the share of human capital brought by immigrants, is $\gtrless 1$.

$$\delta y/\delta M = \frac{a h^{a-1}}{L^2} H_o(b - 1) \quad > o < 0 \tag{21}$$

From this it follows that for a given value of b, more immigration will make the current level of per-capita income increase (or decrease) if b is more (or less) than 1.

The authors estimate the equilibrium value of the stationary state of the parameters for a sample of twenty-three OECD countries from 1960

---

[9] Solow's model, augmented by immigration, has been used. See also Mankiw, Romer, and Weil (1992).

to 1985, getting an estimated value for b of between 1.41 and 0.72. This value is similar to the values obtained for some European countries, with the expected effect of a decrease in per-capita income. Because the immigration flow was exogenous and using the parameters of the model, the authors estimate the effect of immigration on growth. According to the model, an increase of one per thousand in the net migratory flow decreases the equilibrium per-capita income in the stationary state by 1.5% and decreases current income by 0.04%. This outcome, however, is less than the negative impact of population growth on the growth of per-capita GNP.

The theoretical model used to analyze the impact of immigration on a country's growth can be extended to analyze the impact of emigration on a country of origin, and thus it is possible to study how population movements lead to convergence. The theory is that growth in the departure area is favored by the emigration of workers with few skills, whereas the rate of growth in the area of immigration is decreased by workers with few skills, thereby converging the rate of growth and the rate of per-capita income in the two areas (see, for example, Goria and Ichino 1994 and Piras 1995 for Italian regions). Taylor and Williamson (1994) have written an interesting article that assesses the role played by immigration in the United States from 1870 to 1913 – specifically, whether it was a factor that made the incomes of the countries of immigration converge with those of the countries of emigration.

Another particularly interesting article, which treats the topic only in theoretical terms, was written by Davies and Wooton (1992). The authors analyze the effect of the international migration of workers on the distribution of income in the departure country and in the receiving country. This study overturns the traditional assumption that the migration of unskilled individuals reduces the difference in incomes in the departure country and increases it in the receiving country. As in the case of the migration of skilled workers, the authors question the assumption that the variance of the distribution of income in the receiving country is reduced and in the departure country is increased. The authors show that the migration of unskilled workers can have a twofold effect, and they show that although the movement of skilled workers can reduce inequalities in income in the departure country, differences can increase in the receiving country.

Sarris and Zografakis (1999) and Ferri, Gomez-Plana, and Martin-Montaner (2000) analyze Greece and Spain, respectively, adopting a computable general economic equilibrium model and using the most recent data. They consider the effect of immigration on the well-being (income) of the population and find that families maintained by unskilled workers became poorer.

3.1.4 Impact on Social Expenditure

A fourth line of research concentrates on measuring the impact of foreigners on social expenditure. This approach is often reduced to an attempt to supply an overall estimate of the costs and benefits of immigration. Simon (1989) pursues ten lines of inquiry so as to analyze the whole problem correctly. Unfortunately, some of his findings cannot be tested. For example, the impact of immigration on technological innovation is assumed to be positive because a multiethnic society is more willing to adopt innovation.

The more limited field of the effect of immigration on social expenditure has produced numerous theoretical studies and a few empirical ones on specific topics, such as fiscal contributions, the payment of pensions, health contributions, and the use of health services. However, the cross-section analysis that is generally used is not suitable for analyzing an issue that has a life cycle dimension. Errors due to different composition and different quality of the cohorts (vintage and cohort errors) can influence the results.

George Borjas (1995b) used longitudinal data for the United States in a series of empirical studies on this topic. In his 1995 study he used data from the 1970, 1980, and 1990 censuses and showed that foreigners took advantage of welfare programs less than their native counterparts during the initial and final stages of their lives. But this pattern changes with later immigration flows. The turning point is reached when immigrants make greater use of welfare services at all stages of life. Immigrants such as political refugees take advantage of welfare programs more than other working immigrants, and their growth in numbers in the past few years has certainly weighed on the aggregate results: Immigrants account for 8% of the population but 10.1% to 13.1% of social assistance.

In a later paper Borjas and Hilton (1996) used the Survey of Income Programme Participation (SIPP), showing greater differences between groups of immigrants in their use of welfare programs. In part, we can impute the differences to the fact that information about such programs is filtered through the reference community. Most recently Borjas (1999a, 1999b) using data from the 1980 to 1990 Public Use Microdata Sample of the U.S. censuses, concentrates on the possibility that welfare can determine, if not the choice to migrate, at least the choice of where to settle. That is, the immigrants who use welfare more were concentrated in the areas where the benefits were more generous.

From these studies, it is not possible to draw any conclusions for the European case. There are three problems:

- The welfare programs differ – that is, they provide different social guarantees and systems of organization of such guarantees for native citizens.
- Access to welfare differs between natives and foreigners – that is, the extension of the social rights of citizens to immigrants is applied differently in different countries.
- The use of welfare differs and is strongly conditioned by the different reference communities.

Initially, European migration was mostly temporary migration from the south to the north and involved workers who returned to the departure country before they had become vested in a pension but after they had paid some contributions. The possibility of capitalizing a pension and cashing it out when they return home has canceled this kind of benefit for the budget of the country of destination and has made it necessary to analyze what use is made of social services by immigrants in their old age or by their families. The different rates of unemployment and the use of available services by ethnic groups – often greater among the most recent immigrants – lead to the conclusion that lower-skilled immigrants are attracted not only by job market opportunities but also by income subsidies.

Staubhaar and Weber (1994) reviewed the empirical results of studies of costs, taxes, benefits, and transfers made by the state to foreigners.[10] Direct comparisons between countries are almost impossible because different statistical and fiscal definitions mean that items of expenditure are grouped in different ways. However, the conclusion reached in this research, as shown in the summary in Table 3.1,[11] is that immigration does not necessarily have a negative effect on public finances. In fact, in most cases it is neutral or doubtful, and in some cases it is positive.

The results of case studies in Europe are very limited; the studies of Germany and Switzerland are highlighted in Table 3.1. Detailed inquiries have been made into the use of unemployment payments in other countries, such as in the Netherlands and in northern Europe, but these studies are directed more toward examining the unemployment differentials

---

[10] Interesting results regarding the United States, Australia, and Canada are developed in the work by Tapinos and de Rugy (1993, pp. 169–70).

[11] Table 3.1 is taken from the work quoted by Staubhaar and Weber (1994) and has been integrated with recent work quoted by Tapinos and de Rugy (1993), which, however, has not been examined directly because a complete bibliographic reference was not available.

Table 3.1. *Empirical research on the distributional effects of public transfers between immigrants and natives*

Author	Budget positions analyzed	Area of analysis	Transfer effect for the natives
Simon (1984)	Taxes and public transfer payments	United States	Positive
Blau (1984)	Benefits from public welfare and social security programs	United States	Neutral
Muller and Espenshade (1985)	Tax payments and use of public social programs	United States	Neutral
Tienda and Jensen (1986), Jensen and Tienda (1988), Jensen (1988)	Use of public social programs	United States	No general statement possible
Weintraub (1984)	Tax payments and use of public services	State of Texas and its biggest cities	State level: positive City level: negative
Akbari (1989)	Taxes and public transfer payments	Canada	Positive
Kakwani (1986)	Taxes and public transfer payments	Australia	Positive
Whiteford (1991)[a]	Taxes and pensions Other social security benefits	Australia	Positive
Miegel (1984), Wehrmann (1989)	Use of public social programs	Germany	Negative
Ulrich (1992)	Taxes and public transfer payments	Germany	No general statement possible
Wadensjö (1973), Ekberg (1983)	Taxes and public transfer payments	Sweden	Positive
Gustafsson (1981)[a]	Use of public welfare programs	Sweden	Negative
Gustafsson (1990)	Taxes and public transfer payments	Sweden	Neutral
Weber (1993)	Total of monetary and real public transfers	Switzerland	Positive

[a] Unfortunately, these two researches do not have complete bibliographical references in the Tapinos and Weber article.

Source: Straubhaar and Weber (1994), p. 120, and Tapinos and de Rugy (1993), p. 169

between foreigners and natives than the differentials in contribution to social expenditure. Thus, no definite conclusions can be drawn on the issue.

Straubhaar and Weber (1994) try to estimate the impact of foreigners on the Swiss fiscal system using a special inquiry into consumption in 1990. They include, on the income side, payments to the public budget in direct and indirect taxes as well as social payments and contributions for the use of public goods and club goods (education, public health, protection of the environment, etc.). On the expenditure side, the study includes direct transfers to firms and the use of public goods and club goods.

The budget impact turns out to be largely positive for the Swiss government, which received a net transfer per family of about $1,743 in the year under examination. Given the number of foreign resident families, there is a net gain of about $464 million for the Swiss government. The authors conclude that the optimum level of immigration has not been reached in that country, and there is still the possibility of new flows. This result can be attributed in part to the selective immigration policy, which is such that the rate of unemployment of immigrants is higher than for natives, but about 1%.

Migration in Europe also changed a lot in the 1990s, with the immigration from eastern Europe and large inflows of political refugees. Thus, previous results no longer hold because of changes in the nature of immigration itself. Recent research has focused on Germany. The work of R. Riphahn (1998), Fertig and Schmidt (2001), and Bird, Kaiser, and Frick (2001) fundamentally show that immigrants are more welfare dependent because their individual characteristics – lower education, larger families, lower age of the household head – and their lower labor market performance compared with those of natives increase their use of welfare.

Recent research carried out by two teams – one European and one from the United States – tried to reach conclusions about immigration and welfare (Boeri, McCornick, and Hanson, eds., 2002). In the European case they use the information of the European household panel to single out foreigners' welfare dependency. Unfortunately the data do not cover all issues, but the authors did test in ten European[12] countries whether non-EU immigrants have higher predictable dependency than EU natives on unemployment and family benefits. The results are positive in all the countries, with a stronger dependency ratio, for example, for family benefits in the Netherlands, the United Kingdom, France, and Austria. Even if the dataset is unique, it is not

---

[12] Denmark, the Netherlands, Belgium, France, the United Kingdom, Greece, Spain, Portugal, Austria, and Finland.

sufficient to detect welfare shopping by the immigrants at the European level; for the southern European countries, the recent waves of immigrants are probably not sufficiently sampled in the dataset. Thus, no final conclusion can be drawn from these cases.

In the U.S. case, the debate and the research are much more advanced. The results show that the average fiscal impact of immigration is negligible, but the federal government gains from immigration. Many programs used by immigrants are financed at the state level, and because immigrants are negative net contributors to the cost of these programs, some states must bear larger costs. Illegal immigration is an important part of the U.S. research, but very little is said on illegal immigrants' use of public utilities and social services. In contrast, this issue is important in the southern European countries even if its impact on the cost of welfare is likely to be small.

Attempts to analyze the impact of immigration on social expenditure in southern European countries are only now beginning because migration is still a recent phenomenon. Census data are not available to replicate the U.S. study, and there are no longitudinal datasets that can be used to follow the economic integration of foreigners. In these countries, however, the cost of immigration is augmented by the pressures of clandestine foreigners. Illegal entry must be prevented by coastal and land patrols, and illegal foreigners who have already entered the country and have been detected after a stay at a reception center must be expelled, and these policies are all costly for government budgets. The stay of illegal immigrants is a further cost because they use health and welfare services, even if in a limited way. Little can be learned from other European studies about such costs because attention has been concentrated on the impact of legal immigrants.

3.1.5 Effects on the Native Population and on Pension Fund Accounts

Immigration policy is determined not only by economic and political factors but also by demographic factors. Examples are the migrations around 1900 and after the Second World War (Gesano 1994) and, even earlier, the French migratory policy. The French have always had an active demographic policy in that France has always tried to ensure that its army was equal to that of its neighboring enemy, Germany. Immigration represented an alternative source of population growth to native births, allowing the size of the cohorts to be kept under control.

Immigration and emigration today have lost their specific demographic connotation, and economic and political factors have come to the fore.

However, the impact of immigration on the population of the receiving country can still be very important.

The demographic effect of migration depends on the demographic structure of the receiving country and on the way foreigners settle there. The demographic characteristics of the population of the receiving country are influenced by the presence of foreigners because of their effect on the early cohorts, their distribution between genders, and their initial high level of fertility. The effect is much more relevant when it is concentrated in age groups. An example drawn from the history of migration in Italy (Golini 1978) emphasizes that at the end of the large internal migration, the inward flows caused the population of the 20–64 age group to increase by 68% in Turin, whereas the same age group decreased by 40% in Molise.

The study led by Tribalat et al. (1991) reveals that after 100 years of immigration in France, from a demographic point of view, the average age of the male population decreased by 1.3 years and for women by 0.8 years. A study carried out in the Netherlands by Penninx, et al. (1994) showed a decrease in the average age of 0.6 years, and the share of over-65s fell by 0.4 percentage points (Gesano 1994).

Interest in the effect of immigration on the generational composition of the population of the receiving country is no longer primarily demographic but economic. The receiving countries are mainly countries with decreasing fertility, and therefore the size of cohorts of working-age young people is smaller than the size of cohorts of people of retirement age. In industrialized countries, most pension funds are financed on a pay-as-you-go basis – that is, contributions that are paid into the current budget are used to pay current pensions. Therefore, the number of people of pensionable age must be proportionate to the size of the population that contributes to the fund.

As life expectancy in the receiving country increases, there is the risk that the number of pensioners and people of pensionable age will exceed the number of those making contributions. Thus, immigration that is made up of young people whose fertility rate is higher than that of the natives represents a way to increase both the number and the growth rate of the actual population.

From a demographic point of view, the equilibrium of the age cohorts is reached when the population reaches the stationary state. Many studies have been carried out to discover whether immigration can counter aging and a decrease in population caused by a fertility rate that is lower than the *substitution* level – that is, able to maintain the population constant and with the same pattern of age cohorts.

To ensure a constant rate of population growth equal to 1%, the study of Wattelar and Roumans (1991), quoted in Gesano (1994), shows that Canada – a country whose population is not very old – should accept much higher net flows of immigration than the current average: about 500,000 per year until 2050. In the European case, the research of Lesthaeghe, Page, and Surkyn (1991) shows that flows of immigrants should be about one million per year, a figure that is higher than the highest annual level yet recorded.

If instead the aim is to counter the aging of the population with new cohorts of young people so as to maintain the dependence ratio constant – that is, maintain the ratio between the population of working age and those over 65 (the optimum value is 3) – then many inward flows are necessary. Such immigration would cause the initial population to double over sixty years and would create an autonomous demand for new inflows to counter the aging of the immigrants themselves. If instead the aim is to maintain the share of the population of working age, 20–59, constant, there would have to be a relevant growth of population, although less than in the preceding example; but again in this case there would be wide fluctuations.

Admitting immigrants (net of immigrants who return home and emigrants) at a constant rate seems to be the only way, in the long term, that the average age of the population can be lowered in the receiving country without upsetting the preexisting equilibrium. In the case of Italy, Gesano (1994) estimates that the number of immigrants necessary for Italy to have a stationary population is equal to 30% of the native population. This rate of immigration would lead to a maximum population of 69 million in 2039, with a net annual flow of 389,000 immigrants. Smaller inflows would lead to a stationary population, but at a later date. The alternative choice, which is to have a fixed rate of immigration (5.2–5.3%), would lead to slightly smaller flows, and a stationary state would be reached much later.[13]

Using a generational account approach, Coda (2001) writes that in Italy the positive impact of immigration can reduce the public budget deficit by 8%, but that if structural reforms are not introduced, the annual number of immigrants necessary to make up the deficit is the impossible figure of one million. However, the most interesting result that emerges is that temporary

[13] Many of these exercises assume that the fertility of foreigners is the same as that of the natives, but, as is well known, this assumption is not realistic and makes it difficult to forecast the impact of immigration flows. The demographic effect of immigration tends to be underestimated, and the inflows necessary to maintain a stationary population are overestimated.

migration is less attractive than permanent migration because the positive contribution of an immigrant's fertility would be lost.[14] Using a similar methodology in Spain, Callodo, Iturbe-Ormaetxe, and Valera (2002) reach a similar conclusion, although their use of the European socioeconomic panel dataset to build the age consumption profiles is risky given the limited sampling of the survey. In addition, the authors do not specify the interest rate at which the process is discounted, something that probably justifies a more positive presentation of the immigration effect on the national budget.

As Blanchet (1988) emphasizes, immigration policies aimed at bringing the age structure of a population back into equilibrium in the short term create the need for more substantial corrective measures in the long term. There are no short-term solutions, and the best strategy is to adopt a fixed rate aimed at establishing a stable rate in the long term.[15]

3.2 COMPLEMENTARITY AND SUBSTITUTION: EMPIRICAL EVIDENCE

Much attention is devoted to the issue of the competition or complementarity of immigrants in the destination labor market. The debate in the southern European countries is concentrated on this issue, and immigration policy is constantly being revised.

Before we investigate this issue, we must remember that the empirical studies of European countries are limited and difficult to compare. We therefore start by examining the results of studies carried out in the United States, Canada, and Australia so that we can assess the methodological problems and the dynamics, which determine the results, before we consider the cases of northern and southern Europe.

3.2.1 Comparing the United States, Canada, Australia, and Northern Europe

As mentioned previously, there is a big difference between the theoretical approaches to complementarity and substitution of natives and immigrants

---

[14] The assumptions that condition the results can be seen in the study. The same methodology was adopted by Sartor (1997), who also studied the Italian case.

[15] Zlotnik (1981) and OECD (1991) reviewed the models used to estimate the effects of various patterns of migratory flows on the population of the receiving country and discussed the difficulty in identifying the optimum flow that would keep the worker/pensioner ratio constant.

as compared with empirical tests of these phenomena. Most empirical studies – for example, those of the United States – analyze the impact of immigrants on the local (or sector) labor market.[16] They assume closed markets and use a cross-section study among areas (or sectors) where the intensity of immigration varies. Therefore, it is possible to calculate an elasticity between the number of immigrants (or the quota of immigrants) and wages (or employment of native workers divided into homogeneous groups – native whites, young native whites, black natives, young black natives, Hispanic natives, Asian natives – depending on the various studies). The very first study by J. B. Grossman (1982) analyzed the impact of immigrants on employment and wages of three groups of workers: natives, native children (second-generation immigrants born in the United States), and immigrant workers already in the United States. This work reveals that the effects are very weak. An increase of 1% in the number of immigrants led to a decrease in the wages of natives of 0.1%, the wages of the second-generation immigrants decreased by 0.08%, and the earnings of immigrant workers already in the country decreased by 0.23% (the number of natives employed decreased by 0.1%, and the employment of second-generation immigrants decreased by 0.04%). The "new" immigrants hardly competed with the natives, but they clearly competed with the immigrants already in the country because the two groups are more homogeneous. Changes in capital do not seem to affect the results because all the factors of production are complementary.[17] However, these results reveal a common limit to most studies on this topic: They do not allow for differences in "average skills" between natives and foreigners in different areas (or sectors).

Later studies by Borjas (1985, 1987, 1990) reach similar conclusions. Particularly in the work of 1986, Borjas analyzes the effect of different kinds of demand for labor on the results in a cross-section estimate. He finds few differences. However, the time analysis, which uses two censuses, reveals a larger impact than a pure cross-section analysis does. Similar results are found in other studies – for example, the work of Briggs and Tienda (1984), where immigrant workers are complementary to all classes of workers, and competition comes from the women's labor force. Similar complementarity between immigrants emerges from the study by Muller and Espenshade (1985). In this case it is between Mexican and black workers,

---

[16] Borjas (1994) in footnote 30 emphasizes that, in sector and labor market studies, there is no structural interpretation because workers as well as firms can move among sectors and areas.

[17] This result is often contradicted in theoretical models and by some empirical studies.

and surprisingly they are the group of workers who seem to gain most from immigration.[18]

More specific studies of groups of workers who are more at risk show similar results. LaLonde and Topel (1992) analyze the impact that a 1% increase in the number of foreign workers in an area or sector would have on young native workers. The authors find that the annual wages of young Hispanic workers would decrease by 0.2%, and the annual wages of young blacks would decrease by 0.6%.

Similarly, Altonji and Card (1991) find that the effect of immigrants on the employment of low-skilled natives is slight, whereas the impact on their wages varies between −0.3 and −1.2%, depending on the specifications used. These results have been challenged by Borjas (1994) on the grounds that the instrumental variables used were not really appropriate and so should show higher levels. However, the effects are still modest.

The effect of immigration seems particularly reduced if we consider the exceptional emigration of Cubans in September 1980 following Fidel Castro's announcement that anyone who wanted to emigrate to the United States could do so freely from Mariel port. This emigration represented a 7% growth in the labor force of Miami.[19] And as Card (1990) shows, the effect on natives' wages and employment was not significant, and the evolution of wages and employment in Miami was not different from that of cities that did not have any immigration.

Furthermore, illegal immigration does not seem to have a negative effect on workers. Bean, Lowell, and Taylor (1988) assume that Mexican immigrants after 1975 entered illegally, and the authors estimate the effect of this illegal immigration on various groups of workers. The results show that there was no competition even with Mexican immigrants who arrived before 1975, the group that would more easily be competitive than the other groups of workers.

The studies of Canada and Australia are less numerous but tend to reach the same conclusions. The study directed by Swan (1991) for the Economic Council of Canada analyzes only the effect of immigration on unemployment, which seems to be nil. The authors also report a series of results of estimates of aggregate econometric models (p. 56), which forecast that if the labor force increases there will be a corresponding growth of unemployment equal to one-half or one-third of the growth of the labor force. In the case being examined, such empirical evidence could be interpreted

---

[18] For another survey of empirical results regarding complementarity and substitution, see Tapinos and de Rugy (1993) and Borjas (1994).

[19] In the space of a few months, the labor force of Miami increased by 125,000 unskilled workers.

as demonstrating that it is the growth in immigration that induces growth in unemployment. Swan and the other authors of the report are skeptical of such an interpretation because it is not specified who becomes unemployed, and especially because the positive links between immigration and unemployment were not confirmed. On the one hand, the authors emphasize a neoclassical interpretation of the labor market. On the other hand, they draw attention to the importance of a selective immigration policy to improve the way the labor market functions.

In Withers's study of Australia (1986), a survey of the empirical tests on the effects of immigration provide similar results, showing a lack of competition between foreigners and natives with respect to employment and wages both in the short term and in the long term.

In short, the available empirical evidence shows that immigration has a primarily negative, but limited, effect on the wages of various groups of native workers, and more or less no effect on the employment and unemployment of the groups most at risk: young people, those with little skill, and ethnic minorities.

How do the authors explain this somewhat surprising result? In the U.S. case, the thesis is that immigrants have no significant effect on the wages of natives because the natives can "vote with their feet" – that is, they can move to where better jobs and better pay are available. Also in this case the high mobility of the U.S. labor market is considered to have a beneficial effect on the native labor force. This interpretation is reinforced by the research of Filer (1992), which analyzes the impact of a flow of immigrants on native mobility in a local market. He finds a significant negative relationship between the immigration flows[20] and the net flow of native migration, a result that can be explained by natives moving when general prospects worsen. There is a larger negative impact on the wages of earlier immigrants already in the country, and this is attributed to the limited internal mobility of foreigners, who tend to settle where there are important ethnic communities. This is shown by the fact that 70% of the Mexicans who live in the United States are in California or Texas (Martin and Midgley 1994).

At this point we should consider a methodological aside. If, on the one hand, internal mobility decreases the negative effect of immigrants on native wages, on the other hand, it spreads the immigrant effect to other areas and so reduces the ability of this cross-section approach to measure the effect it has on native wages and employment.[21]

---

[20] Net migration grows if the inflows (+) are greater than the outflows (−).
[21] This weakness of the approach is pointed out in more detail in Borjas (1999b).

In the Canadian and Australian cases, the lack of any significant effect of immigration on wages and employment of natives – which, if anything, has had a positive impact – is attributed both to the mobility of workers and to the high selectivity of the immigration policy, which can choose and attract workers who, on average, are more skilled than immigrants in the United States. It is well known that Canada and Australia use a strict point system to authorize entry, which is linked to labor demand and the age of the population. The countries' geographic positions – not bordering other countries with strong emigration pressure – has meant that it is not necessary to make a strong effort to apply a restrictive immigration policy. This system favors workers whom the labor market actually needs. Furthermore, U.S. migratory policy was, with the 1965 Amendment Act, centered on family reunification, whereas the policy in Canada, with the 1962 Immigration Act, removed national restrictions but focused attention on "skill requirements"; and in Australia, only during the 1980s was family reunification emphasized (Borjas 1988). With such laws Canada and Australia managed to select flows of more skilled immigrants who more directly reflected the needs of the market.[22]

This agreement in the results, however, conflicts with the contribution made by Borjas, Freeman, and Katz (1992), who, instead of using "micro" studies, use an aggregate approach. They use an *implicit labor supply*, which includes the quantity of human capital embodied in legal and illegal immigration and imports of intermediate and semifinished goods. The increased implicit supply of labor was due to one of two things: (a) the deficit in the balance of payments during the 1980s and therefore to imports from developing countries, which were 1.5% for the whole economic system and 6% for the manufacturing sector, or (b) immigration, which represented 0.3% of the labor supply per year. Because both trade and immigration implicitly cause the amount of unskilled labor to increase more than that of skilled labor,[23] the increase in these components was the cause of the increase in wages of skilled workers[24] and the cause of the decrease in the remuneration and employment of high school dropouts (for an amount equal to 30–50% of the remuneration between 1980 and 1988). This result

[22] See Green and Green (1995) for information regarding the efficiency of the point system used in Canada.

[23] The reduced impact of immigration takes into account its continuation and its increases over time.

[24] The 1985 balance of payments deficit caused the number of high school dropouts to increase compared with graduates by 5–12% for men and 10–17% for women. In 1988 immigrants accounted for 20% of the high school dropouts.

emphasizes that at aggregate levels immigration and the balance of payments deficit led to a choice of growth model that induced a decrease in unskilled wages.

It is difficult to reconcile such contrasting results; to do so we must assume that the local markets adjust to the new flows of immigrants very rapidly or that immigration creates added demand sufficient to offset the effect very quickly. We must also assume that at the aggregate level a process is set off that slows the modernization of traditional unskilled jobs and that decreases their wages. This aggregate approach also emphasizes the competitive effect both of immigrants and of trade.

Now let's examine the European results. As we have emphasized, they are difficult to compare because they refer to different countries and different periods and because the researchers used different data. The results shown in Tables 3.2 and 3.3 are strangely conflicting. A number of studies show keen competition between foreigners and natives and especially unskilled natives, whereas others favor complementarity.

In the German case, the five studies that we know of do not provide similar results. De New and Zimmermann (1994), who used the GSOEP from 1984 to 1989[25] for only male workers, reveal, using a random effect model and an industry specification, that an increase of 1% in the foreign labor force produces a decrease in native hourly wages of, on average, 4.1%, with decreases of as much as 5.4% for blue-collar workers and an increase of 3.5% for white-collar workers with little experience.[26] The work of Hatzius (1994a) analyzes the impact of immigration on a regional cross section using data from 1984 to 1991. Following Altonji and Card (1991), Hatzius uses a two-stage estimate. First, an estimate is made of wages (both wages and earnings) and individual unemployment,[27] with regional dummies based on the data of the GSOEP. Then he estimates how the regional dummies vary by using variables that include the share of immigrants. He distinguishes between those who come from eastern European countries – having high human capital – and the others, and he finds complementarity in the former case (+2.%) and high substitution in the latter (−7% for a 1% growth in the foreign labor force).

---

[25] The panel was cleansed of managers, self-employed persons, and civil servants so as to create more homogeneous conditions.

[26] At a sector level there are positive elasticities for some sectors, such as commerce, but they are mostly negative.

[27] It is measured as the probability of being unemployed and is later changed into the regional probability of a typical case: a 40-year-old married male with a low level of education and 20 years' experience in the labor market.

Table 3.2. *Wage and employment effects of immigration in northern Europe*

Study	Country, period, data	Dependent variable	Type of analysis	Variable used to measure immigrants	Analysis dimension	Instrumental variables (if any)	Results
De New and Zimmermann (1994)	Germany, 1984–89, GSOEP	Log hourly gross individual wage of natives	Random effects panel model (individual-specific component in the error term) $w_{it} = \alpha + \beta' X_{it} + e_{it} + u_i$	Foreign workers for each major industry	10 industrial sectors	Industry dummy, industry growth rates, overall and industry-specific time trends	1% increase in foreign share produces a reduction of 4.1% of aggregate native wages and higher reduction for blue-collar workers (5.9%). Foreigners have positive effect on wages of white-collar workers with less than 20 years experience (3.5%).
Hatzius (1994a)	Germany, 1984–91, GSOEP, Aggregate (regional) published data	**1° stage:** a1. Log indiv. real wages a2. Log indiv. real earnings b. Indiv. unemployment **2° stage:** Coefficients of region-by-period dummies of the 1° stage	**1° stage:** OLS regression on wages or earnings, logit regression on indiv. unemployment. Inclusion of the only variables exogenous to any labor market adjustments brought by immigration	a. Foreign labor force relative to initial total labor force by region b. East German immigrant labor force relative to initial total labor force by region c. Ethnic German immigrant labor force relative to initial total labor force by region	10 regions	a. Lagged immigration values to instrument the current immigration values b. Lagged values as explanatory variables	**Unemployment:** No form of immigration appears to affect native unemployment in all analyses. **Earnings:** a. 1% increase in lagged foreign share produces a reduction of native earnings (−7%) using GSOEP data. No statistically

Study	Data	Dependent variables	Method	Migration variable	Area	Controls	Results/Comments
			2° stage: Equation with lagged dependent variables and time dummies estimated (with heteroschedasticity-consistent std. errors) using; a. The dynamic panel data estimator (Arellano) b. Anderson and Hsiao first difference-estimator			(personal variables but *Not* industry, occupation, position in a company)	significant effect using aggregate data. b. East German immigration appears to raise native earnings: +2.5% using GSOEP; +1.1% using aggregate data. c. Coefficient for ethnic Germans is never significant. **Wages:** Results on wages look very suspicious. Probably data on wages are not trustworthy, and it is better to use data on earnings.
Pischke and Velling (1997)	Germany, 1985–89, aggregate data from various statistical sources	a. Employment-to-population, ages 15–64; b. Employment-to-population, ages 15–64 (Germans only); c. Unemployment rate	a. Mean reversion model $u_{it} = b_1 u_{it-1} + b_2 \Delta f_{it} + e_i$; b. Differences (OLS) $\Delta z_{it} = \alpha \Delta f_{it} + x_{it-1}\gamma + \varepsilon_{it}$ (z = labor market performance of natives); c. Differences (IV)	a. Change in the foreign share between 1985 and 1989 (working age population); b. Foreign inflow (outflow) from (to) abroad and Germany for each year from 1986 to 1989	167 labor market regions	Foreign share in 1985 and its square	Little evidence of displacement effect due to immigration, in particular for unemployment rate. No effect of migrant inflows on native migration pattern.

(*continued*)

129

Table 3.2 *(continued)*

Study	Country, period, data	Dependent variable	Type of analysis	Variable used to measure immigrants	Analysis dimension	Instrumental variables (if any)	Results
Pischke and Velling (1994)	Germany 1984 German Federal Research Institute for Regional Geography and Regional Planning	d. Change in log manufacturing wage	Earning function approach	All foreigners and Turks only	167 labor market regions	Change in foreign share in 1985 and its square	Foreign share seems to have a large and positive effect on the log manufacturing wage (+1.8–3.3%), but no significant effect considering Turks only. The authors believe that these results are likely to be spurious.
Haisken–De New and Zimmermann (1999)	Germany (males only), 1985–92, GSOEP	a. Log real monthly individual labor earnings b. Mobility dummies variables (change of occupation; intrafirm mobility; interfirm mobility)	a. Random effects panel model (earnings equation) b. Probit model with time-specific fixed effects using pseudo R2 (mobility equations). "Moulton problem" solved by employing industry-specific fixed effect.	a. Foreign share in the labor force by region and sector (merged to the micro data by industry, state, and year) b. Trade deficit ratio ((import-export)/ output) by industry	Foreign share by region and sector (34 values). All the other aggregate variables are at industry level.	Growth of industry value added, industry dummies, time dummies, and industry-specific time trends	Trade is more relevant than immigration on both wages and mobility: Immigration has a positive effect on the overall wages (+0.6%), no effect on the wages of low-skilled workers, but a positive effect on the wages of high-skilled blue collars (+1.4%). Trade deficit ratio

(continued)

Study	Country, year, data	Methodology	Immigration measure			Results
						has a negative effect on wages (−0.11, for white collars −0.35). Immigration reduces intrafirm mobility only. Trade deficit ratio has a negative effect on occupational mobility and intrafirm mobility, positive effect on interfirm flexibility
Bauer (1997)	Germany, 1990, German Labour Force Survey	a. Factor share (relative share of income accruing to factor I) b. Translog production function a. Cross section assuming strong separability between capital stock and all other inputs. b. Six subgroups: native and foreign low-skilled blue collars, native and foreign high-skilled blue collars, native and foreign white collars	Log (foreign low-skilled blue collars) Log (foreign white collars)	62 industries	None	White-collar immigrants are substitutes to low-skilled blue- and white-collar natives. Low-skilled blue-collar immigrants tend to be substitutes of low-skilled blue-collar natives. All other groups are complementary. The effect of immigration on wages of all native groups is negligible.

131

Table 3.2 (continued)

Study	Country, period, data	Dependent variable	Type of analysis	Variable used to measure immigrants	Analysis dimension	Instrumental variables (if any)	Results
Winter-Ebmer and Zweimuller (1996)	Austria, 1988–91, Sample of young employees from social security records	a. Log individual monthly earnings for male blue-collar natives below 31 b. Joint determination of log individual monthly earnings (male blue-collar natives below 31) and share of aliens in the firms' workforce c. Individual earning growth between May 1988 and May 1991	a. Wage regression with Heckman correction (probability of being blue vs. white collar). Crosssection 1991 b. Simultaneous equations following Nelson and Olsen framework and Heckman correction c. Equation on wage growth with Heckman correction (probit employment equation)	a. Share of foreign workers in an industry and in a region b. Foreign share at firm's level c. Change of the share of foreign workers	a. Industries and regions b. Firm's level c. Industry level; region level; firm level d. Separately, movers and stayers	a. Foreign share in 1981, employment growth 1981–91, share of blue collars 1991, share of women 1991 (regional or industrial basis), mean foreign wage b. Foreign share lagged one or two, share of blue, women, and expected mean wage of immigrant at firm level c. Foreign share in 1988	Immigration has a positive effect on native wages (+2.1–3.7% at regional level; +0.2–1.0% at industry level). Immigration has a positive effect on wages (+0.1–0.5%) especially in large (>50) firms. Increase in the share of foreign workers: • Lowers wage growth at firm level (stayers only) • Is insignificant at regional level • Raises earnings at industry level

(continued)

Study	Data	Dependent variable	Methodology	Explanatory variables	Subgroups	Additional variables	Results
Winter-Ebmer and Zweimuller (1999)	Austria, 1988–91, sample of young employees from social security records	Probability of unemployment entry within one year (1, 0)	a. Probit analysis pooled cross sections (with and without instruments) b. Random effects analysis	Share of immigration in industry and share of immigration in region	a. 46 industries b. 76 regions c. Different subgroups: men, women blue, whites seasonal, nonseasonal foreigners already employed	Lagged foreign share, share of women and blue-collar workers, mean wage of immigrants at regional as well as industry levels	Increase in the share of foreign workers (both at industry and regional level) reduces earnings of stayers (−0.5–2.9%), is not significant or positive for movers. Modest impact of immigration on the unemployment risk for native young employees. Seasonal workers and foreigners already employed are more affected by immigration. The negative effect is always shown by the share of immigrant at industry level; the share at regional level, when significant, always has a positive effect.

Table 3.2 (continued)

Study	Country, period, data	Dependent variable	Type of analysis	Variable used to measure immigrants	Analysis dimension	Instrumental variables (if any)	Results
Winter-Ebmer and Zimmermann (1999)	Austria and Germany, 1985–94 (A), 1987–94 (G), aggregate (industry) data	a. Employment growth b. Native employment growth c. Wage growth	Reduce-form equation: weighted regression with sectoral employment shares as weight	a. Variation in the log foreign share (A) b. Variation in the log foreign share (G) c. Variation in the log eastern Europe foreign share (G) d. Variation in the log share of ethnic Germans (G) e. Russian share X f. Variation in the log share of ethnic Germans (G)	a. 30 industries (A) All and 3 subsamples: low-wage, high-import, high immigr. b. 12 industries (G) All and 3 subsamples: low-wage, high-import, high immigr.	a. Lagged levels of immigrant shares, lagged levels and changes in minimum wages, shares of blue-collar workers, EU output (A) b. Lagged levels of immigrant shares, lagged levels and changes in union wages, shares of blue-collar workers, EU output	Immigration has no impact on employment at large (A). Immigration reduces native employment, expcially in high-immigration industries (−.13%) (A). Immigration reduces overall wages (−0.16%) (A). Immigration has an unclear effect on employment at large (G). • Total foreigner significant and positive only for high-import industries • Negative for Russian ethnic • Positive for eastern Europe

Study	Data	Dependent variable	Method	Key variable	Period		Findings
Butare and Favarger (1995)	Switzerland, 1950–90, national statistics	Native employment	CES, translog, Zellner estimate method	Number of foreigners in the labor force	30 years	None	Foreign labor is complement to native labor. Elasticity 0.51–0.35; foreign labor and capital 0.06, and native labor and capital 0.11–0.08.
							Immigration has a negative effect on domestic employment except for high-import industries, positive for eastern Europe (G). Immigration (especially eastern Europeans) has a positive (but significant only in few cases) effect on wages (G).

(continued)

135

Table 3.2 *(continued)*

Study	Country, period, data	Dependent variable	Type of analysis	Variable used to measure immigrants	Analysis dimension	Instrumental variables (if any)	Results
Kohli (1999)	Switzerland, 1950–90, national statistics	Residents' wage and unemployment	Production theory approach: cost function and GNP function translog	Number of nonresidents that includes only recent immigrants. Old immigrants are considered as natives.	30 years	None	Nonresident workers depress the wages of residents, but the impact is very small. The effect of foreign workers on natives' employment is negative (elasticity −0.2%), but this is imputed to the fixed-wage hypothesis. More important, foreigners and trade always complement each other.
Gang and Rivera-Batiz (1994)	1988–92 Eurobarometre, northern European Countries	Individual's wage (Wi) is made up of physical labor (bu) plus a return for education (Edi) and experience (Exi). $Ln(Wi) = bu + bdEdi + bxExi + ui$	Production theory, translog, SURE	Immigrants by origins: Portugal Po, Spain Sp, Turkey Tk, Italy It, North Africa AF, Asia As, Ireland Ir	Cross region	None	The effect on the average worker's wage in France is −0.07 by NA, −0.11 AS, −0.04 Po, −0.03 Sp, and −0.01Ir; in the Netherlands −0.01 Tk, −0.07 Po, −0.06 Sp, −0.04 It, −0.03 Ir; in Germany −0.01 Tk, −0.05 Po, −0.02 Sp. The results are greater for unskilled workers, but the sign changes for workers with some schooling.

Source: Venturini and Villosio (2002c)

Table 3.3. *Wage and employment effects of immigration in southern Europe*

Study	Country, period, data	Dependent variable	Type of analysis	Variable used to measure immigrants	Analysis dimension	Instrumental variables (if any)	Results
Hunt (1992)	France, 1962–68, census	Unemployment rate among natives, and wages	Cross-section OLS, GLS, and IV wage both level with fixed effect and first differences (1968–62)	Share of repatriated from Algeria (skilled labor)	Cross-departments	Temperature and early repatriates	1% increase in the number of emigrants returning from Algeria causes a 1.3% decrease in wages, in the VAR Department −5.7% (where they were concentrated 7.5%), an aggregate increase in unemployment 0.3 and in Var 1.4%.
Garson et al. (1987)	France, 1985, employment survey	Individual wage	Léontief and translog with regional control variables	North Africans, southern Europeans, and other immigrants	–	Employed in each group	A 1% increase in Algerians, Tunisians, and Moroccans increases native wages by 0.03;[a] 1% increase in Spaniards, Turks, Portuguese, and Yugoslavs by 0.09, whereas competition exists between groups of immigrants and elasticities are −0.01, −0.04.

(continued)

Table 3.3 (continued)

Study	Country, period, data	Dependent variable	Type of analysis	Variable used to measure immigrants	Analysis dimension	Instrumental variables (if any)	Results
Gross (1999)	France, 1974–94, quarterly data	Native unemployment rate	VAR model	a. Immigration rate (IR) b. IR adjusted by the foreigners regularized in 1981 (IRA) c. Immigration rate of family members	40 observations	None	Unemployment falls with immigration in the long run. Family-reunified immigrants reinforce the negative impact because they reinforce the additional demand effect. In the short run, by raising aggregate wages (low-skill immigrants are complement to high-skill natives) an increase in the labor force produces an increase in temporary unemployment.

Study	Data	Variables	Method	Immigration measure	Sample	Instruments	Results
Carrington de Lima (1996)	Portugal, mid-1970s, aggregate data, district data	a. Aggregate wage b. Aggregate wage and unemployment c. District wage in the construction sector	a. Compare trends in wages in Portugal with France and Spain b. Regression of 1962–81 wage and unemployment c. Cross-regional analysis of wages in the building sector	Returnados from Angola and Mozambique in three years, more skilled than domestic labor force	18 years and 18 districts	None	Wage trend is similar to French and Spanish ones. Small effect on unemployment. Districts with the highest population growth show lower construction wage growth.
Dolado, Jimeno, and Duce (1996)	Spain, 1990–92, administrative register of work permits	$\Delta \ln w_u$ (wage of unskilled) $\Delta \ln w_s$ (wage of skilled) $\Delta \ln N_u$ (employment of unskilled) $\Delta \ln N$ (total employment)	Cross sectional equation in differenced forms $\Delta Y_j = c\Delta m_j + \Delta X_j b + e_j$ ($j = 1, 2, \ldots 50$)	Change in the proportion of immigrants in each province (out of total employment)	50 provinces and two groups of natives: skilled and unskilled	Lagged immigration rate and its square to instrument the immigration rate change; lagged unemployment change to instrument current unemployment change	The effect of immigration on wages of unskilled workers is small but positive (between 0.024 and 0.036), not significant on the wages of skilled workers. The effect of immigration on employment of unskilled workers is negative but not significant. The effect of immigration on total employment is positive (elasticity of 0.05).

(continued)

Table 3.3 (continued)

Study	Country, period, data	Dependent variable	Type of analysis	Variable used to measure immigrants	Analysis dimension	Instrumental variables (if any)	Results
Gavosto, Venturini, and Villosio (1999)	Italy, 1990–95, administrative data on dependent employees (INPS)	1° stage: Δ Log indiv. real wages 2° stage: Coefficients of the joint regional and branch dummies for 5 years from the 1° stage	Two-stage procedures à la Moulton on repeated cross sections	a. Rate of inflow of immigrants into employment (difference in the share of employed immigrants to natives between two periods) b. Cumulative inflow of immigrants into employment starting in 1989 divided by the amount of native employment and its square	Branch (20) and region (20) jointly	None (lagged foreign share, share of women and blue-collar workers in the workforce)	Inflow of immigrants raises the wages of native manual workers; larger effect in small firms and in the north (overall elasticity +0.01). The cumulative inflow of immigrants is positive but nonlinear (it increases at a decreasing rate). The threshold is reached when the share of immigrants reaches 7.7% of total employment – 10% in small firms and 12.2% in the north.

140

| Venturini and Villosio (2002a) | Italy, 1993–97, individual data from the Labour Force Survey | a. Probability of finding a job (transition from unemployment to employment) b. Probability of losing a job (transition from employment to unemployment) | a. Logit estimation, with White heteroschedasticity consistent estimator b. Linear probability model with a two-stage procedure, à la Moulton | Foreign share by branch and region in the dependent employment | a. Region (19) b. Branch and Region (19 × 5) | Lagged foreign share, share of women and blue-collar workers in the workforce, mean wage of immigrants at regional and branch levels | The share of immigrants has no effect on the native transition from employment to unemployment and on the transition from unemployment to employment for workers looking for a new job; for people looking for a first job (the young), the negative effect is limited in amount, restricted to the first year and to the south, whereas the effect is positive in the most recent periods and in the north. |

Source: Venturini and Villosio (2002c)

Pischke and Velling (1994) analyze a slightly earlier period (1985–89)[28] and test a county cross section by using a different source of data: the Office of Federal Statistics. The authors are very careful in presenting their results. After controlling for the changes in the regional unemployment rate, this work shows that immigration has little or no effect on the wages and unemployment of natives. The authors attribute the diversity of their results with respect to those of De New and Zimmermann (the only ones available) to the different periods examined. They analyze a period of expansion, whereas the other authors look at a period of recession. Furthermore, Pischke and Velling analyze differences, whereas the others analyze levels. Finally, they suggest there might be endogenous problems due to the self-selection of immigrants. Another result of this work differs from the U.S. results of Filer (1992): the absence of any immigration effect on the internal mobility of German workers.

In a later work on the German case, Haisken–De New and Zimmermann (1995, 1999) again use the individual data of the GSOEP but for a longer period (1985–92) and test a monthly earnings equation with a random effect model. And using region-specific foreign shares by industry, they find that the latter variable has a positive effect on native earnings; they have no effect on low-skilled wages but have a positive effect on high-skilled wages. The authors also introduce trade variables and find that a trade deficit has a negative effect on wages in all specifications.

Bauer (1997) also analyzes the German case but with a translog production function for 1990 in a cross-industry approach. He finds competition between white-collar immigrants and blue- and white-collar natives, as well as between low-skilled blue-collar immigrants and highly skilled blue-collar natives; in the other cases, however, complementarity prevails. The author stresses that even when competition prevails, the coefficients are extremely small, and thus the effect of immigration is limited.

It is difficult to reconcile such varied results, but it might be useful to remember that foreigners are usually in low-wage sectors. Therefore, with sector analyses such as the ones by De New and Zimmermann (1994) and by Bauer (1997), it is consistent to find that competition prevails, but because immigrants generally settle in high-wage regions, a cross-region analysis concludes that there is complementarity. This finding is confirmed by

---

[28] In a later work published in *Review of Economics and Statistics* (1997), the same authors report only employment figures. This is a great pity because there is agreement between the effect of immigration on employment levels in Germany, whereas different results were obtained for the effect on wages, measured as wages and earnings.

Pischke and Velling (1994). However, this interpretation is not sufficient to solve the puzzle because a cross-regional analysis carried out by Hatzius (1994a) reveals a competitive relationship, whereas Haisken–De New and Zimmermann (1995, 1999), considering different regions in a cross-sector study that brings together both aspects, do not find competition.

The results of Gang and Rivera-Batiz (1994) show the same trend, even though the size of the effect is much smaller. They break a worker's wage into two components – education and experience – and, using the data from a survey by EU Eurobarometro, they calculate the cross elasticities between the various components of wages and the impact of various kinds of immigrants on natives having different characteristics. In the Netherlands, France, Great Britain, and Germany, a negative cross elasticity prevails between immigrants of different nationalities and the "average worker," with small exceptions. The relevant result is, however, that the elasticities are never higher than −0.1. In France and Germany they are lower than in the Netherlands, with values that are frequently equal to −0.02. There are examples of complementarity between immigrants and natives only in education, but (in Table 3.3) negative signs prevail.

It is natural to compare the case of France – where Hunt (1992) analyzes how immigrants returning home from Algeria in 1962 affected the local market[29] – with the work done by Card (1990) on Cuban immigrants. The effect on wages at an aggregate level is found to be high: an elasticity of −1.3%, with a peak of −5.7% in the Region of Var, where immigrants returning home were concentrated. The effect on unemployment was also negative – that is, at an aggregate level the estimated elasticity was 0.3%, and in Var it was 1.4%. The differences are surprising because they show opposite results for similar percentages of density of immigration. In the Region of Var in 1968, 7.1% of the labor force was made up of immigrants returning home from Algeria, just as in Miami 7% of the labor force was made up of immigrants from Cuba. The lack of data regarding prices at a local level (and therefore the need to use nominal wages) can lead to overestimation of the effect of competition between foreigners and natives. Still, the difference between the two cases is substantial.

Returning to the case of France, the research done by Garson et al. (1987) seems, in contrast, to suggest complementarity between foreigners and natives. Using the individual data of the National Survey of INSEE of 1985 with a regional cross section, the authors propose a Leontief model, which

---

[29] Immigrants returning from Algeria in 1968 numbered 900,000 and represented about 1.6% of the labor force.

reveals weak complementarity between immigrants and natives. The elasticity of the wages of natives to the growth of various groups of immigrants varies from 0.03 (in the case of Algerians, Tunisians, and Moroccans) to 0.009 (in the case of Spanish, Portuguese, Yugoslavs, and Turks). In contrast, there seems to be slight competition between groups of immigrants, with a negative wage elasticity that varies between −0.01 and −0.04. This result, which contradicts the one presented in the previous case (Hunt 1992), shows that the French labor market reacted very slowly to immigration. However, in the long term it seems to have been absorbed into the internal market.

This conclusion is also reached by the fine study of Gross (1999). Using a general equilibrium approach, Gross tested[30] the long- and short-term relationship between unemployment and immigration in France from 1974 to 1994. She finds a net demand effect because unemployment falls with immigration in the long term. She also finds that the introduction of family-reunified immigrants reinforces the negative effect of immigrant workers on unemployment, highlighting their lower probability of getting a job. In contrast, in the short term, by raising aggregate wages (that is, low-skill immigrants are complementary to high-skill natives), an increase in the labor force produces an increase in temporary unemployment during the adjustment period.

Butare and Favarger (1992) analyzed the situation in Switzerland using an aggregate production function and found clear complementarity between native and foreign workers. Depending on the specifications, it fluctuates from 0.5 to 0.35. The study uses an aggregate approach similar to the work of Borjas, Freeman, and Katz (1992), and its results contradict those prevalent in Europe, such as those of the authors mentioned earlier for the United States. The study generates another surprising result in that complementarity between foreigners and capital is repeated in all the specifications used. There is either very low complementarity or net competition between capital and native workers. The authors point out that the foreigners' high average human capital may be the result of grouping sectors with low human capital for foreigners and sectors with high human capital, a combination that may mask composition effects. Similar conclusions are reached by Ulrich Kohli (1999) using an aggregate production function approach for the same period. Nonresident workers depress the wages of residents, but the impact is extremely small. Moreover, the effect of foreign workers on natives' employment is negative (elasticity −0.2%), but that is to be imputed to the

---

[30] The methodology used is the traditional Johansen time series.

fixed wage hypothesis more than to the foreigners themselves. It is more important to note that foreigners and trade always complement each other. However, trade can be a substitute for domestic labor.

A comparison of the results in Europe and the United States shows two different examples: one where there is an example of competition at least in the short term (Hunt, Hatzius) whereas in the long term complementarity dominates (Bauer, Garson et al., Butare and Favarger); and one where complementarity prevails in the short term but competition seems to prevail in the long run.

The first possible explanation is the reduced flexibility of the European labor markets, especially the difficulty for native workers to vote with their feet because of the high costs of moving, the rigidity of the housing market, and the linguistic barriers to jobs as white-collar workers. This interpretation appears to confirm the results of the study by Pischke and Velling (1994) and especially those of Winter-Ebmer and Zweimuller (1996) for Austria. The authors reveal that the effect of immigration on natives' wages between sectors and regions is negligible. When workers are divided into job-stayers and job-changers, the impact of the former is negative, whereas the latter is positive, confirming the proposed interpretation.

These differences in mobility between European labor markets and the U.S. labor markets are well known. The OECD study (1990, p. 85) clearly shows that the number of people who change region of residence within the country from 1970 to 1987 is limited, but the values are more than double in the case of the United States compared with Europe. The values decrease (from 1970 to 1987) from 3.6% to 2.8% in the United States, and from 1.8% to 1.1% in Germany, and from 1.8% to 1.3% for France.[31] Canada and Australia also show greater internal mobility than the European countries, but it is rather limited: 1.6% and 1.5%. In such cases, it should be remembered, the interpretation of complementarity was based on successful selective migration policies. The case of Switzerland can be aligned with the Canadian and Australian cases, where the migration policy is selective both in theory and in practice.

The results for Europe are conditioned by the period of economic recession, where competition between groups of workers can be stronger. If the research had referred to the 1960s or the early 1970s, the results would be more homogeneous, with a general complementarity among the various segments of the labor force.

---

[31] In Europe, only the northern countries of Norway and Sweden show values that can be compared to those in the United States.

3.2.2 Implications and Evidence for the Southern European Countries

There are few empirical studies or estimates for the southern European countries that can be compared to those presented for the northern European countries and North America. The reason for this is simple: The migratory phenomenon is still too recent. There have been many regularization measures in Italy, Spain, and Portugal, and one in Greece. Foreigners are underrepresented in the labor force surveys, and so the data are not reliable.

Local Research

In all the countries of recent immigration there are numerous and accurate local and local sector studies. However, these studies have many limits in their use in interpreting complementarity or substitution between workers.

First, the local dimension does not facilitate an analysis of the effects of immigration on the labor market as a whole because the effects cannot be extended to other professions or localities. In addition, the continuous evolution of the migratory phenomenon causes the area of reference to change quickly. Research carried out in the area of Trento (Borzaga, Carpita, and Covi 1995) serves as an example. It shows that in one year, immigration of political refugees from Yugoslavia introduced irregular activities that had never been offered to African immigrants in the region, and this has overturned the conclusion that there was not any irregular work in the area.

Most of these studies have another methodological problem: They generally analyze only the economic activity of foreigners. In Figures 3.2a and 3.2b, for example, they analyze the segment $N'iEi$ and $NiEi$, from which it is not possible to infer anything about native employment; it might have remained the same, or it might have decreased or increased. The general tendency in these studies is to conclude that there is complementarity between foreigners and natives. We do not claim that this is impossible, but we do claim that it cannot be sustained by the arguments made so far.

Two Laws from Previous Experiences

To analyze the role of foreigners in the labor market of the southern European countries, we can use the experience of countries where there has been immigration for a long time: the United States, Canada, Australia, and northern Europe. Two laws have been shown to be relevant in determining the effect of immigrants in the U.S. and European contexts: the more restrictive the migratory policy of the receiving country and the more flexible the labor market, the less the competition between foreigners and natives. In the case of southern European countries, the two laws lead us to predict that competition between low-skilled immigrants and low-skilled natives is likely.

1. The "immigration" policy of the southern European countries, as is shown by the repeated amnesties in Italy, Spain, and Portugal and in Greece, has been neither selective nor planned. If a system of selected access – in which immigration is coordinated with the needs of the national labor market – is foreseen by the laws of these countries, it, in fact, has not been achieved because legal access was "closed."[32] If there is a relationship, it is only through the informal market, and it is outside legal control.

2. The labor market in the southern European countries is shown to have less interregional flexibility compared with the U.S. labor market. The only other country considered in the previously mentioned OECD study (1990) is Italy, where interregional mobility involves only 0.6% of the population. In the Spanish case the research of Bentolila and Dolado (1991) shows similar values to those in Italy (0.6% of the population) for the 1960s, and even lower values (0.4%) for more recent periods (1976–86), and there has been no sign that the trend has been reversed.

Bentolila and Dolado (1991) trace the limited mobility of the labor market to the possibility of the unemployed receiving support from their families – support that would be lost if they moved. Faini, Galli, and Rossi (1996) and the same three authors with Gennari (1997) come to a similar conclusion for Italy, where, in conditions of wide differences in unemployment, internal mobility is discouraged by the higher cost of living in the possible destination areas. When the rate of unemployment also increases in the possible destination area, the probability of finding work decreases, and so internal mobility[33] is decreased even further.

There is low internal mobility in Portugal, too (Baganha 1998), and there are large variations in the rates of regional unemployment. The rate of unemployment in the region of Alentejo in 1993 was 8.1%, almost double

---

[32] In Italy in 1995 it was possible to get an authorization to enter to do domestic work, and later annual and seasonal quotas were set.

[33] In addition, Antolin and Bover (1993) underline a change in the nature of the internal migration during the 1980s and the discouraging role played by the structure of the unemployment benefits.

the national average (4.9%), and yet internal mobility was limited. The level of unemployment also varies widely in Greece. In 1995 it reached 11% in Attica, whereas it was only 4% in Crete and 7% in Tessalia (Eurostat 1995b).

If the relationships found in the United States, Canada, Australia, and northern Europe are valid in the case of the southern European countries, then the impact of foreigners on the local and domestic labor markets should be neither limited nor positive.

Effect on Natives: Characteristics of Foreign Employed and Native Unemployed

The high level of unemployment in the southern European countries might lead us to conclude that perhaps the supply of foreign workers willing to accept worse working conditions than those accepted by the natives means that firms are discouraged from undertaking restructuring processes. The process that the foreigners introduce into the productive system seems to be similar to indirect competition in the Dell'Aringa and Neri model (see section 3.1.1): In this model, the presence of foreigners decreases the employment of the more highly skilled natives, and the lower wages attract capital to the low–human-capital-intensive sectors employing fewer skilled workers. If this process actually takes place, the presence of foreign workers willing to do certain unpleasant work discourages the modernization of such processes. Fewer nurseries and more immigrants from the Philippines results in less mechanized agriculture, fewer skilled agricultural workers, and more seasonal work in agriculture, often irregular.

In an attempt to explain the role played by foreigners in the labor market, the previous analysis suggests that foreign workers are generally complementary to natives when the high demand for labor is not satisfied by natives and when the migrants' skills are complementary to those of the natives. Therefore, it is necessary to clarify the characteristics of the foreign labor force in the four countries being examined before we try to suggest an interpretation.

Immigration to the southern European countries in the 1980s and the early 1990s has the following characteristics:[34]

- The immigrants are mostly unskilled, or if skilled they do not use their skill or their qualifications in the job they are doing in the receiving country.

---

[34] For a more detailed specification see Chapter 1.

- The sectors where they are concentrated are agriculture, traditional industrial production, and building and, in the service sector, catering and hotel services and domestic work. Irregular activities also follow this pattern, particularly in the services and agriculture (except in Portugal).
- The firms that use foreign labor are mostly small or medium-sized. Large firms in the industrial sector have gone through a long crisis or modernization, so they do not need unskilled workers. What is more, in their case the strong presence of trade unions increases negotiation costs and discourages the employment of foreign workers. Modern firms that have restructured production processes with significant capital-intensive investment do not use labor to counter the economic cycle, and if they do they need highly skilled labor. The firms that take on foreign workers are traditional firms that cannot find unskilled workers on the labor market or respond to positive fluctuations in the economic cycle by taking on workers and not by investing.

Can such characteristics displace weak native workers – young people, women, or manual workers who are excluded from the productive process? In the southern European countries, and especially in Italy and Spain, the level of unemployment of young people (15–24) is very high. In Spain it passed from 25.4% in 1980 to 32.3% in 1990, 31.1% in 1991, 34.6% in 1992, 42.4% in 1993, 45.1% in 1994, and 37.1% in 1997 (OCDE figures). In Italy it was 25.2% in 1980, 25.7% in 1990, 32.4% in 1994, and 33.6% in 1997, with wide territorial variations: higher values in southern Italy and lower in the north.

In Portugal unemployment of young people reached 15.2% only in 1994; previously it had always been lower (10% in 1990), but it remained at the higher level in subsequent years. Unemployment of young people in Greece was 21.9% in 1985 and 21.5% in 1990; then it increased to 27.7% in 1994 and reached 31% in 1997 (OECD figures).

Unemployment for women in these countries is very high, about twice that for men. In 1990, 1994, and 1997, in Spain the levels were 24.2%, 31.4%, and 18.4%, respectively; in Italy the percentages were 17.1% (12.8% according to OECD figures), 15.7%, and 16.84%; and in Portugal, 6.3% and 8.1%, and it stayed at a similar level (7.9%) despite a sharp rise in the employment of women. In the same years the levels in Greece were 10.8% and 13.7%, with a further increase to 15.1% in 1997 (OECD figures). Unemployment for workers of working age (25 to 54) – and at this age unemployment usually means having lost a job – increased only in Greece and Italy; in the other countries it decreased slightly, depending on the respective levels.

The high levels of unemployment for women and young people might lead to the conclusion that foreigners have displaced the weak segments of the labor force. If young people and women's unemployment is caused by structural change rather than economic change, then foreigners might have increased this exclusion by stealing jobs from the natives.

Effect on Natives: Spain and Italy

As was pointed out in the theoretical section, competition between native workers and immigrants is highlighted by a fall in wages and employment in labor markets that have flexible wages, and such a reaction was found to be weak in the United States and sometimes stronger in Europe.

In their study on Spain, Dolado, Jimeno, and Duce (1996) try to identify the effect of the 1991 regularization on overall employment, on low-skill employment, and on wage differentials between skilled and unskilled workers. Using a cross section of fifty regions, they consider changes in the relevant variables between 1990 and 1992. They determine the percentage of foreign workers by comparing the number of work permits issued with total employment in each region.

As the results in Table 3.4 show, the effect on unskilled workers' wages (Wu) is positive in all the estimates, whereas the effect on skilled workers' wages (Ws) is positive and not significant. The effect of immigration on the employment of unskilled workers (Nu) is negative but never significant, whereas it is positive and significant for total employment.

It is a surprising result because it contradicts all previous expectations and rules as well as international experience. However, similar results are repeated in a study of Italy by Gavosto, Venturini, and Villosio (1999) using different data and methods.

The authors first gather from individual administrative records (INPS) data on the number of foreigners legally employed in the private sector from 1987 to 1995 and the percentage of foreigners employed compared to natives by region and sector. They then make a two-stage estimate of the individual wage changes of native workers. In the first stage, they insert region–sector dummies. In the second stage, the coefficients of the dummies from 1989 to 1995, corrected as in Bonjour and Pacelli (1998), are explained not only by aggregate demand control variables but also by the percentage of foreigners by joint region and sector. Surprisingly, the results concur with those of Spain: Foreigners seem to have a positive effect on unskilled workers' wages

Table 3.4. *The effect of immigration on the Spanish labor market*

Variable/Estimation	(OLS)[a]	IV[b]	(IV')[c]
1. $\Delta \ln W_u$	4.19	4.23	3.47
	(1.39)	(3.57)	(1.77)
2. $\Delta \ln W_s$	1.38	1.84	1.60
	(1.48)	(1.79)	(2.02)
3. $\Delta \ln N_u$	−3.84	−2.70	−0.88
	(2.22)	(3.78)	(1.74)
4. $\Delta \ln N$	5.75	6.85	6.24
	(2.14)	(2.94)	(2.63)

[a] Equation estimated with OLS
[b] Equation estimated with IV for the level of unemployment and the rate of change of immigration (instrumented by the constant, the migration rate lagged one year, its square, the lagged unemployment rate, and predetermined variables)
[c] As in equation (2), with the lagged rate of change in immigration, which, being exogeneous, is not instrumented.
Source: Dolado, Jimeno, and Duce (1996)

and a positive and not significant effect on nonmanual workers' wages. Furthermore, in the areas where foreigners are concentrated most – small firms and in the north – their effect is complementary: They have a positive effect on workers' wages in that area. Gavosto, Venturini, and Villosio (1999) use different measures to get the percentage of foreigners (see Table 3.5), both for the rate of change and for the stock – that is, changes from the beginning of the period up to a certain year and its square. The first two measures are always positive, whereas the square of the stock has a negative sign and is significant. The level at which the variables change sign is about 7–8%.

The authors, making allowance for the regularizations that took place during the period and the small dataset, tentatively suggest that a small share of foreigners has a positive effect caused by the high level of demand in the system. In Italy the percentage of foreign workers, on average, is about 2–3%, but if the percentages are higher – for example, equal to the percentage of foreigners in Germany – then a negative effect will be set in motion.

Both the Spanish and the Italian authors propose this interpretation, but there are other possible explanations of why immigration does not appear to affect the wages of native workers, as expected, from the empirical study. First, a regularization is not a natural event, and it can be foreseen. Important regularizations, as occurred in both Spain and Italy, meant that many immigrants had been working illegally in the country for some time,

Table 3.5. *The effect of immigrants on natives' wages – various groups in Italy*
(t-statistics in parentheses)

Group	Share of foreigners by branch and region[a]	Square of share of foreigners by branch and region[a]	Changes in the share of foreigners
All	0.22	−0.034	0.09
	(3.1)	(−3.4)	(1.8)
Blue collars	0.48	−0.08	0.118
	(6.1)	(−5)	(2.)
White collars	0.08	−0.02	0.047
	(0.9)	(−1.3)	(0.7)
Dim 0–50	0.80	−0.10	0.15
	(7.6)	(−4.8)	(2)
Dim > 50	0.17	−0.03	−0.011
	(1.6)	(−1.5)	(−0.15)
North	0.73	−0.08	0.19
	(4.7)	(−3.7)	(1.9)
Center	−0.14	0.01	0.06
	(−0.7)	(0.3)	(0.5)
South	0.10	0.17	−0.067
	(0.8)	(0.3)	(−0.6)

[a] Regression instrumented by share of employed foreigners in the earlier period by region and sector, share of women employed by region and sector, share of workers employed.
Source: Gavosto, Venturini, and Villosio (1999)

and it is possible that the wages had already incorporated such an effect. The effect of a regularization on native wages would therefore develop during the years before the actual regularization. However, there is the opposite argument, which suggests that the effects of a regularization should be spread over the years that follow the law because labor markets are slow to adjust in that wages are fixed by negotiation for more than one year, and so on.[35]

Such arguments regarding tight regulation of southern European labor markets and strong trade unions lead to the conclusion that there will be a greatly reduced elasticity of wages because of exogenous changes. Thus, one could imagine labor markets in which prices are so rigid that changes are brought about by changes in quantities such as employment.

[35] Gavosto, Venturini, and Villosio (1999) try to allow for the fact that the effect of the regularization will be spread over time in their model, which uses the percentage of the stock of foreigners. Such a variable reflects the difference between the stock in a given year and its size before the regularization in 1991. Because the number of regular immigrants increases mostly in that year, its effect is carried over into later years.

Table 3.6. *Probability of transition from unemployment to employment for those looking for their first job in northern and central Italy*

Category of worker	1993	1994	1995	1996	1997
All	−0.35 (−2.5)	−0.03 (−0.3)	0.01 (0.1)	0.20 (1.3)	0.27 (1.9)
High education	−0.37 (−1.3)	−0.44 (−1.6)	0.06 (0.2)	0.22 (0.8)	0.19 (0.8)
Medium education	−0.48 (−2.9)	0.13 (1.0)	0.10 (0.6)	0.18 (1.1)	0.19 (1.2)
Low education	−0.25 (−1.6)	−0.14 (−1.1)	−0.11 (−0.6)	0.21 (1.2)	0.36 (2.3)

Relative coefficient of the share of foreigners employed (t-statistics in parentheses)
Probit regression
Source: Venturini, and Villosio (2002a)

The results reported by Dolado et al. (1996) for Spain show that the effect on overall employment is positive, and it is significant for unskilled workers. Venturini and Villosio (2002a) use ISTAT's quarterly labor force survey (from 1992 to 1996) to analyze the effect of the percentage of foreigners in the labor force on the probability of those employed losing their jobs and those unemployed finding jobs, using annual probit cross-section estimates (see Table 3.6). The percentages of foreigners and the other aggregate variables are fixed, respectively, at regional and sector levels in the former case and only at a regional level in the latter.[36]

When the probability of natives becoming unemployed is considered, it is found that the effect of the percentage of foreigners on the regions and sectors in which natives are employed is either negative – that is, the probability of losing a job is reduced – or is not significant. Similarly, the effect on unemployed workers looking for a new job, usually adults, does not appear to be competitive, although there is a slight competitive effect on young people looking for a first job in the first few years. Looking more closely at a territorial distribution, there are traces of such an effect in northern and central Italy only for the medium-educated, and in fact it turns out not to be significant for the two other education groups.

Such results do not contrast with high native unemployment. Some 85% of the foreign population in Italy is from Africa and eastern Europe, and immigrants settle where the demand is highest: There are relatively few immigrants in the south (10%) and many in the north (65%), where the

---

[36] To counter the aggregation bias (different levels of aggregation were present in the equation: individual, sector, and region) in the probit equation, a heteroschedasticity-consistent estimator has been used and, in the linear probability model, a two-stage procedure, as suggested by Bonjour and Pacelli (1998). To check for the endogeneity of a migrant's choice of location, the share of foreigners was instrumented by lagged foreign share, the share of women employed, the share of blue-collar workers employed in the region, and the average wage among immigrants.

level of unemployment (6.7%) is half the national average (11.9%), which is almost half the level in the south (21%). If a simple correlation between the unemployment rate and the percentage of foreigners holding a work permit is calculated for each region, the result is –0.7.

In Spain – where there is, as in Italy, a high level of unemployment (28.2% in 1997, OECD) and a high regional spread, even though it is less than in Italy[37] – the link is not so strong. The flows of Africans and Asians[38] in the past decade were concentrated mainly in four regions: Catalonia, Madrid, Andalusia, and Comunità di Valencia. The rate of unemployment in 3 regions out of 4 was lower than the national average in the 1990s.[39]

The correlation between the best proxy for immigrants who came to work in the past few years – that is, the percentage of Africans – and the level of regional unemployment is only –0.2 (in 1990 and in 1991). According to Jimeno and Bentolila (1998), the regional markets were not very responsive to the level of unemployment, and the adjustment between regions was weak. Spanish unemployment is largely caused by deep structural changes that can be traced to post-Franco economic reform – which opened protected markets to competition[40] – and to the economic recession of 1992–93. Added to this is the increasingly frequent and widespread use of temporary contracts, which have transformed employment in the Spanish labor market. In 1991, 32.2% of dependent employment was made up of temporary contracts, compared with 5.4% in Italy (OECD 1993). According to Jimeno and Toharia (1992), the introduction of these contracts was not a factor in increasing efficiency. They seem to be linked negatively to productivity, which after 1985 reversed its procyclic trend.

The immigrants of the 1980s do not seem, however, to compete with native workers: On the one hand they are mostly low-skilled workers, and the percentage of unemployed Spaniards with low school qualifications (without qualifications or with only elementary schooling) decreased from 70%

---

[37] The figure for the unemployment rate in Italy is almost half what it was in Spain. For example, in 1987 it was 11.2% for Italy and 20.1% for Spain. But the standard deviation, considering twelve regions in the former and eleven in the latter, was 0.47 and 0.24, respectively.

[38] The overall figure by area is not very representative because it includes a large number of U.S. and European tourists and retired people.

[39] Unemployment in Catalonia and Madrid is 30% lower than the national average, whereas for the Communità of Valencia it is slightly lower and for Andalusia 40% higher.

[40] Jimeno and Toharia (1994) describe the situation of the labor market in this way: "Thus the foremost cause of employment losses in the 1975–85 period is a structural one, whose viability was based on the existence of cheap labour and lack of competition and the change in the economic environment."

of the total in 1976 to 40% in 1988 and settled at this level (Blanchard et al. 1995, p. 30).

On the other hand, the impact of young people on long-term unemployment decreased in the 1980s for the 14–29 cohort, decreasing from 57% in 1979 to 40% in 1989 to 34% in 1991. Later it increased following the economic recession of 1992–93. But in that period, fewer work permits were granted as well.

It therefore appears that the groups of workers – young people and foreigners – followed the same trend in demand during the expansion of the 1980s and during the recession of the last year of the decade, 1990.

Effect on Natives: Portugal and Greece

There are no empirical investigations into the impact of recent immigration on the Portuguese economy. De Lima and Carrington (1996) analyze the impact of Portuguese returning from Angola and Mozambique in the mid-1970s. These immigrants accounted for about 10% of the labor force (in three years) and had a higher level of human capital than the national average. The scarcity of data led the authors to adopt three lines of approach. First, they compared the trend of wages in Portugal with the wages in the neighboring European countries: Spain (which, like Portugal, had undergone important political changes) and France. These comparisons did not reveal any relevant differences in the trend of wages, and even though the difference in the rate of growth of unemployment in Portugal after 1975 is evident, the unemployed were absorbed rapidly, and it does not appear to have had any permanent effect on the Portuguese labor market.

The second line of approach was to perform a regression analysis of a time series of data from 1962 to 1981. This test shows that the lagged immigration rate had a positive effect on average Portuguese wages. The effect was complementary, but, at the same time, there was a positive effect on unemployment, indicating competition. The limited data available, however, discourage the authors from considering the results to be conclusive.

The third approach used a cross-regional analysis of the effect of the level of *returnados* on the trend of wages in the building sector. It was found to be strongly negative, but this is interpreted circumspectly. Although the results tend to favor the conclusion that workers returning to Portugal had a competitive effect – similar to that of workers returning to France from Algeria; see Jennifer Hunt (1992) – the authors are less confident in suggesting that immigration has a negative effect.

In any case, whatever lesson can be learned from the study carried out by De Lima and Carrington (1996) on the *returnados* in Portugal, it is a special case, for two reasons: because the flow lasted so long and was so large, and because of the high quality of the workers returning home. The more recent immigration into Portugal is very different.

Recent immigration into Portugal is made up of skilled European workers and Brazilians as well as immigrants coming from the former colonies (PALOP[41]) who do low-skilled work, often in the informal urban sector. Moreover, immigration accounts for only 2.5% of the labor force (Baganha 1998; Baganha, Ferrao, and Malheiros 1998). As Maria Baganha (1998) points out, the European and Brazilian workers were employed in the rapidly growing modern sectors of the economy and were complementary to the low-skilled domestic labor force (about two-thirds of the Portuguese have a junior school certificate or less). The latter group are concentrated in the metropolitan area of Lisbon (MAL), which grew less than the rest of the country (0.45% compared with 0.6% per year from 1981 to 1991), and are mostly unskilled or self-employed. They find regular or irregular work in sectors that native Portuguese have left so as to take advantage of opportunities offered by the EU. Brazilian workers work in the building sector, traditional industries, commerce, catering, and domestic service, often without a proper labor contract. Baganha emphasizes that the immigrants from the old Portuguese colonies compete with low-skilled native workers for urban jobs, but not in agriculture, where native workers are still predominant. However, elements of competition have also appeared recently between skilled foreign workers and young, highly qualified Portuguese in the professions, such as medicine and dentistry (Baganha et al. 1998). These comments on the situation in Portugal come from a sociological analysis that favored single cases, but they are not incompatible with the results described earlier for Spain and Italy, which offer an overall picture of the phenomenon and do not in any way exclude cases of individuals or groups of workers being replaced.

The southern European countries have a long history of irregular employment that partly attracts illegal immigrants, as in the case of Greece. The research, of Lianos et al. (1996), which investigates the role played by foreign workers in the north of Greece, shows a very high presence of foreigners, especially in the area bordering Albania (17% of the population). This means that the number of temporary as well as permanent immigrants in the labor force increases to 13%, of which about half are irregular. The foreigners who

---

[41] PALOP stands for African countries that have Portuguese as their official language.

work irregularly are concentrated in this area because the national average, again according to the estimates of the research, is around 4.5%.

The strong presence of regular and irregular foreign workers leads us to believe that a displacement effect takes place between native workers and foreign workers. The interviewees were asked to estimate the direct substitution and gross substitution, as defined by the authors, of natives by foreigners in employment – that is, how many jobs previously done by Greeks were now occupied by foreigners. The values obtained were very high: about 12.7% with reference to regular immigrants, and about 21% for irregular immigrants. These values, however, constitute an overestimate of the phenomenon because they do not take into account changes in supply – that is, the fact that many Greek workers are no longer willing to do certain jobs or tasks. Cleansed of that value, the rate of gross substitution would be almost nil, whereas the rate of net substitution for regular workers would be 0.5%, and 5.8% for irregular workers.

This result is not surprising because in the irregular market, competition is certainly stronger, wages are more flexible, and it is easier to replace workers. Foreigners receive a lower wage than natives, but it is interesting to note that the difference is proportionate to the worker's lower productivity.

In the agricultural sector, for example, Lianos, Sarris, and Katseli (1996) found about 20% substitution and even higher levels of complementarity. About 34% of skilled work and 18% of unskilled work would not be done if the foreign workers were not available. Thus, it is calculated that they make a net contribution of immigration to income growth of about 3%.

The competition of foreign workers in Greece is also the subject of an empirical study by Tsamourgelis (1995). Using Eurostat data on net migration from 1977 to 1990, the author finds a positive link with the rate of unemployment and a negative but insignificant link with wages.[42]

Effect on Natives: The Non-Regular Foreign Workers

Most empirical research in all European countries is concentrated on the effect of regular foreign employment on the native wages and employment (sections a and b in Figure 3.1). But this is only part of the story. Especially in southern European countries, where the flow of immigrants into the legal

---

[42] Tsamourgelis's work is very interesting for its theoretical model, from which the empirical version is derived. The results obtained, however, are not very convincing because the study uses a time series of net flows – net of returns to the country of origin – which include not only the net flows of foreign immigrants but also the flows of Greeks who have returned to Greece. Thus, it is implied that Greeks who return home have the same effect as foreign immigrants, and that invalidates their significance for the study of immigration.

labor market was affected by amnesties, the impact of illegal immigration is also an important part of the picture (sections c and d in Figure 3.1).

To see whether irregular immigrants displace those who do irregular work with respect to regular employment, Venturini (1999) uses ISTAT estimates of units of irregular labor to measure whether irregular immigrants "replaced" regular employment in Italy. ISTAT estimates are split into various items, including foreigners, who, since 1987, have been the fastest-growing component. To find out the effect of irregular labor on regular employment, the author tests a production function differentiated by sector from 1980 to 1995 (a cross-section time series). The employment of regular workers is a function of regular workers' wages, the total number of workers (regular and non-regular native workers as well as non-regular foreigners), output, and lagged employment.[43] The aggregate results show that the activity of workers in the informal sector is one of substitution; it has a negative effect on formal employment, but this impact is extremely small. In the long term, when it is at its peak, it reaches only −0.01; if the activity of non-regular foreigners increases by 1%, regular employment falls by 0.01%. This effect, as well as being small, is also less than the effect on regular workers of native workers who work in the informal sector, which is −0.02; that is, if the native non-regular activity increases by 1%, regular employment falls by 0.02%. This result is not surprising because natives who work irregularly are more homogeneous with regular native workers. It is therefore reasonable to conclude that their competitive effect is greater.

This kind of analysis was repeated for the main macro-sectors: agriculture, industry, building, and tradable and nontradable service sectors, and a breakdown by sector gives varying results. As shown in Table 3.7, the negative effect of non-regular employment is not distributed uniformly. For example, in agriculture and building it is negative or even, whereas in nontradable services it is positive. The higher elasticities in the two sectors are not surprising because irregular employment is traditionally strong in these sectors.

Competition is strongest in the agriculture sector. The effect on the regular employment of natives who work irregularly is −5.5, and the effect of foreigners is −3.8: These figures are lower than for agriculture in northern Greece (−5), as shown in Lianos, Sarris, and Katseli (1996).

The high values of the coefficients confirm that there is competition, but perhaps the substitution caused by irregular work is overestimated. It is

---

[43] For a discussion of the ISTAT estimates of non-regular labor, see Venturini (1999) and ISTAT (1993).

Table 3.7. *Long-term elasticity between regular employment and irregular employment by sector in Italy*

Group	Agriculture	Industry	Building	Tradable services	Nontradable services
OLS					
Foreigners	−2.78	−0.19	−0.68	−0.10	0.38
Natives	−5.01	−0.07[a]	−1.77	−0.20	1.22
IV					
Foreigners	−3.82	−0.14	−0.23[a]	−0.08	0.03[a]
Natives	−5.50	−0.16	−1.37	−0.14	2.39[a]

[a] Not significant.

Source: Venturini (1999)

possible to identify a form of discouragement in which natives, both men and women, voluntarily leave agricultural work.[44]

Slight competition prevails in the other economic sectors, and the long-term elasticities vary from −0.08 to −0.2 for non-regular foreigners, and −1.8 to −0.14 for non-regular natives. There is a degree of complementarity between non-regular foreign workers and natives in the sector of nontradable services.

The sector analysis shows that the effect of non-regular work done by foreigners varies greatly depending on the economic sector. It also shows that the overall view hides compound effects of different signs. However, the negative effect of foreigners doing irregular work is always smaller than that of natives who work irregularly, although it exists and amplifies the effect of irregular natives.

The strong segmentation of the labor markets conditions the effect of irregular foreign workers, which follows the prevalent trend in the sector. Foreigners who entered these markets later did not change the productive structure, but they probably reinforced the prevalent methods of production. They are employed in the sectors that show greater responsiveness to changes in labor costs and less responsiveness to changes in production and "slower" adjustments in the regular labor market. This finding highlights either the specificity of these activities or the choice of production methods.

---

[44] It is difficult to distinguish between, on the one hand, leaving employment voluntarily and, on the other hand, discouragement due to the worsening working conditions that follow from the presence of foreigners working in such activities. These conditions become unacceptable to natives who consume in the destination country.

Research into Spain carried out by Blachard, Jimeno, et al. (1995, p. 23) concludes that "unrecorded employment is not likely to be a significant explanatory element of the high Spanish unemployment." As pointed out earlier, this phenomenon was caused by structural changes. Because irregular foreigners do not represent a significant share of irregular labor, they, too, will have little effect on native employment.[45]

There are other forms of indirect and direct competition that have not been researched, so other approaches can be proposed. Little can be said about direct competition between natives and foreigners in the informal sectors, something that is particularly important in southern European countries, where irregular activities are substantial and often constitute an important part of the family income.

The lack of competition in the regular labor market and competition in the irregular labor market can hide relevant effects of poverty growth in important segments of the population that are already marginal. This topic can be described only by field studies and detailed interviews conducted by privileged observers. Such studies have not yet been done.

Similarly, little can be said about indirect substitution between productive sectors or territorial areas. In fact there is little evidence whether domestic mobility and productive relocation (sections e and f in Figure 3.1) are slowed by increases in the number of foreign workers in areas where territorial mobility for both workers and firms is low and the demand for labor is growing.

The method chosen to measure wage and direct employment effects is based on a territorial cross section (and sector). This method uses territorial variations to measure the effect foreign workers have in areas where they are most concentrated, so it cannot reveal territorial or sector displacement.

Effect on Natives of Testing a Macroeconomic Model: Greece and Spain

Another way to investigate the effect of illegal immigration (illegal presence in the territory) or irregular labor (which can also take place when the worker has only a valid residence permit) has been proposed by Sarris and Zagrafakis (1999) and by Ferri et al. (2000) using two computable

[45] According to labor force surveys, the level of unemployment, after allowing for informal activities, should be 4–5% lower; but the authors, after careful examination of other sources, including self-employed work, reach the conclusion reported.

general economics (CGE) models; the former is applied to Greece, and the latter to Spain. The big advantage of these models is that they can be used to explain macroeconomic relationships and therefore trace the overall effect of growth in the labor supply and repercussions on the labor market. In particular, these models make it possible to analyze sector and territorial competition introduced by immigration. The results of these models are strictly dependent on the hypotheses on which they are based. In both models, wages are flexible, foreign workers are unskilled and substitute unskilled native workers, and they are complementary to skilled native workers. The wages received by irregular unskilled foreign workers are 40% less than those paid to regular unskilled workers. Irregular foreign workers send about 50% of their earnings to their country of origin, a practice called *remittance.*

The Sarris and Kografakis model assumes that the effect of immigration on wages and native employment levels depends on the balance of payments. If there is a surplus (exports are greater than imports), the increase in employment and the decrease in unskilled wages cause the prices of goods to decrease. An increase in exports leads to an increase in domestic demand, canceling the negative effect on wages and employment of unskilled native workers. If there is a balance of payments deficit, the decrease in wages and prices is accompanied by a smaller increase in domestic demand, an increase that is not sufficient to offset the negative effect on unskilled native workers' wages and employment. Remittances abroad, which are equal to imports, make the macroeconomic picture worse.

The results of the basic model conform to the working hypothesis of the model. The workers' annual income increases by 1.5%, and real wages decrease by 36%, as does native employment. The latter decreases by 47,000 units per annum, about one-third of the total new flows of immigrants. The decreases in wages and employment are concentrated in agriculture and in unskilled employment, whereas wages and employment for skilled workers increase (see Table 3.8).

Various hypotheses are compared to this basic case. If native workers' wages are fixed, there is a smaller increase in wages and there is a greater degree of substitution of unskilled native workers. That is, unemployment increases for Greeks,[46] whereas if foreign workers are regularized they receive the same wage as natives and there is no change with respect to the reference case.

---

[46] This specification describes an unusual effect on income distribution, where total wages bill would not change because the loss in jobs is offset by there being no loss in wages.

Table 3.8. *Macroeconomic effects of illegal immigration in Greece*

Factor	Reference value	Base scenario change
GDP at factor cost	8,239,762[a]	1.47%
Consumer price index	1.13	−2.04%
Real wage	0.69	−6.22%
REAL WAGES[b]		
Agriculture	0.48	−36.50%
Unskilled urban	0.74	−28.27%
Semiskilled urban	0.81	5.40%
Skilled urban	1.15	3.18%
GREEK EMPLOYMENT[c]	3992	−47.10
Agriculture	70	−6.24
Unskilled urban	982	−64.67
Semiskilled urban	766	16.64
Skilled urban	433	5.56

[a] Million Drac
[b] Employees
[c] Thousands of employees
Source: Sarris and Zografakis (1999)

This result is highly relevant to the Greek debate, where it was feared that the regularization of foreigners would have a negative effect on income growth. Both the fear and the results are repeated in the Spanish study.

Ferri et al. use a slightly more complex model, which assumes that the public sector is always in equilibrium. They analyze the effect of an increase in the Spanish labor force of 875,000 units and get results similar to those for Greece (see Table 3.9). However, because the table shows aggregate employment levels, there does not appear to be any substitution of employment for unskilled natives in this case.

As immigrants are only unskilled workers who are perfect substitutes for unskilled native workers and as total illegal immigration accounts for about 13% of unskilled labor, in the Spanish case if all the immigrants were employed, there would be a substitution of natives of about 8% (13% minus 5%), which is equal to an elasticity of −0.01 around 100,000 units.[47] The authors distinguish between illegal and legal immigration and show that, when there is legal immigration, only the wages of unskilled workers decrease; income, employment, and wages of skilled workers all increase. If wages are rigid, the loss in wages of unskilled natives is less (0.8 in the case

[47] I wish to express my thanks for this specification, which was provided by the author at my specific request.

Table 3.9. *Macroeconomic effects of changes in the rate of legal and illegal immigration in Spain*

Factor	Illegal immigration	Legal immigration
GDP	1.93	2.56
Price index	0.01	1.21
Unskilled employment	5.09	6.34
Skilled employment	2.32	2.89
Unskilled workers' rent	−1.48	−1.79
Skilled workers' rent	0.94	1.22
Return on capital	3.26	4.50
Wage differentials unskilled/skilled	−2.39	−2.97

Source: Ferri et al. (2000)

of illegal immigration and 1 in the case of legal immigration), but the other variables are worse, when compared with the basic model.

Extreme care should be taken in interpreting these results because their reliability depends on how well they can measure all the interrelationships in the economic system. The results are interpreted as long-term effects under the conditions measured by the models. For example, in the Sarris and Zografakis study, the public sector is not considered, and in the work of Ferri et al. the public sector is always in equilibrium, which could alter the results. But the message is clear: If the economy is open and wages are flexible, the effect of immigrants on natives' wages and employment depends on the trend in the goods market, and in an open economy this means dependence on exports and imports. The more rigid wages are, the smaller will be the decrease in wages for low-skilled workers, but the benefits for the other branches of production will also be less. Analysis of the models shows that overall, income distribution gets worse for unskilled urban workers in Greece, whereas in Spain, it remains the same for families whose breadwinners are not skilled workers. In the latter case, living conditions are worse when there is illegal immigration than when it is legal. This conclusion allayed fears of regularization, if anything providing arguments in its favor.

The models also carried out an important analysis of the effect of immigration on sector growth and the sector growth of skilled and unskilled employment. The hypothesis of perfect mobility of labor between sectors, however, means that such results are interesting as a possible scenario but are not realistic in countries, such as the southern European countries, where mobility is limited.

3.3 CONCLUSIONS

It is clear from this survey that it is difficult to extend the general working rules of the migratory phenomenon taken from different economic and historical contexts. Territorial contexts differ, and local labor markets are strongly segmented.

The southern European countries serve as ideal candidates for countries where there will be competition between immigrants and natives. First, the unemployment rate in those countries is high, and internal mobility is low because of institutional, economic, and social ties. In addition, there have been repeated amnesties. These regularizations highlight a nonselective migration policy and, what is more, access to the labor market through informal activities, where competition is higher or "unfair."

More specific studies have shown that the migrant who works in the formal market in Spain and Italy has a positive effect on the wages of unskilled native workers. These studies also show a competitive but not significant effect on the level of employment of unskilled workers in Spain, and on the transition out of unemployment for young people looking for their first job in Italy. In Portugal, only recently has competition between skilled immigrants and highly skilled young Portuguese become apparent (sections A and B in Figure 3.1). Numerically, however, it has been very limited. A more important form of competition is found in the informal labor market, which is a characteristic of more or less all the southern European countries (sections C and D in Figure 3.1).

Empirical studies show that in Greece and Italy there is competition between irregular labor and regular labor. However, it is limited in absolute terms, albeit higher in agriculture. Irregular work by foreigners in Greece, in contrast, causes high product growth in the sectors where foreigners are employed and seems to be a complement to the more skilled segments of the labor force.

If wages in the labor market are fixed by national contracts, the possibility of wage competition is reduced. Furthermore, if businessowners discriminate slightly – that is, if they employ foreigners only when there are no native workers, when the foreigners offer a better product or service than the native workers for the same wage, or when immigrants accept working conditions that native workers will not accept – there will be limited competition.

In the irregular labor market, where there are no contracts and the cost of getting rid of workers is nil, production costs are lower, and, in theory, competition is stronger. However, the fact that competition is weak can be explained by the segmented demand for labor. There is effective competition with regular workers in only two sectors: agriculture and, in some cases, building. In these two sectors, no specific human capital is needed and turnover costs are low, and this means that employers can choose those workers who are willing to work at the lowest cost.

The role played by foreigners depends on the structural characteristics of the productive sector in which they work. Strong competition in agriculture is probably due more to the type of technology, which determines the kind of work demanded, than to the characteristics of the foreign workers. Depending on their specific human capital, foreigners find work in sectors that already employ a similar labor force, and they adopt the same recruitment procedures, either regular or irregular.

In general, the effects of immigration on the local labor market are viewed optimistically, and this can be traced to the limited incidence of foreigners in such local markets. Where there is competition, it is limited and similar to that described by Dell'Aringa-Neri – that is, it reflects the continued use of inefficient traditional production methods that do not attract capital because of the cheap labor supply.

This is probably what emerges from general economic equilibrium analyses, which describe a clearer picture of competition. This transformation, however, is not rapid. Rather, it takes place over time in economies that always accept new flows of unskilled labor at low wages and poor working conditions. Similar conclusions seem to have been reached in research into the past 100 years of immigration into France (Tribalat et al. 1991), where the complementarity found between foreigners and natives hides the overall effect of slowing the modernization process.

Foreigners may therefore cause a kind of technological unemployment, which is the opposite of traditional opinion. Added to traditional unemployment caused by labor-saving technology at high levels of industrial growth, a lack of technological innovation would result in insufficient demand for skilled labor and therefore unemployment or discouragement in an industrial country with a skilled labor force. Available evidence, however, does not seem to confirm this view. Even if the high unemployment in the southern European countries is not concentrated in the low-skilled groups, neither is it prevalent in the groups of those with an intermediate level of education. To discuss this possible effect of immigration it would be necessary to know the number of additional jobs that the most modern technology can create. It is difficult to get an overall view of such a situation because it varies greatly among economic systems, sectors, and periods. General economic equilibrium analyses have highlighted, both in Greece and in Spain, how the effect of immigration on the local labor markets depends on changes in the overall economic system; the labor market settles at lower wage levels for native workers with the same skills as immigrants, and there is a possible and probable competitive effect for jobs – but all that depends strictly on the balance of payments deficit.

The southern European countries, however, have yet another reason to be careful in their choice of migration policy. On the one hand, the level of unemployment for natives is high, especially in Italy and Spain, but high unemployment is concentrated in areas where the demand for labor is lower; immigrants, who are more mobile, satisfy any excess demand where it exists. A possible competition could take place between immigrants in high-demand areas and natives in low-demand ones, but no evidence is available of possible discouraged internal mobility of natives due to the presence of immigrants (section E in Figure 3.1). Immigrants in high-demand areas could discourage the decentralization of production in high-unemployment areas (section F in Figure 3.1) and thus could play an additional competitive role. In turn, this would lead southern European countries toward a more restrictive migration policy.

On the other hand, immigration discourages the decentralization of production in foreign countries, thus keeping traditional production in southern Europe. What is more, these countries are experiencing a decrease in population due to a low birth rate, something that would lead them to favor an open migration policy. The downward trend of a nation's population creates a potential demand for additional labor. This demand could be satisfied in part by growth in female labor, but it also creates a demand for foreign labor.

In a flow model of the labor market, the rate of generational replacement identifies how many jobs are created for those who enter the labor market generationally (the 16–65 cohort) by those who leave the labor market generationally (the 65 and over cohort). Generational replacement reaches 0.94 in the decade 1990–2000, and 1.98 in 2000–2010 for the countries of the northern basin of the Mediterranean (Portugal, Spain, France, Italy, and Greece) (Bruni and Venturini 1995). This means that for every person who enters the labor market, in theory, there will be a job waiting for him or her, if only for generational reasons. Thus even if the economic system is not able to create additional jobs, young people will have jobs to go to. In the north of Italy, this phenomenon will be even more evident; for every male who entered the labor market in the five years from 1996 to 2001, there were 1.5 jobs available (Bruni 1994).

The level of unemployment, however, can increase in terms of quality, not quantity, if there is a mismatch between demand and supply that can be satisfied by workers whose skills and aspirations differ from those of the natives. This reduces the incentives to adopt technology in line with the supply of labor.

Empirical research does not reveal strong competition between natives and foreigners, and immigrants do not seem to be the cause of increased unemployment and reduced wage growth among native workers. Analyses based on the general economic equilibrium models reach opposite conclusions, but they look at the long term and are based on simplifying hypotheses. Thus, the elements of competition revealed are different from those in previous studies and do not contradict them. Instead, they identify a basic trend in the economic system that has not yet been established and perhaps never will be established but that is an underlying tendency.

At this point, it is worth reflecting again on the famous "rules" that favor complementarity between foreigners and natives. If there are no clear signs of competition between natives and foreigners in the short term, the general characteristics of a migration policy (not very selective) and of the labor market (not very flexible) can in the long term offset the positive effects revealed up to now and favor a radical change in the role of immigration.

For these reasons, the "indications" offered by the experience of countries having a long tradition of immigration suggest that less restrictive migration policies should be adopted in order to discourage irregular immigration. As has been seen, this is the most difficult to control. But any policies should be selective so as to favor the economic integration of immigrants.

4

The Effects of Emigration on the Country of Origin

This chapter examines how migration affects the departure country. We have adopted a *domestic* view, which considers only those people who remain in the country of departure. In contrast, a *national* approach would also include the specific benefits that an emigrant gains by going abroad. This latter definition, especially if long-term migration is being considered, is not wholly appropriate for measuring the effect of migration in the departure country, and therefore only those variables that relate to the departure country have been considered.

Researchers have tried to measure the effect of migration on economic growth in the departure country, bearing in mind that a decrease in population should produce an increase in per-capita income, whereas the loss of human capital through emigration could, instead, decrease the rate of income growth. However, these effects are accompanied by a flow of remittances, which should favor economic growth. This is because such payments help to reduce financial constraints on productive activities and encourage household consumption. In the longer term, migration of the most educated could foster investment in education by those who remain. This could stimulate economic growth, and some workers, having increased their human capital abroad, could be persuaded to return, something that should also favor economic growth.

Attempts to construct an overall balance sheet of the consequences of migration have often been hampered by the lack of information. Most research therefore has been concentrated on the effect of emigration on the population in the departure country and on the country's human capital, as well as the effect of emigrants' remittances on economic growth, income distribution, and the education level of those who stay behind.

4.1 EMIGRATION AND GROWTH

During the past few years the effect of emigration on a departure country's economy has become the center of the debate in both Europe and the United States. During the 1980s, immigration into Europe involved an increasing number of countries, including Italy, Spain, Greece, and Portugal. Having had a history of emigration, these countries wanted to tackle the problem of regulations and economic growth in a new way. They wanted to identify how much and what kind of aid was necessary to decrease migratory pressure and so avoid the need to erect high barriers. In the Americas, too, the signing of the agreement for the free circulation of goods (NAFTA) between the United States, Canada, and Mexico has been welcomed as a way of increasing the movement of goods and wealth, thereby decreasing the rate of emigration.

The link between migration and growth is part of a wide-ranging study of the link between population and growth. There are two opposing theories. One suggests that the lack of population is a limit to economic growth, and therefore immigrants are welcome; the alternative view suggests that overpopulation slows economic growth, and so emigration is welcome (Tapinos 1994). These two diverse opinions assume that there is a dynamic link between the resources available in a country. In the former case, resources increase as population grows, whereas in the latter case, they are destroyed by population growth. A classic example of the former is the United States, whereas the latter refers to the experience of some developing countries, where population growth prevents part of one year's production being saved for the following year. Both scenarios are possible, and it is important to identify which of the two stages the departure country is passing through.

Initially doubts were expressed about the effects of emigration on economic growth in the departure country. In the traditional models proposed by Lewis (1954), emigration from an area of low wages and low capital per worker, under decreasing returns to scale, causes marginal productivity and average productivity per worker to increase. Thus, available capital is spread among a smaller number of workers, favoring an increase in per-capita income and economic growth in the departure country (see Figure 4.1).

Empirical evidence has shown that this is not always so (Paine 1974). There are three reasons. In such countries emigration is accompanied by a *high birth rate*; therefore, population growth is much higher than the reduction due to emigration, and this means that there is no significant

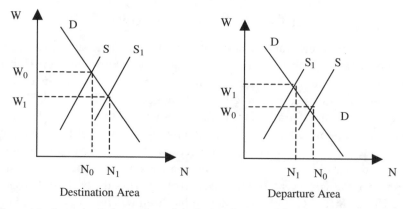

Figure 4.1. A neoclassical growth model of migration. N = labor force, N_0 = number of people employed before migration, N_1 = number of people employed after migration, W = real wage and labor productivity, DD = demand for labor, SS = labor supply before migration, SS_1 = labor supply after migration

redistribution of capital or land (or both). Furthermore, as modern growth theory emphasizes (see section 3.1.3), if per-capita income growth also depends on the *human capital* of those who have emigrated and if, as many empirical surveys show,[1] the people who emigrate have more initiative and are better educated than those who stay behind, emigration decreases the rate of growth in the departure country. Where this happens, it is often inappropriately called a "brain drain." A positive link between this so-called brain drain and incentives for pursuing education (and thus increasing average human capital) is also possible, but for the moment no strong empirical evidence of this link exists.[2] Finally, if returns to scale in production are not decreasing but increasing, the reduced size of the market for goods following emigration can have the opposite effect. In the example presented by Layard et al. (1992, p. 82), in conditions of increasing returns in production, the slope of the demand curve for labor is positive and emigration leads to a decrease in domestic wages (see Figure 4.2).

Such a possibility, quoted by the authors in the case of some eastern European countries, also appears to be true for the Mediterranean area, where there have been increasing returns to scale. For example, the production function is not homothetic for Greece from 1970 to 1980.[3]

[1] See, for example, Vijverberg (1993).
[2] See, for example, Beine, Docquier, and Rapoport (2001, pp. 275–89). This is the only empirical attempt to test a positive relation between migration, education, and growth, but it found no such relation.
[3] See Palaskas and Christopoulos (1997).

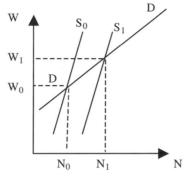

Figure 4.2. Migration in a goods market with increasing returns to scale. N = labor force, N_0 = number of people employed before migration. N_1 = number of people employed after migration, W/P = real wage and labor productivity, DD = demand for labor, SS = labor supply before migration, SS_1 = labor supply after migration

If, on the one hand, Lewis's model seems to be optimistic about the induced effects of emigration – that is, available capital is redistributed over a given population – on the other hand, it fails to take into account both the enrichment of local human capital when the emigrants return home and the positive effect of emigrants' remittances. In fact for some countries, such as Morocco, Turkey, and Tunisia, remittances represent an extremely high proportion of the balance of payments. Therefore, from a financial point of view, they are a precious source of foreign currency. However, these funds are rarely used productively; instead, they are invested in houses, land, and consumer goods.

In the medium term, emigration creates a link between the two areas: The frequent contacts reduce linguistic and cultural differences and favor international trade, investments abroad, and tourism. Such indirect consequences are certainly important and relevant. If, in the short term, emigration can be seen as an inevitable choice, a country must export workers because it cannot export sufficient goods to guarantee employment for local workers; in the long term, it can be seen as a strategy to favor foreign investment and other positive items in the balance of payments, and these favor economic growth.

The complexity of the problems related to development and underdevelopment in many departure countries as well as the shortage of available data has meant that, most empirical research has been concentrated on only two aspects: the emigrants' human capital and their remittances.

The general theme of the effect of emigration on economic growth in the departure country is often linked to the effect of economic growth on emigration. The question to be asked, in fact, is whether emigration induces growth, and whether this growth later discourages or encourages migration.

The traditional economic growth theories – that of Lewis and that of Heckscher and Ohlin regarding international trade – forecast that as growth increases, migration will decrease because income differentials will decrease and thereby reduce the desire to emigrate. Mobility studies, however, show that migration increases even when there are constant differentials in income between two areas (see, for example, Faini and Venturini 1994a, which analyzes the experience of the Mediterranean countries), and doubts have been raised regarding the negative linearity of the relationship between growth and emigration.

The creation of NAFTA, involving the United States and Mexico, has also raised the question of whether such trade agreements discourage or encourage growth and emigration. Martin and Midgley (1994) unequivocally conclude that the migratory flow from Mexico to the United States will increase. In the short term, it will contribute to an extraordinary growth of emigration. In fact, as a result of the trade agreements on agricultural prices, many Mexican farmers will not be able to grow crops at competitive prices. They will leave the countryside for the city and so will increase the number of potential emigrants.

Martin (an agricultural economist) offers a structural explanation. He argues that NAFTA will set off a process of modernization in agricultural production, which will create a substantial number of redundant workers, who will leave the land and choose emigration. Therefore, in the short term, the size of the outward flows will increase. Only in the long term, when the modernizing process is completed, will the outward flows slow or even stop.[4]

Faini and Venturini (1993, 1994a) came to the same conclusion after adopting a different approach. The Faini and Venturini model, described in section 2.1, emphasizes that two conditions must be satisfied if there is to be emigration: First, those who want to emigrate must be able to do so. Second, anyone wishing to emigrate must possess the necessary financial resources and level of human capital, and not all potential emigrants have them. Because these resources are positively linked to growth in income, they will be more accessible as income grows, and thus an ever-increasing number of people who want to emigrate will be able to do so. Thus, growth in income in poor countries initially favors emigration, and only when

---

[4] The article of Markusen and Zahniser (1999) approaches the same issue within the international trade theory.

per-capita income has reached a relatively high level will the income effect[5] stop or slow emigration.

The difference between the two approaches is that, in the latter, growth in migratory flows does not necessarily depend on a negative shock. In fact, in such a case, impoverishment caused by people being forced to leave the land could also slow emigration. However, both approaches consider the link between development and emigration to be initially positive. Only later, at a certain level of income (or growth), is it negative.

4.2 POPULATION AND THE LABOR MARKET

4.2.1 Population

The effect of emigration on the population of the departure country can be summarized in a quotation from Oreste Bordiga: "Only women, boys, white-haired men and resigned people are seen in the processions."[6] The effect of emigration on the stock of the population and its growth rate is usually limited, and sometimes it cannot easily be traced in aggregate data because the figures refer to countries and areas where there is a high natural rate of population growth. As is well known, population growth is given by natural growth (births minus deaths) plus net migration (immigrants minus emigrants), and the difference between the two determines the size of the net change. Because emigration was from southern European and North African countries, areas with high fertility rates, its effect is not apparent at an aggregate level.

Table 4.1 shows that in the early 1970s, of the southern European countries only Portugal registered a decrease in population due to the outflow of emigrants. This exceptional finding reflects the concentration of high levels of emigration into a short period. Such a finding cannot be repeated for the other Mediterranean countries, where the natural increase in population was almost thirty per thousand in the 1960s but fell to twenty per thousand in the 1990s, and where, for example, one million Turks would have to emigrate each year to offset new births net of deaths.

---

[5] As consumption in the departure country produces greater utility, for a given wage differential, the increase in income means that the more expensive good – staying home with relatives – can be bought.

[6] Oreste Bordiga gave evidence about Campania to the commission inquiring into the conditions of farm workers in 1908 and is quoted in an excellent study by Sori (1979, p. 189). The original quotation was in dialect: "Femmene, guaglioni, cape janche e cape scocciate."

Table 4.1. *Rate of natural population growth (Tin) and net migration rate (Tmn) (per thousand)*

Country		1960	1970	1980	1990	1997
Greece	Tin	11.5	8.1	6.3	0.8	0.1
	Tmn	−5	−4.4	5.2	7	2.1
Italy	Tin	8.8	7.2	1.8	0.5	−0.4
	Tmn	−1.9	−0.9	0.1	0.7	2.7
Portugal	Tin	13.5	9.7	6.5	1.3	0.4[a]
	Tmn	−7.7	−14.5	4.3	−6.1	1.3
Spain	Tin	13	11.1	7.4	1.7	0.3[a]
	Tmn	−4.6	−0.5	0	0.8	1.2

[a] 1996

Table 4.2. *Population change as a result of emigration flows*

Country	Effective population		Expected population at the end of the period	Net migration	% change due to net migration
	1950	1970	1970		
Italy	47.1	53.8	56.4	−2.6	−39
Spain	28	33.8	35.5	−1.7	−30.3

Source: Golini and Strozza (1998).

Emigration certainly has an important impact on the population. In an interesting study, Golini and Strozza (1998)[7] compare the actual population in Italy and Spain in 1970 with the projected population had there been no emigration between 1950 and 1970. As can be seen in Table 4.2, the effect of emigration means that the actual population is lower than in the closed model.

The effect is seen even more clearly when smaller areas – for example, regions such as Basilicata, Abruzzo, and Molise – are examined during periods of mass exodus, such as between 1910 and 1911. In these cases, net decreases in the population – 0.98% in Basilicata, and 3.58% in Abruzzo and Molise – were recorded. The largest imbalances caused by the traditional emigration of young males looking for work are not evident in aggregate data but can be seen in the decrease in the percentage of males and in the change in the shape of the age cohort pyramid.

---

[7] Details regarding the methodology used can be found in the work.

4.2.2 Male Share

As the quotation from Bordiga shows, initial emigration from the southern European countries comprised mainly males looking for work abroad. Initially it was temporary, but it could become permanent, in which case other members of the family (women and children) joined them. Sometimes whole families left, but this happened mainly when the destination was far away, such as the Americas, Australia, and Canada. However, even to these destinations most of the emigrants were men traveling alone. Emigration within Europe from the southern European countries was considered temporary, and therefore most emigrants who left were males, with their families joining them only if the move proved to be successful.

This kind of southern European migration changed the male/female ratio in the departure country. Golini and Strozza (1998), comparing the actual population with the "closed" population in Italy and Spain from 1950 to 1990, calculate that the percentage of males (male population/female population per 100) clearly decreased because of emigration. The change in Italy was –1.3, and in Spain it was –0.8.

If another, more specific example is taken from Italian emigration figures, it can be noted that in Italy there were more men than women: 1,002 and 1,005 for every 1,000 women in 1861 and 1871, respectively. There was a regional imbalance that revealed an internal flow of male emigration from the south to the north: 1,021 and 1,026 in the north, and 979 and 984 in the south. After the great exodus in 1911, the national average decreased to 967, with 979 in the north and 948 in the south. This emphasizes that Italy had become a country of male emigration that initially was temporary, with the men leaving first.

In 1881 adult men between the ages of 20 and 50 represented 40.1% of the cohort in Calabria, 38.9% in Basilicata, and 38.8% in Abruzzo and Molise; the national average was 40.2%. Thirty years later in 1911, the percentage of males between the ages of 20 and 50 in Calabria had fallen to 29.5%, in Basilicata to 31.6%, and in Abruazzo and Molise to 29.3%, compared with a national average of 36.6% (see Sori 1979, p. 191). The big exodus occurred at the beginning of the twentieth century, when emigrants left both northern and southern Italy, with some regions being hit more than others.

The social consequences of this phenomenon are not considered here, but it is sufficient to remember that women, young boys, and old people had to replace those who had left in agriculture and other sectors, leading to feminine emancipation and other social changes.

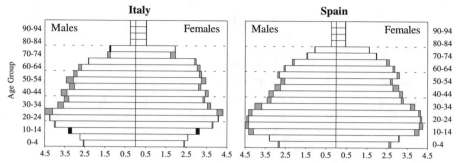

Figure 4.3. A comparison of the age structure of the population with emigration from 1950 to 1990 and the actual population in 1990. Positive net emigration is shown in black, and negative in gray). *Source:* Golini and Strozza (1998)

4.2.3 Age Cohorts

At the aggregate level, emigration does not seem to have a big impact on the population of departure countries that usually have substantial population growth rates, but it does affect the structure of the population of the departure country and the size of the age cohorts.[8] Golini and Strozza (1998) drew up an index of the structure of the population of working age (the age 40–50 population over the age 20–39 population per 100) for the period 1950 to 1990, with an open and a closed population. The index for the closed population for Italy is 1.5% higher, and for Spain it is 1.6% higher, indicating a loss in the labor force in the 40–50 cohort during that period.

These figures would certainly be higher if the figures for only the first twenty years were calculated. The effect is even more evident if changes in the shape of the age pyramid are considered. In Figure 4.3 (taken from Golini and Strozza), the gray area indicates a population outflow in that age group.

Another way of highlighting changes in the size of the age cohorts has been adopted by Le Bras (1991). In the case of Italy he compares the closed population and the open population between 1950 and 1981. Figure 4.4 shows that there were larger reductions in the size of the cohorts for men than for women and that emigrants tended to return to the departure country at the end of their working life. Even though the size reduction was limited, it means that such figures take on a positive sign.[9] Concentrating on the

---

[8] The effect of immigration on the population structure in the receiving country is discussed briefly in section 3.1.5 of this book.

[9] The effect of immigration on the age cohorts in the receiving country is positive for the initial and central groupings. The effect gradually decreases for the older age groups.

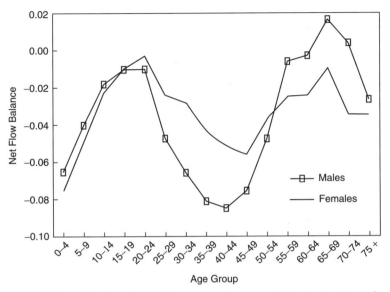

Figure 4.4. Effects of emigration and return on the age and female structure of Italy, 1981. *Source:* Le Bras (1991)

effects of emigration on the demographic structure of the population and on the labor market means that some relevant effects – such as those on consumption, educational needs, savings, investment, and birth rate, to mention only a few – are ignored.

4.2.4 Population of Working Age

Another way to analyze the effect of emigration (and eventually immigration) on the labor market of the departure country is suggested by Bruni and Venturini (1995). They propose a labor market model expressed in terms of stock and inward and outward flows. If the closed model is opened and inflows of emigrants (eventually immigrants) are added, it is possible to measure the impact of migration. Labor supply in the form of a flow (Sf) that depends on the level of participation of the working age cohort – those who enter the market at a given time – is offset by a flow of demand for labor. This demand is made up of the replacement labor demand (Ds) – that is, the demand created by those leaving the market for retirement – and an additional (new) demand for labor (Da).

$$Sf - Ds + Da = ExSi \qquad ExSi \geqslant 0$$

Table 4.3. *Marginal rate of absorption*

	Morocco		Tunisia		Turkey	
	1980–85	1985–90	1980–85	1985–90	1980–85	1985–90
Marginal rate of absorption of workers abroad	0.10	0.17	0.10	0.14	0.07	0.12

Source: Bruni and Venturini (1995)

If the flow of demand and the flow of supply coincide, there is no unemployment. But if supply is higher than demand, there will be an excess domestic supply of labor, *ExSi*. Broadening the flow model so that we can introduce a flow of labor demand abroad (*De*) helps to bring the two internal flows closer (*ExS*, total excess supply) and makes it possible to calculate the importance of migration for the labor market of the departure country.

$$Sf - Ds + Da + De = ExS \qquad ExSi \geqslant 0$$

Such a model has been applied to the Mediterranean case, and the percentage of the flow of workers who were absorbed abroad was calculated for Morocco, Tunisia, and Turkey from 1980 to 1990 – that is, the relationship between the number of emigrants during the period and the potential number of workers entering the labor market (see Table 4.3). The rate at which the market for foreign workers absorbed the flow of workers who entered the labor market varied between 7 and 17%, and on average it was higher in the later period.

Giubilaro (1997) reconsiders the empirical application of this work for a longer period and extends it to Algeria. More important, figures for illegal immigration or those who work abroad illegally are introduced, and the results show a higher degree of foreign absorption in the case of Tunisia, the same for Morocco, and a lower figure for Turkey. In all these cases the excess labor supply remains very high even when foreign absorption has been allowed for because it is very limited and is certainly not sufficient to offset the excess supply of domestic labor.

4.2.5 Labor Markets in the Departure Countries

If it is possible to measure the effect of emigration on the population as a whole and on the population of working age, it is more difficult to measure its effect on employment. An attempt to study the effect of emigration on the labor market can be made by splitting it into the direct and indirect effects: the direct effects due to a reduction in the labor force and therefore the potentially unemployed, and the indirect effects of remittances and the additional demand for labor (see Courbage 1990).

It is worth noting that the reliability of employment data and other labor statistics varies greatly from country to country. For example, although employment and unemployment data for Turkey are readily available, only historical time series of labor force data are available for Morocco, and unemployment figures are limited to urban workers. Moreover, the contribution of women workers is often underestimated in labor force data.[10]

According to a study by Barazik (quoted in Courbage 1990, p. 26), flows of legal emigrants from Turkey absorbed about 15.2% of the surplus workers. If there had been no emigration between 1962 and 1982, the unemployment rate would have been 36.5% higher.[11] This figure increases to about 44% if illegal emigration is taken into account.

Again in the case of Egypt, pioneering research by Hansen and Radwan (1982) tries to measure the effect of emigration on employment from 1960 to 1976. If there had been no emigration, the unemployment rate would have been twice as high, increasing from 7.7% to 15%. The most recent estimates made by Courbage (1988) refer only to men. He shows that if Egyptian emigrants from 1976 to 1986 numbered about 46,000, then without this outflow the unemployment rate would have been 3.1 percentage points higher than the already high figure of 10.1%.

Similar results are obtained in a study of Morocco. Courbage (1988) has drawn up various scenarios, assuming that emigrants have different activity rates if they remain in the departure country. Courbage suggests that the unemployment rate in 1982 – if there had been no emigration – would have been 2.3% or 4.5 percentage points higher.

These aggregate studies reveal that emigration has substantial positive effects on the labor market, and the greater the emigrants' activity rate, the greater the effect. It should be remembered, however, that the figures include family members – women and children – joining the worker. In addition, these conclusions are based on simplifications and do not take into account

---

[10] One example is the 1986 census in Egypt, which reports double the number of working women (2.1 million) compared with the UNO estimate (1.25 million) in 1988.

[11] Courbage (1990) quotes Barazik's work, but he does not give a full reference in the bibliography nor does he explain the methods used to get the results. Labor supply without emigration was probably estimated, and then the demand for labor (with suitable assumptions made about elasticities to changes in wages, which are already at subsistence level) was compared to it so as to get the excess labor figures.

a foreigner's human capital, skills, age, and so on. Therefore, they offer only a rough indication of the possible impact of the restrictive immigration policies being adopted by some receiving countries.

4.2.6 Human Capital

If the labor supply is reduced and therefore the potential unemployment rate decreases, that is not sufficient to conclude that emigration has a positive effect on the labor market of the departure country. It also depends on the economic role that the emigrant plays or would have been able to play in his or her own country; that is, it depends on the emigrant's *human capital.*

Economic growth in the departure country is affected by the loss of human capital at different stages. First, human capital is lost at the time of the emigrant's departure. Then the loss is reduced and can turn into a gain if the emigration of the more educated stimulates the education of those who remain. Finally, human capital is regained when the migrant returns.

1. There have been exceptional cases of brain drain – for example, the migration of Asian and Indian doctors, engineers, and professional people, who account for a high proportion of immigrants in the United States (about 500,000 in the 1970s). Generally, however, the loss of human capital in the departure country depends on the position migrants hold relative to the average level. It has been mentioned that in the endogenous growth models, if the human capital is greater than the national average, the effect on income is uncertain. The positive effect of a decrease in the labor force is added to the negative effect of the loss in human capital, and the eventual impact depends on which of the two elements is greater.

Sociological research[12] suggests that migration is a selective process, or rather, a self-selective process. Only those who have enough resources emigrate; that is, emigration is positively linked to educational levels[13] and to the intangible concept of ability. This includes the ability to learn and to adjust to new professions and new environments.

2. A recent branch of the migration literature points out the possible positive effect the brain drain can have on the average level of education in the country of origin.[14] If the probability of emigration, and thus of getting a

---

[12] See Reyneri (1979) and Calvanese and Pugliese (1988) for discussions of the situation in Italy.
[13] For example, see Zimmermann (1994).
[14] See, for example, Miyagiwa (1991); Mountford (1997); Stark, Helmenstein, and Prskawetz (1997, 1998); and Beine et al. (2001).

higher wage abroad, is higher for the more educated workers, emigration in the short term reduces the level of the stock of human capital in the country of origin (brain drain) but fosters the acquisition of more education among the ones who remain (brain gain). Emigration can thus enhance a higher average level of human capital and a higher level of growth in the country of origin. As Oded Stark (2002) points out, this reversed positive effect of the brain drain holds only if a restrictive immigration policy limits the outflows from the country of origin and if the brain gain induced by the emigration is larger than the brain drain produced by the emigration.

This new and more optimistic view of the brain drain does not apply, however, to the southern European case, for at least two reasons. First, most emigrants from the southern European countries had little skill. It is sufficient to remember, that the introduction of a literacy test to enter the United States was sufficient to force aspiring Italian emigrants to change their destination or even to give up the idea of emigrating (Sori 1979). A brain drain existed, but it was intangible. The more able – those with entrepreneurial talents – migrated. These abilities often are not correlated with education level, and in any case they cannot be replicated. Second, the emigration flows were very large. Thus, even if the ex post positive effect of emigration on average human capital existed, it was overwhelmed by the ex ante brain drain effect.

When people emigrated not only to find work but also, and especially, to get away from a political regime, as happened in certain periods in Portugal and Greece, some of the immigrants were highly qualified, but their numbers were so small that they do not show up in the statistics. For example, there is no trace of skilled Portuguese workers moving to France, and, more important, they had no relevant effect on economic growth.[15]

3. The human capital emigrants accumulate abroad is not easily transformed into a similar enrichment of domestic human capital when they return home. In fact they have raised their specific and general human capital while abroad, and when they return home they could, at least in theory, use it to add to the growth of national income.

However, foreign workers who return to the departure country seldom manage to use their specific human capital. This is because the productive structure that they return to is too different from that in the receiving country. Thus, they find it difficult to get a job or set up a business because the necessary infrastructure is not available. For example, see Paine's pioneering work for Turkey (1974) and that of Glytsos for Greece (1995).

---

[15] See Baganha and Pereira (2000).

Glytsos's valuable work[16] draws on a wide range of literature in Greek regarding emigrants returning home. He points out that more than half of those who returned between 1971 and 1986 were men, 52% of them of working age (15–44 years old), and they had a lot of difficulty in finding jobs. In fact, their unemployment rate was 10.4% compared with 6.9% for nonemigrants. For ex-emigrants, 60% of the unemployed were between 30 and 60 years old whereas for natives it was half that figure (Petroupolis 1990, quoted in Glytsos). Similarly, in Portugal more than one million people returned from overseas, causing unemployment to increase from 2.1% in 1974 to 4% in 1975 (Carrington and De Lima 1996).

Considering the Italian situation, Cerase (1967) discusses the return of southern emigrants with plans to start their own businesses or with new projects. Instead of being welcomed, they were excluded and prevented from introducing innovative projects (licenses, permits, and so on were not granted). Thus, they were relegated to the largely unproductive role of owner of poor, infertile land. Cerase points out that 43.5% of the Italian workers who returned from the United States did no work at all, 32.3% farmed independently, 11.4% did other self-employed work, and only 10% found jobs in firms. Those who wanted to innovate did not find a receptive environment, at least in southern Italy, for they were not able to stimulate behavior that was different from the prevalent conservatism.[17]

After returning, the only human capital that emigrants were able to use was general human capital. This meant that they set up businesses in the import/export sector or in the tourist trade, or they used the specific human capital that they had possessed before leaving the country and so entered agriculture. Much more frequently, however, foreign workers return when they have retired, and so their activities are marginal or very limited.

4.3 EMIGRANTS' REMITTANCES

There are at least four channels for sending remittances to departure countries:

- Official financial transfers (such as so-called money transfers) through banks, post offices, and other offices that offer financial services. Such

---

[16] Glytsos's work (1995) is valuable not only for its clarity but also because of the wealth of material he quotes from Greek sources, which otherwise would not be available to the wider public.

[17] Cerase, referring to employment, quotes returning emigrants who complained that they were treated as foreigners by their countrymen, who tried to cheat them as they would do with a foreigner.

transfers are registered in the balance of payments statistics of departure countries.

- Unofficial transfers using various channels in unofficial networks that collect and transfer moneys. These channels are organized by the emigrants themselves, with their savings being delivered personally when they return home.
- Buying and sending goods directly to the departure country.
- Transfers by means of a system of financial compensation. An emigrant pays for certain goods and services received by someone in the destination country. That person, in turn, pays an equivalent sum to the emigrant's family in the departure country. This form of transfer is adopted especially when there are restrictions on the foreign exchange markets.

The available data regarding emigrants' remittances come from each country's balance of payments figures supplied by the IMF. These data hugely underestimate the phenomenon – an optimistic estimate suggests that 60% of total remittances are recorded in this way – and perhaps also its evolution.

The way remittances are sent depends on the dispersion of the banking system and on which channels are favored. The possible ways of sending remittances and their growth have been carefully analyzed by Garson and Tapinos (1981) and Garson (1994) in studies centerd mainly on the French–Maghreb case. Their findings, however, can easily be extended to other cases, where sums of money are sent through intermediaries using financial compensation and often the delivery of semidurable goods.

The available information is expressed in current dollars and is very interesting. The growth of remittances from 1968 to 1997, shown in Figure 4.5, offers many insights into how emigrants handle their savings. It can be noted immediately that remittances to Italy no longer make up a relevant part of a citizen's wealth. In contrast, migration from Portugal reached its peak at the end of the 1960s and the beginning of the 1970s, and there was a constant increase in total remittances until the beginning of the 1990s, when the maximum point was reached, twenty years after the outflow of migrants had peaked.

In the southern Mediterranean countries, despite many fluctuations there was a gradual rise in the total of workers' savings sent home. The fluctuations were greater in Egypt because of changes in the migration policies of the receiving countries. Emigrants were influenced by these changes, but there was an underlying rising trend.

Two aspects of emigrants' remittances have been the subjects of research: why migrants send money back home and the effects of remittances.

a.

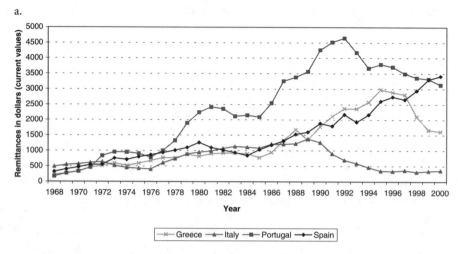

b.

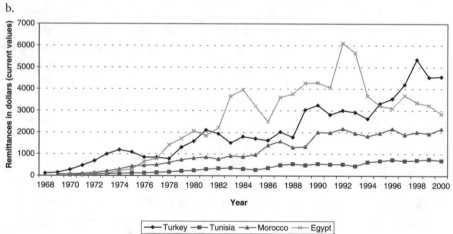

Figure 4.5. Trends of remittances in current dollars for the Mediterranean countries, 1968–2000. *Data source:* IMF, *Balance of Payments Statistics Yearbooks*

4.3.1 Reasons for Sending Remittances

The reasons emigrants send part of their income back to the departure country are many and complex. In general, it can be explained by two main factors: one is *self-interest*, and the other is *altruism*.

The altruistic explanation sees emigrants maximizing their own utility as well as that of their families. An increase in purchasing power due to a devaluation of the currency in the departure country will encourage them not to reduce the amount they send home (see, for example, Bhattacharyya 1985).

The self-interested approach argues that emigrants send money to their families because, as Lucas and Stark (1985) suggest, they hope to inherit family property. They want their land in the departure country to be looked after properly, and they want to keep on good terms with relatives should they decide to return.[18] Alternatively, remittances are a kind of insurance in case the emigrant is forced to return for some reason.[19] If there is devaluation, remittances are reduced, although the purchasing power of those remittances remains the same.

Lucas and Stark (1985) also describe a self-interest contractual model. The decision to send remittances home can be explained by an implicit agreement between the emigrant and the family. The individual repays the family the costs that the family bore for his or her upkeep and education. However, after the emigrant is abroad he or she might not honor the contract or might stop sending money when the debt has been paid off. Alternatively, the emigrant will honor the contract and continue to send money home for various selfish reasons.[20]

A third approach does not explicitly follow either of the two previous approaches. This approach, as in Katseli and Glytsos (1989), interprets emigrants' remittances as a *portfolio choice*: How remittances are allocated is mainly a function of return differentials.

Looking at the empirical approach, there is a series of empirical studies that use *macro data* to analyze what determines the size of emigrants' remittances. There are at least four studies of this phenomenon. Here we consider one by Faini (1994), a second by Lianos (1997),[21] a third by Straubhaar (1986b), and a fourth by Chillemi and Gui (1977).[22] The first

---

[18] In a theoretical study, Subramaniam (1994) suggests that emigrants engage in selfish behavior in that they send remittances only if the funds are invested in agricultural growth and therefore can increase their inheritance.

[19] See Rempel and Lobdell (1978).

[20] Individual data is necessary to test such hypotheses. The one proposed by the authors is that the richer families pay for further education for members of their family because it enables the recipients to earn more, and consequently it is the richer families who receive most remittances.

[21] Reference is made to the earlier works of Glytsos (1988) and Katseli and Glytsos (1989) on remittances to Greece.

[22] A 1984 study by J-P Garson, quoted in a more recent article (1994), analyzes the impact of macroeconomic variables on remittances from France to Portugal. This empirical analysis shows that the real exchange rate is highly significant in explaining changes in the variables; when the Portuguese currency is devalued, remittances increase, thus confirming both the altruistic reasons for wealth flows and the significance of the 1974 dummy introduced for the change in French migration policy, which made it possible to account for the 15% decrease in remittances after that date. The author points out that it was not possible to introduce the interest rate.

study uses aggregate data for the period 1977–89 and analyzes remittances to the Mediterranean countries (Morocco, Tunisia, Turkey, Yugoslavia, and Portugal) as well as remittances from Germany to Greece, Italy, Spain, Portugal, Turkey, and Yugoslavia. The second analyzes remittances to Greece from Germany, Sweden, and Belgium between 1961 and 1981, and the third considers the flow of remittances to Turkey from 1963 to 1982, mainly from Germany. The fourth, using aggregate data, analyzes remittances from Italian workers in Germany between 1964 and 1973.

Although the periods and countries overlap, it is not possible to compare the cases of Turkey and Greece directly because Faini analyzes them together with other flows. Therefore, the cases that are quite similar are compared in Table 4.4: remittances from Germany to the Mediterranean countries in the case of Faini, remittances again from Germany to Greece in the case of Lianos, and remittances to Italy mainly from Germany in the case of Chillemi and Gui. The explicative variables used in the four studies are different, especially in Straubhaar,[23] who uses rates of change for both explicative and dependent variables.

In the first three studies the emigrant's income (Ym) is significant and has a positive sign, whereas in the work of Chillemi and Gui (CG) the authors express doubts regarding the quality of the data available, and they do not include income variable in their regression equation.

In the work by Faini and Lianos, family income in the departure country (Yf) is not significant, and the stock of immigrants ($SMIG$) has a positive effect. CG try to allow for the size of the family abroad by using the relationship between inactive and active workers (In/Lav). As can be expected, this reduces the flow of transfers.

However, the findings regarding some key variables, such as the actual rate of exchange, are contradictory. In study 1 (Faini), it has a positive sign, whereas in 2 (Lianos) it is negative, and in 3 (Straubhaar) it is not significant. The work done by Faini suggests that if the real rate of exchange in the departure country increases, emigrants choose to increase their remittances because they are able to buy more goods in the departure country (a substitution effect prevails). However, in the Greek case illustrated by Lianos, the income effect seems to prevail, with a decrease in remittances.

The rate of interest is important in the first three tests, but in study 1 it is only one variable made up of the difference between the real rate of interest in the receiving country (rm) and the real rate of interest in the departure

---

[23] The dependent variable is the change in the real value of flows of remittances, corrected by U.S. price changes and changes in the foreign exchange rates.

Table 4.4. *Estimates of what determines remittances from Germany*

Variable	(1) Faini 1967–89		(2) Lianos 1961–81		(3) Straubhaar 1963–82[a]		(4) Chillemi and Gui 1964–75	
		t		t		t		t
Ym	1.24	6.5	63,955	4	–	–	2.74	2.7
Yf	−0.4	0.13	−47,836	0.97	–	–	–	–
$SMIG$	0.3	4.3	464	2.6	–	–	–	–
IN/LAV	–	–	–	–	−1.23	5.3	–	–
RER	0.44	7.3	−6,600	5.01	−2.6[b]	2.7	0.72	1.37
Rm-rf-dev	0.11	1.2	–	–	–	–	0.22[c]	0.6
Rf	–	–	34,958	2.05	–	–	–	–
Rm	–	–	−9,448	1.01	–	–	–	–
$Infl$	–	–	32,102	2.49	–	–	–	–
Vb	–	–	–	–	4.7	5.6	–	–
Un	–	–	−17,370	1.8	–	–	–	–
ΔLF	–	–	–	–	–	–	4.5	3.44
Rem_{t-1}	0.16	3.2	–	–	–	–	–	–
Policy	–	–	–	–	–	–	47.9	6.12
Inflation in Yugoslavia	−0.01	5	–	–	–	–	–	–

[a] Rates of change variables; the dependent variable is the rate of change of actual remittances after allowing for the U.S. inflation rate and changes in the exchange rate, which affect purchasing power.
[b] Static expectation of changes in the exchange rate
[c] Differences between real interest rates

Dependent variable remittances in terms of country of origin: (1) Log (Rem); (2) Rem; (3) Δ Rem; (4) Log (Rem)/Y

Ym = Emigrant's income in receiving country, Yf = Income of family in country of origin, RER = Real rate of exchange, SMIG = Stock of immigrants, IN/LAV = Inactive immigrants over workers, Rm-rf-dev = Nominal rate of interest abroad, (Rm) less nominal rate of interest in the country of origin (Rf) after allowing for nominal expected devaluation, dev, Infl = Inflation in the country of origin, Vb = Relation between the official and unofficial exchange rates, Un = Level of unemployment in Germany, ΔLF = Changes in the labor force in Germany, Rem$_{t-1}$ = Remittance lag, Policy = Dummy for the years when there was no change of government, t statistics

country (rf) minus expected inflation (dev), and it is not significant.[24] This is also the case in study 3, which uses only the differences between the real rates of interest. In study 2 the two variables for the rate of interest appear separately but have opposite signs: positive and significant for Greece,

[24] The change in the regression with the Mediterranean countries is significant and positive; see Table 4.2.

which can be interpreted as an incentive to send savings back home, and negative and insignificant for Germany, which is the opposite of what was expected.

Lianos has introduced inflation in the departure country (*infl*) as a separate variable, and it turns out to be significant and to have the expected positive sign. In study 4, the authors (CG) introduce the expected exchange rates as a ratio between the average rate of exchange between the lira and the German mark in one period and in the preceding period. This new variable has a negative sign, indicating that if the lira is devalued remittances decrease, again showing an income effect. Furthermore, to measure the advantage of transfers CG have introduced a variable they call "cost of bank-notes" (*vb*). This measures the relationship between the quotation for lira bank-notes (the unofficial market) and the currency quoted on the Zurich market. This variable seems to be highly significant in all cases.

Each study has its own specificity: Lianos also introduces the unemployment rate (*Un*) in Germany, which is significant and has the expected negative sign. Straubhaar introduces the rate of growth of the labor force (ΔLf), and this variable turns out to be positive and very significant. He also introduces a dummy that allows for the years in which there were no changes in government and no new incentives to send remittances. The latter variable is very significant and indicates that the flow of savings to Turkey increases during times of political stability.[25]

Furthermore, Lianos suggests that there are various reasons that the propensity of emigrants to send part of their income home varies in different periods. One reason may be the rural or urban origin of the successive migratory waves. He splits the period being examined into shorter periods and gets ever-decreasing positive and significant coefficients for the emigrants' income. According to the author, these results reveal the tendency of emigrants to decrease the share of their income sent as remittances the longer they stay in the receiving country. This decrease in remittances, in turn, tends to encourage more emigration, adding new people to the ever-increasing flow.

An interesting study by Elbadawi and de Rezende Rocha (1992) discusses the factors that influenced remittances from European countries to the Mediterranean countries (Morocco, Tunisia, Turkey, Portugal, and the

---

[25] Other studies – for example, Rodriguez (1996), a study of the Philippines – show that policies have little effect in encouraging flows of remittances. Studies of economic history clearly show how important it is to create a network of banks to facilitate remittances and to avoid cheating and theft. See Moreno (1995) for Italy.

former Yugoslavia) from 1987 to 1991. This study covers a particularly important area because it refers to countries that actually export labor, and therefore during that period the remittances they received were relevant. The authors explain the trend of remittances in relation to a weighted average of per-capita income in the receiving countries (Ym), the stock of workers ($SMIG$) or the population abroad, inflation in the departure country ($infl$), the difference between the black market exchange rate and the official exchange rate, and a proxy for the length of the individual's stay abroad.

Because it is impossible to distinguish between the receiving countries and the departure countries, the results of the empirical estimates in Table 4.4 have not been included. Again in this case, however, the emigrant's potential income is significant and has the expected positive sign, and the stock of labor or population abroad is positive and significant, whereas the premium obtained by dealing on the black market decreases remittances. This latter variable is very similar to the one used by CG in the study of Italian emigrants in Germany, but this time it is positive. The two results, however, are less contradictory than they might seem at first sight. In the study by CG the big advantage of the exchange rate or the black market favors sending larger remittances, whereas in the more recent study by Elbadawi and de Rezende Rocha, it is discouraged – but perhaps only through the official channels. The inflation variable in the departure country has a negative sign and is significant; this is the opposite of what Lianos found, but it is difficult to compare the results because other variables, such as the interest rate and the exchange rate, are missing in the test. The proxy for the length of stay abroad is significant and has the expected negative sign only if the time dummy is not included; otherwise, it is not significant, which suggests that a better proxy is needed.

The picture that emerges from these empirical studies is not unequivocal because it is strongly influenced by the availability of information and by the authors' reference models. However, there is clear evidence that three kinds of effects matter: effects due to expected wage levels in the receiving country and in the departure country, that is, wage and labor market variables; the return on investments, that is, the real rate of interest weighted for the rate of exchange; and characteristics of migration deduced either from the stock of immigrants or from the number of active immigrants compared to the inactive immigrants.

Another series of studies with *individual data* analyzes what determines the size of remittances. These studies include not only the income variables but also variables such as education, the status of the breadwinner, the number of children, the length of stay abroad, and ownership of property. This approach was used in the survey carried out by Rempel and Lobdell (1978), in the work already mentioned by Lucas and Stark on Botswana (1985), the research done by Mohammad, Butcher, and Gotsch (1973) on Pakistan, that of Johnson and Whitelaw on Kenya (1974), and that of Brown for Pacific Island (1997).

The variables that seem to be crucial in this context are the length of stay abroad, ownership of property, and the number of members of the family in the departure country. The level of education also provides data that can be used to check the theoretical model of Lucas and Stark presented earlier.

There are only three studies that concern southern Europe: research by Kuncu (1989) into emigrants' remittances to Turkey from Germany, based on an survey carried out by the Turkish Central Bank in 1985,[26] an article by Merkle and Zimmermann (1992) based on data from the German socioeconomic panel of a sample of immigrants interviewed in 1988 (Turkish, Italian, Greek, Spanish, and Yugoslav) in Germany,[27] and a chapter of a book by Conti, Natale, and Strozza (2003) that uses data from a survey of four communities in three areas of Italy. All these studies concentrate on the individual factors that favor the decision to send remittances (see Table 4.5 for a summary of the variables).

Kuncu's work concentrates on families in which the breadwinner is an employee; it does not consider self-employed people or the very few families in which the breadwinner is a woman. He distinguishes between immigrants who are of urban or rural origin. The latter have a higher propensity to save (the marginal propensity to save is between 0.21 and 0.48) than the former, whose marginal propensity to save is between 0.24 and 0.38. He also examines which family characteristics appear to lead to the decision to send remittances.

Various hypotheses have been tested empirically, and the Heckman correction for errors in choosing the sample was applied to the estimates. The variables that favor the flow of remittances toward the departure country are, as expected, income, intention to return, and ownership of property abroad. The number of family members abroad is not significant, whereas being married and being young had negative effects on savings. The latter is probably because young immigrants have many fixed expenses, which reduce possible savings.

---

[26] The survey covered 1,593 families, 625 of them urban dwellers and 968 rural.
[27] A total of 721 people were interviewed.

Table 4.5. *Individual reasons for sending remittances*

Kuncu 1989	Urban, rural	Merkle and Zimmermann 1992		Conti, Natale, and Strozza 2003	
		Sex male	(+)	Sex male	(+)
Married breadwinner	(−),(−)	Married breadwinner	(+)	Married breadwinner	(+)
Size of family in Germany	(°),(°)	Size of family in Germany	(−)	Relatives in Italy	(−)
Age	(−),(−)	Age	(+)	Age	(+)
		Age squared	(+)	Residency status legal	(+)
Planned return	(+),(°)				
		Length of stay abroad	(−)	Temporary intention of stay abroad	(+)
Family income	(+),(°)	Family income	(+)	Family income	(+)
Family income squared	(+),(+)			Consumption in destination area	(−)
		Education or training in the receiving country	(°)	Dummy for area of destination	
		Wives or children in the departure country	(+)	Dummy for country of origin	
Ownership of property in the departure country	(+),(+)	Ownership of property in the departure country	(+)		
		A dummy for Turkey	(+)		

° Non-significant coefficient, + Significant coefficient positive, − Significant coefficient negative

Similarly, the work of Merkle and Zimmermann (1992) is interesting because of the originality of the dataset, which enables immigrants' savings as well as their remittances to be studied. This work seems to suggest two reasons for the choice to send remittances. Either the migration is part of a planned temporary absence from the departure country where the family still lives and where the emigrant owns a house, or there is a possibility of future return and a wish to maintain links and property. The dummy for Turkey provides a way of checking the higher propensity of Turks to save and remit to the departure country.

Conti, Natale, and Strozza (2003) analyze survey data on four immigrant communities (Albania, the former Yugoslavia, Poland, and Morocco) in three areas (Veneto, Rome, and Campania) in 1995–97.[28] The authors use

---

[28] The number of foreigners interviewed is 1,718 (279 from Albania, 264 from the former Yugoslavia, 410 from Poland, and 765 from Morocco).

this dataset to inquire into saving and remittance behavior to see whether it depends, as expected, on the employment status (legal or illegal) of immigrants, their income, whether their families are with them or in the origin country, their migratory plans, or other specific effects related to origin or area of destination. What emerges is that the behavior differs depending on community of origin – something that reflects different migratory plans – and on whether they were males or females. Legal status plays a completely different role: Legal males remit more, whereas legal females remit less, probably because in the latter case, legal status comes at a more permanent stage of migration.

There are also numerous and interesting *historical studies* of migration, in which representative cases of emigrants and their savings and remittances to the departure country are examined. It emerges, for example, that in 1972, 70% of the breadwinners in Germany sent remittances to the departure country (see Chillemi and Gui 1977), whereas in France during the same period only 57% did so. In the latter case it was probably because there was a large percentage of permanent, long-term immigrants. Immigrants in both Germany (ILO 1976, quoted in Reyneri 1979) and Switzerland (Cinnari 1975) who sent remittances sent about one-third of their earnings home, whereas in France it was a little less (24%) (Ministere del L'Economie, quoted in Reyneri 1979), for the reasons mentioned earlier.

4.3.2 The Effects of Remittances on Income Distribution in the Departure Country

In his theory of rural/urban migration, Oded Stark (1991; Stark, Taylor, and Yitzhaki 1986) considers migration as a form of family insurance that is undertaken for both altruistic and selfish reasons. He also investigates the effect of remittances on the distribution of income in the departure country.

Using Gini's coefficient as a function of covariation between income (y_0) and its cumulative distribution $F(y_0)$, we get equation (1), where G_o represents Gini's coefficient of the village's total income, and μ_o is the average income of the village.[29]

$$G_o = \frac{2cov[y_o, F(y_o)]}{\mu_o} \tag{1}$$

---

[29] In the equation, the 2 indicates that the set has been divided into two parts. In a more general formulation in v parts, the expression between the square brackets would be raised to $(v-1)$.

Using the properties of covariance, equation (1) can be rewritten as in (3), where S_k represents the component k's share of income compared to the total income of the village. $S_k = \bar{Y}_k/\bar{Y}_o$, G_k represents Gini's index corresponding to component k of income, and R_k (2) represents Gini's correlation of the component k with total income.

$$R_k = \frac{cov[y_k, F(y_o)]}{cov[y_k, F(y_k)]} \tag{2}$$

Equation (2) enables the impact of remittances on the country's income disparities to be split into three parts. The first part identifies the size of the remittances with respect to total income, the second identifies the inequality in the remittances, and the third specifies the correlation between the remittances and total income.

$$G_o = \frac{2\sum_{k=1}^{k} cov[y_k, F(y_o)]}{\mu_o} = \sum_{k=1}^{k} R_k G_k S_k \tag{3}$$

An exogenous variation that causes every component j of family income to change by the factor (e) gives equation (4).

$$\frac{\delta G_o}{\delta e} = S_j(R_j G_j - G_o) \tag{4}$$

When related to G_o, equation (4) shows that the relative effect of a marginal change in the component j on inequality can be split into two elements: the relative contribution made by the component j to total income disparities minus the relative contribution to total income – in other words, the marginal importance of such income to total family income and its average importance to total income.

Empirical studies made in two Mexican villages with internal migration and flows of emigrants to the United States show that both domestic and international remittances reduce these disparities. The specific role played by the two flows of remittances – domestic and international – was not the same in the two villages. Where migration to the United States is a limited phenomenon, remittances from that source are an important cause of income disparities. In contrast, where international migration is widespread, the contribution of remittances from the United States is very limited and amount to only one-third of domestic remittances. In a later work (Stark, Taylor, and Yitzhaki 1988) the authors reveal that the positive effect of international remittances is reduced if more weight is given to the poorer families.

Adams (1994) carried out similar studies for Egypt (and for Pakistan), but there are none for southern European countries. Instead, for these countries there are historical studies that follow the experience of single emigrants, families, or small villages. Research into Italian emigration, which occurred primarily from the south to the Americas and Europe, has revealed that remittances were used mostly to satisfy the basic needs of the families that stayed behind and seem to have decreased poverty.[30] This does not necessarily mean that the disparities were reduced because other poor were created. However, the suffering of many families was relieved (Moreno 1995). When it was possible for the recipient family to use remittances as savings, they were held as bank deposits and did not produce any positive effects on the local economy.[31] If receiving remittances did not represent a source of renovation for the productive system in the emigrant's home country, they were the cause of an important social revolution in that they served to give importance and financial autonomy to the mostly illiterate women who remained at home in small agricultural villages. Having a bank account was therefore a very relevant source of wealth and represented a big social change (Moreno 1995).

4.3.3 The Effect of Remittances on Income and Employment

Empirical research seems to suggest that the effect of remittances on the economy of the departure country is contradictory. On the one hand, remittances increase consumption by those who stay behind because they loosen the limits on agricultural credit, making it easier to purchase household goods and real estate. Remittances also are a positive item in the balance of payments, enabling machinery, important for growth, to be purchased. On the other hand, remittances stimulate nonproductive consumption, often of imported luxury goods, and this worsens the balance of payments. Remittances also encourage speculation in buildable land, and that can cause inflation. In fact, remittances do not seem to have been invested in the productive sectors, and therefore their effect on economic growth is limited, in some cases distorting economic growth (Swamy 1988).[32]

---

[30] See, for example, Sori (1979).

[31] As Adams (1994) shows in his study of Pakistan, reducing income differentials does not necessarily have a positive effect on growth. In fact, in this study the remittances from international emigrants were received by the richest groups in the village, and therefore income differentials had a greater effect on local growth because these groups had a higher propensity to invest.

[32] Rivera-Batiz (1986) has written an interesting, exclusively theoretical article that analyzes in a traditional model of international trade (with constant returns to scale, minimum costs, perfect

In a survey of immigrants in Germany from six countries, Kondis (1990) (quoted in Glytsos 1995) revealed that 35% of their savings were used to buy a house, an apartment, or household equipment, and only 7.3% was invested in vehicles, agricultural machinery, or small businesses. According to Martin (1991), Turkish emigrants returning home used their remittances to buy agricultural machinery and to extend irrigation systems and therefore add to cultivated land – all actions, that should have a positive impact on local production. However, the effect was modest because the money that was received was first spent on consumption (20%) or on purchasing houses (24–33%), and only after such expenditure was it used to buy agricultural land or small enterprises (Barisik, Eraydin, and Gedik 1990).

Similar evidence for Italy can be found in research carried out by D'Amore et al. (1977) and Signorelli, Tiriticco, and Rossi (1977). Initial optimism due to more than half of the remittances (56.7–73.1%) being used to buy a house in the home country is accompanied by regret that only 13%–16% was allocated to productive activities.[33] Reyneri (1979) points out that emigrants are acting rationally because any productive activity they might start would produce goods that would not compete in cost and quality with those that could be imported. De Castro (1994) emphasizes that remittances were high in Portugal, too, but they do not seem to have led to any appreciable economic growth.

Such considerations of the immediate effects that remittances – which are primarily allocated to consumption – have on income are based on reports that can be found in the history of emigration of any country. In his study of Greece, Glytsos (1993) tries to calculate both the immediate effect and the multiplier effect of remittances on the economic system of the departure country. Following an approach applied by Adelman and Taylor (1990, 1991)[34] and Massey and Parrado (1994) to Mexico[35] for the same

---

competition, etc.) the effect of emigrants' remittances on the welfare of the departure country, income distribution between factors of production, and inflation. Although the increase in prices reduces the positive effects of remittances, migration has an overall positive effect on wealth in the departure country, and there is a shift in the distribution of income in favor of labor.

[33] Signorelli et al. (1977, p. 258).

[34] There is a slight mystery about the bibliographical reference that appears in the work by Durand, Parrado, and Massey (1996) regarding an article by Aldelman and Taylor. In the Durand et al. article the date 1992 is associated with the Adelman and Taylor article. However, in the bibliography the publication date of the article, titled "Is Structural Adjustment with a Human Face Possible? The Case of Mexico," is shown as 1990, not 1992. In 1991 the same authors published in the same journal an extension to the previous article with the added title "New Evidence for Mexico" (pp. 154–63). But the quotation used by Durand, Parrado, and Massey is in neither article, so they were probably referring to a provisional version that was cut for publication.

[35] These findings were used and elaborated in an article by Durand et al. (1996).

period, Glytsos initially distinguishes between individual consumption before and after receiving remittances and shows that consumption increases on average by 91%. The growth of some items in the consumption basket is much higher; for example, expenditure on education increases by 226%. Even when remittances lead to large increases in consumption by the families who receive them, the increased consumption that they induce at an aggregate level amounts to only 3–4.4% of total consumption. If consumption induced by remittances is introduced into an input/output matrix, then the production that it induces can be calculated using an average multiplier of expenditure of 1.7 – which is higher in industry but not so high in services – and produces income growth of about 4.1%. The remittance multiplier calculated in the Greek study is lower than the one calculated for Mexico (3.25, according to Durand, Parrado, and Massey 1996, p. 442), but in both cases remittances, when indirect production is taken into account, have a very positive effect on the departure country's productive system. In particular, expenditure on housing has a higher than the average multiplier. Thus, the conclusions drawn in most of the literature regarding the effects of remittances are questioned because they are based on immediate effects while they should emphasize total overall effects, which depend on the origin country's multiplier.

No similar research has been carried out on the Italian situation, and remittances are now a thing of the past. Similarly, Spain and Portugal have been ignored. However, because the situation in Greece is typical of the northern Mediterranean countries, the conclusions can be extended to the whole area.

Another useful attempt to estimate the effect of emigrants' remittances was made by Courbage (1990) in his study of Morocco. He argues that between 1970 and 1985, remittances helped to create 15,000 jobs per year, which is equivalent to a 0.4% annual growth in income and 0.2% in employment.

Such growth in consumption could cause inflation, at least in the sectors where it is concentrated, such as the building industry, thereby decreasing its benefits to economic growth. Again in such cases the evidence is contradictory. Martin (1991), in his study of Turkey, shows that remittances have little effect on inflation because if demand increases, the supply of goods also increases. Although inflationary pressure could have been created in the Greek building industry, no evidence of it was found by Glytsos (1993).[36] As stated earlier, these results should be interpreted with extreme care.

[36] See Russel (1992).

4.3.4 The Effects of Remittances on the Balance of Payments in the Departure Countries

At an aggregate level, the departure country stands to gain by encouraging migration not only for the reasons we have mentioned – *probable* positive effects on income growth and increased employment (or lower unemployment) in the home country – but also for the *certain* and *immediate* positive effects of remittances on each country's balance of payments. Figure 4.6a shows the experience of the southern European countries from 1968 to 2000. The calculations are based only on figures for remittances that were officially transferred through the banking system,[37] so there is an underestimation of the actual flows to the departure countries. As the figure shows, these remittances were used to pay for a large share of imports.

Figures for Portugal, where there was a period of intense migration[38] from the 1970s to the 1980s, fluctuate between 40% and 10%, whereas the average figure for Greece was 15%. It was lower for Spain and Italy, where migratory flows were decreasing or had in fact come to an end. In contrast, Figure 4.7a emphasises that remittances are still important for the southern Mediterranean countries. For example, at the end of the 1960s and the beginning of the 1970s, remittances enabled Turkey to offset its balance of payments deficit and stave off its economic crisis until 1973.[39] Comparing imports is, however, less revealing than comparing exports for the various countries. Figure 4.6b shows that in the southern European countries the trend is more or less the same. Remittances were no longer an important item in the balance of payments for Italy and Spain, and their importance for Portugal was decreasing. But as Greece went through an economic recession, remittances made an important contribution to exports and increased in the past few years.

In the case of the southern Mediterranean countries (Figure 4.7a 4.7b), Turkey seems to have replaced or at least integrated the emigration of its workers with increased goods exports. Morocco's policy has not been equally successful, and remittances account for 30% of all exports. The case of Egypt is completely different. The country does not seem to have replaced the emigration of workers with the export of goods. The decrease in remittances

---

[37] The data come from "Workers' Remittances and Current Account Merchandise: Imports f.o.b. and Exports f.o.b.," IMF *Balance of Payments Statistics Yearbook* for various years.

[38] De Castro (1994), in his study of Portugal, highlights the role played by the spread of Portuguese banks – for example, in France, their role in the growth of emigrants' remittances, which are sent through official channels.

[39] See Barisik et al. (1990).

a.

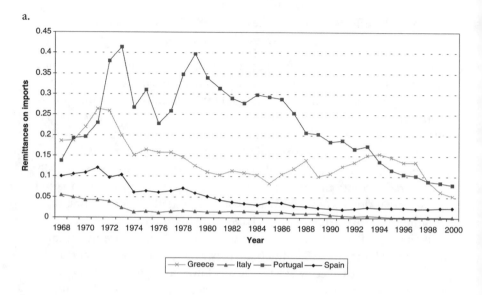

b.

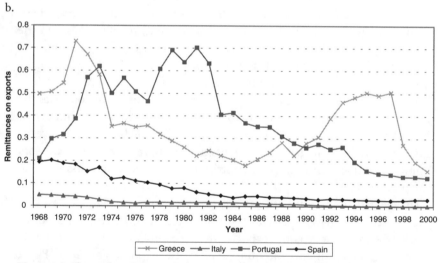

Figure 4.6. Share of remittances on imports and exports for Greece, Italy, Portugal, and Spain, 1968–2000. *Source:* IMF, *Balance of Payments Statistics Yearbooks*

in the 1990s was caused by exogenous factors: the economic recession, wars in the Arab countries, and the replacement of Egyptian workers by cheaper Asian workers. It was not because Egypt had become less dependent on that source of foreign currency.

a.

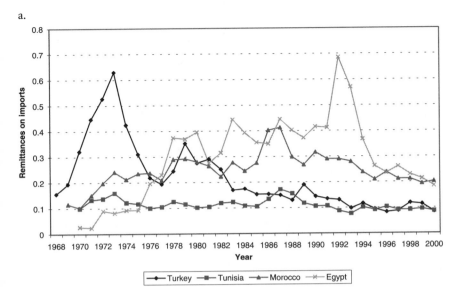

b.

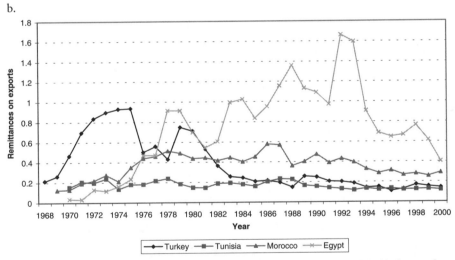

Figure 4.7. Share of remittances on imports and exports for Egypt, Tunisia, Turkey, and Morocco, 1968–2000

The trend of remittances (Figure 4.5) reveals that remittances to the southern European countries continued to increase until 1989 for Italy, 1992 for Spain, 1994 for Greece, and the following year, 1995, for Portugal. Remittances seem to lag twenty to thirty years behind flows of emigrants.

Table 4.6. *Share of exports, imports, and remittances over GDP*

	Spain			Portugal			Italy			Greece			Turkey			Tunisia			Morocco			Egypt		
	E/Y	I/Y	R/Y	E/Y	I/Y	R/Y	E/Y	I/Y	R/Y	E/Y	I/Y	R/Y	E/Y	I/Y	R/Y	E/Y	I/Y	R/Y	E/Y	I/Y	R/Y	E/Y	I/Y	R/Y
1968	5.61	10.82	1.09	14.54	22.21	3.05	11.68	10.40	0.57	0.49	1.32	0.24	2.74	3.79	0.59	12.92	17.86	0.00	0.00	0.00	0.00	0.00	0.00	0.00
1969	5.86	11.26	1.18	14.50	22.44	4.30	12.20	11.56	0.57	4.93	13.33	2.49	2.64	3.57	0.69	12.87	19.84	0.00	13.25	14.29	1.64	10.71	12.75	0.00
1970	6.61	11.51	1.25	14.86	23.99	4.69	12.21	12.44	0.53	5.07	12.51	2.76	3.29	4.76	1.53	13.13	20.43	2.02	12.31	15.77	1.59	10.63	14.11	0.38
1971	6.95	10.61	1.28	14.89	24.93	5.75	12.21	12.12	0.53	4.69	12.91	3.42	3.94	6.14	2.75	12.64	19.76	2.61	11.43	14.57	2.18	10.26	13.65	0.33
1972	6.66	10.52	1.02	14.98	22.37	8.52	12.46	11.89	0.47	5.04	13.05	3.38	3.77	5.99	3.15	12.87	18.64	2.55	11.65	12.87	2.54	8.55	12.30	1.10
1973	6.17	10.16	1.05	11.73	17.52	7.25	11.14	13.00	0.31	5.22	15.19	3.03	4.07	5.80	3.65	12.78	19.11	3.04	12.27	13.94	3.36	8.72	12.47	1.02
1974	6.73	13.22	0.80	12.45	23.30	6.23	13.31	17.08	0.24	6.48	15.06	2.28	3.41	7.47	3.17	20.45	22.79	2.76	18.43	18.30	3.89	15.42	26.88	2.47
1975	6.11	11.77	0.76	9.45	17.25	5.36	13.41	13.86	0.20	6.36	14.01	2.32	2.47	7.45	2.31	15.20	23.56	2.75	14.03	20.77	4.89	11.29	28.38	2.63
1976	7.17	13.00	0.80	8.73	19.31	4.43	15.22	15.95	0.19	7.06	15.59	2.46	3.19	7.30	1.60	15.02	27.37	2.73	11.64	21.54	5.11	10.43	24.91	4.90
1977	7.44	11.81	0.77	11.57	20.71	5.37	15.90	15.95	0.25	6.83	15.37	2.43	2.46	7.13	1.38	13.02	26.89	2.82	9.95	21.86	4.56	11.55	23.63	5.43
1978	7.30	9.52	0.69	10.67	18.63	6.48	14.96	14.18	0.25	6.24	13.55	1.98	2.72	4.78	1.17	12.40	23.76	2.97	8.98	15.86	4.60	10.43	25.51	9.54
1979	7.22	9.45	0.56	11.81	20.57	8.16	14.91	15.11	0.24	6.51	14.82	1.88	1.91	4.07	1.43	16.56	26.57	3.05	9.42	15.79	4.61	10.34	25.60	9.44
1980	7.41	11.63	0.59	12.26	23.03	7.82	14.15	16.05	0.21	6.47	15.26	1.68	3.25	8.39	2.31	18.94	27.50	2.80	9.86	15.39	4.30	12.92	22.85	9.04
1981	9.57	14.16	0.59	12.32	27.65	8.65	15.96	18.44	0.24	9.03	19.23	2.01	5.61	10.22	2.97	24.66	34.34	3.60	12.67	21.31	5.62	14.49	28.69	7.90
1982	10.65	15.28	0.56	14.01	30.48	8.86	16.45	18.46	0.27	8.04	17.32	1.98	8.27	11.96	3.00	22.02	34.83	4.14	11.99	22.41	4.99	14.22	27.37	8.63
1983	12.64	17.54	0.60	21.96	32.05	8.90	17.29	17.89	0.27	9.70	19.84	2.18	9.45	14.24	2.42	22.16	35.01	4.30	14.74	23.64	6.56	13.13	29.32	13.03
1984	14.31	17.00	0.53	23.64	32.84	9.77	17.87	19.28	0.27	10.75	21.09	2.20	12.02	16.80	2.94	21.52	35.49	3.84	16.95	27.99	6.84	12.61	32.89	12.93
1985	14.27	16.78	0.62	24.01	30.16	8.83	17.92	19.35	0.26	10.60	23.09	1.91	12.06	16.41	2.50	—	—	—	16.67	27.29	7.51	11.06	26.09	9.26
1986	11.59	14.42	0.51	19.63	24.08	6.93	16.02	15.27	0.20	9.46	18.73	1.97	9.84	13.84	2.12	20.21	30.52	3.22	14.22	20.52	8.25	7.34	19.98	6.98
1987	11.47	15.90	0.45	22.16	30.72	7.78	15.31	15.35	0.16	10.01	19.82	2.38	11.84	15.55	2.32	19.55	29.92	4.00	14.87	20.58	8.49	7.69	19.98	8.90
1988	11.50	16.72	0.44	22.65	34.15	7.04	15.31	15.35	0.15	9.18	18.57	2.59	13.13	15.09	1.95	21.67	29.18	5.01	16.34	19.75	5.90	7.90	26.76	10.76
1989	11.39	17.83	0.42	24.60	34.01	6.89	16.11	16.36	0.16	8.94	19.94	2.01	10.99	14.93	2.84	23.76	34.63	5.39	14.50	21.85	5.85	9.47	28.80	10.73
1990	11.32	17.25	0.38	24.48	34.42	6.34	15.52	15.45	0.12	7.68	19.98	2.14	8.64	14.99	2.15	24.50	40.97	4.83	16.38	24.54	7.77	9.10	23.89	9.93
1991	11.41	17.16	0.34	21.17	31.11	5.84	14.73	14.77	0.08	7.76	19.02	2.38	9.05	13.91	1.87	28.60	42.25	4.48	18.30	24.64	7.15	11.86	28.01	11.55
1992	11.42	16.70	0.38	19.31	29.19	4.89	14.60	14.34	0.06	6.17	17.92	2.40	9.36	14.51	1.89	28.27	37.44	4.02	17.54	26.17	7.60	8.95	21.71	14.89
1993	12.96	16.08	0.40	18.80	28.30	4.93	17.17	13.84	0.06	5.54	16.93	2.56	8.65	16.50	1.62	25.95	39.02	3.41	18.37	26.06	7.29	7.56	21.15	12.07
1994	15.33	18.40	0.45	21.43	31.00	4.22	18.81	15.31	0.05	5.41	16.84	2.61	14.08	17.30	2.01	25.55	39.63	3.04	18.26	25.20	6.02	7.82	19.34	7.10
1995	16.71	19.97	0.47	24.91	34.15	3.93	21.39	17.30	0.03	5.16	17.72	2.60	12.83	20.55	1.94	29.67	39.68	4.02	20.47	27.87	5.87	7.90	20.76	5.46
1996	18.24	21.09	0.49	25.30	34.56	3.68	20.77	15.75	0.03	4.79	17.40	2.35	18.28	24.24	2.00	30.41	41.47	3.78	18.78	24.76	5.90	7.06	19.47	4.59
1997	19.63	22.14	0.50	24.23	33.58	3.42	20.80	16.71	0.03	–	–	–	17.19	25.29	2.21	28.17	36.65	3.76	21.00	26.57	5.65	7.31	18.72	4.89
1998	20.19	23.93	0.53	23.96	35.38	3.14	20.46	17.46	0.03	6.33	19.55	1.73	15.72	22.89	2.70	28.71	39.50	3.62	20.09	26.61	5.66	5.32	17.68	4.08
1999	21.48	27.26	0.63	25.33	39.04	3.31	22.68	20.43	0.03	6.82	21.14	1.33	14.78	20.05	2.28	27.93	38.12	3.62	21.45	28.44	5.54	5.88	17.03	3.63
2000	20.75	26.66	0.62	23.56	37.02	2.98	22.23	21.23	0.03	9.06	27.02	1.43	15.84	27.03	2.28	30.01	41.58	3.60	22.25	31.95	6.48	7.15	15.58	2.89

E/Y = Exports over GDP
I/Y = Imports over GDP
R/Y = Remittances over GDP
Data Source: IMF; Balance of Payment Statistics, and International Financial Statistics

a.

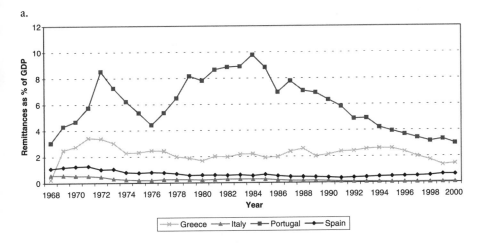

b.

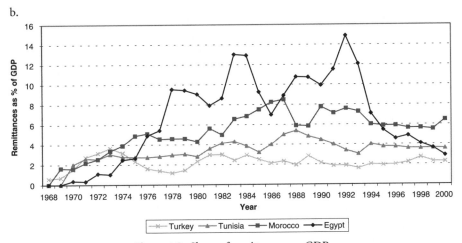

Figure 4.8. Share of remittances on GDP

Remittances continue to increase even when emigration is decreasing. Only when contacts with the home country become less frequent – when the family is united or when they are second-generation emigrants – does the flow of remittances begin to decrease. Such a decrease is not yet apparent in any of the North African countries (Figure 4.5) except for Egypt, where the flows of remittances, as has been noted, were affected by economic and political crises in the receiving countries rather than by the evolution of the migratory phenomenon.

Table 4.7. *Relationship between flows of remittances and direct investment in the country of origin*

Time period	Spain	Portugal	Italy	Greece	Turkey	Tunisia	Morocco	Egypt
1970–75	–	–	0.86	–	11.65	2.11	34.31	–
1976–80	1.01	17.30	1.33	1.62	29.08	1.11	10.80	2.71
1981–85	0.56	11.91	1.01	1.90	22.43	0.18	4.21	4.33
1986–90	0.20	2.85	0.32	1.85	6.04	6.57	16.06	3.45
1991–97	0.26	2.74	0.15	2.47	4.23	1.72	3.91	6.44
1998–2000	0.16	1.04	0.05	2.06	5.87	1.01	203.67	2.78

Data source: IMF, Balance of Payment Statistics

The contribution of remittances to GDP also indicates which migratory phase a country is passing through, and it confirms how important it is for some countries to export labor. In Spain and Italy (see Figure 4.8 and Table 4.6), where the migratory phenomenon is almost over, remittances in the 1960s accounted for about 1% of GNP and today are irrelevant. In Portugal, in contrast, remittances in the 1980s accounted for 8% of GNP, but nevertheless the underlying trend was downward. In Greece the percentage was lower (about 2%) and was reasonably stable – more stable than, for example, exports. It is interesting to analyze the situation in the southern Mediterranean countries, where remittances sent to Tunisia, Morocco, and Egypt represent an important part of total income. Remittances reached their peak toward the end of the 1980s, with values of 5%, 8%, and 10%, respectively, and then gradually decreased, whereas in Turkey remittances accounted for a quite stable but reduced share of GNP.

The real importance of remittances to emigration countries can be understood by comparing the contribution they make to each country's economy with that of direct investment.[40] Surprisingly, remittances on average are multiples of direct foreign investment in all Mediterranean countries except Spain and Italy, where they were very small.

At the end of the 1970s and the beginning of the 1980s, the flow of remittances to Portugal was 10–17 times as high as foreign direct investment (see Table 4.7), and during this period remittances represented about 8% of GNP. Equally high rates were recorded for Turkey, whereas for

---

[40] To avoid inappropriate comparisons between direct foreign investment and remittances, annual averages have been calculated for the period and have been compared to the annual average flow of remittances. The data were taken from the IMF *Balance of Payments, Statistics, Annual Yearbook.*

Tunisia and Egypt, remittances represented multiples that varied from 2 to 6 times direct foreign investment as late as the 1990s. Morocco shows an incredible jump of remittences' role at the end of the 1990s, due to a large reduction in direct investment.

Remittances also can be compared to the departure country's foreign reserves. According to an OECD study (1998), in some periods remittances have accounted for very high levels of a country's foreign reserves. For example, in 1970 in Greece they represented 225% of the foreign exchange reserves, in 1980 in Portugal they were about 400%, and in 1980 in Morocco and Turkey, they were 250% and 200%, respectively, later settling at levels of about 50–60%, as in Tunisia.

Even though all these values should be treated circumspectly, data regarding remittances and direct foreign investment as well as foreign reserves can be improved. These comparisons show that in addition to having an effect on real wealth, remittances represent a valuable source of finance for the departure country and can provide overall benefits that are much greater than those enjoyed by the individual families. It is clear that there are many reasons a departure country should encourage the flow of remittances in addition to the benefits enjoyed by the individual families that receive them. There can be economic reasons an emigrant should be discouraged from integrating culturally into the receiving country and should be encouraged to maintain links with the departure country long after leaving it.

5

The Effectiveness of Migration Policies

This chapter focuses attention on how receiving countries can handle the problem of immigration by passing suitable legislation. Immigration is a complex phenomenon because it affects a number of core issues, such as national identity, sovereignty, and so on. It also has demographic, economic, and social effects. The receiving country will therefore want to control the flow of immigrants according to its political, social, and economic priorities. It is perfectly right that a country should do this, as recognized in the 1977 Helsinki agreement, which states that the "right to emigrate" is not matched by a symmetric "right to immigrate." Immigration – that is, accepting an immigrant – is left to the "mercy of the nation state" (Garson 1997), and the policies adopted by each state should be considered in this light. The multiplicity of the consequences of immigration forces "immigration policy, in its strictest sense" – that is, the laws that regulate entry into and residence in a country and an immigrant's assimilation or eventual deportation – to be supplemented by norms that define who is considered to be an alien.

The widespread dissatisfaction with immigration policies is due in part to the numerous aspects that are involved. They range from the difficulty of anticipating changes in flows to the need to solve the conflicts that can arise. This may mean adopting measures that go against the basic principles of a modern democracy or that are extremely expensive. Immigration policies based on the same principles can have different effects because situations that are similar at the outset are subject to different exogenous shocks. Moreover, an individual's decision to emigrate depends on reasons and conditions that are outside the influence of an immigration policy.

This section has two aims. First, it aims to identify the effects of an immigration policy in its strictest sense: entry into a country, the issue of residence permits and work permits, and the fight to reduce illegal immigration. Second, we wish to draw attention to other policies that affect an alien's status or facilitate assimilation within a country: literacy programs, training, and professional integration.

The topic is vast, and there is a wealth of legal and institutional literature available, so attention is focused here on the effectiveness of such measures and the dynamics they set off. A detailed description of the policies is not given here but can be found in the works of Stalker (1994) and Salt, Singleton, and Hogarth (1994), in the European Commission of Europe and the European Union reports, and more concisely in the OECD *Trends in International Migration* publications.

5.1 IMMIGRATION POLICY IN ITS STRICTEST SENSE

Immigration policy is defined as the set of regulations that govern (a) a foreigner's entry into a country whether or not he or she wishes to work, (b) the immigrant's legal status in that country, and (c) the action to be taken when entry has been illegal. First, the prerequisites of entry are specified. When there are more potential immigrants than the country wants to accept, the prerequisite of a visa is introduced. It must be obtained in the country of departure before leaving and can be granted for tourism, study, or work. This requirement was introduced by the southern European countries, which became the destination of many immigrants in the unexpected wave of immigration in the 1980s. Italy introduced the measure for immigrants from Nigeria, Senegal, and Morocco. Spain, Portugal,[1] and Greece also introduced a visa requirement for other countries. A number of countries require an entry visa.[2] The different treatment reserved, for example, for Peruvians,

---

[1] In Portugal in 1994, a circular was issued that reduced the cases not requiring a visa for some ethnic groups.

[2] Citizens of certain countries must produce a visa to enter the European Union. Here is a common list for the European Union countries (decided on 25 September 1995): Afghanistan, Albania, Algeria, Angola, Armenia, Azerbaijan, Bahrain, Bangladesh, Belarus, Benin, Bhutan, Bulgaria, Burkina Faso, Burundi, Cambodia, Cameroon, Cape Verde, the Republic of Central Africa, Chad, China, Comoros, Congo, Ivory Coast, Cuba, Gibuti, Dominican Republic, Egypt, the Republic of Yugoslavia, Equatorial Guinea, Eritrea, Ethiopia, Fiji, Gabon, Gambia, Georgia, Ghana, Guinea, Guinea Bissau, Guyana, Haiti, India, Indonesia, Iran, Iraq, Jordan, Kazakhstan, Kirgikistan, Kuwait, Laos, Lebanon, Liberia, Libya, Madagascar, Falkland Isles, Mali, Mauritius, Mauritania, Moldavia, Mongolia, Morocco, Mozambique, Myanmar, Nepal, Niger, Nigeria, North Korea, Oman, Pakistan, Papua New Guinea, Peru, Philippines, Qatar, Romania, Russia, Rwanda, San Tomé e Principe, Saudi Arabia, Senegal, Sierra Leone, Somalia, Sri Lanka, Sudan, Suriname, Syria, Tajikistan, Tanzania, Thailand, Taiwan, Togo, Tunisia, Turkey, Turkmenistan, Uganda, Ukraine, United Emirates, Uzbekistan, Vietnam, Yemen, Zaire, Zambia.

The following countries are included on the Schengen list but not on the European Union list: Antigua and Barbados, Bahamas, Barbados, Belize, Botswana, Dominica, Granada, Kiribati, Lesotho, Marshall Isles, Micronesia, Namibia, Nauru, North Marianna Isles, St. Christopher and

compared with people from neighboring countries, can be explained by Peruvians' high propensity to emigrate. This has led the receiving countries to introduce stricter controls on such flows.

An entry visa can be granted to political refugees, for work, for family reunification, for study, for tourism, and for other numerically less important reasons and is followed by the issuance of a residence permit. As shown in Table 5.1, in Italy most residence permits were granted for work (which represented a little more than 60% of the non-EU applicants in the 1990s),[3] for family reunification, and for political asylum. The number for the latter two has increased considerably in the past few years.

As well as defining the necessary conditions to enter a country, immigration policy determines the number of permits to be issued and therefore the size of the flow that the receiving country is willing to accept. It also determines its composition, which depends on which categories of immigrants are allowed in. As has been done in the United States, the law can fix the number of entry permits to be issued every year or can set up a commission to establish the number according to the country's economic and political priorities.

There are numerous conditions to be satisfied in the case of residence permits for people looking for work. In European countries there is a widespread preference to employ native workers, and a foreigner is employed only when no native worker is willing to do the work and there is no foreign worker already in the recipient country who is unemployed and has the necessary skills.

Some countries, such as Australia and Canada, tailor immigration to their program of domestic growth by adopting a point system that combines the goal of achieving a demographic balance with that of ensuring their

---

Nevis, St. Vincent and the Grenadines, Santa Lucia, Samoa, Seychelles, Solomon Isles, South Africa, Swaziland, Tonga, Trinidad and Tobago, Palau, Tuvalu, Vanuatu, Zimbabwe.

The following countries have no visa requirement both for the European Union and the Schengen Agreement: Andorra, Canada, Czech Republic, Island, Japan, Liechtenstein, Malta, Monaco, New Zealand, Norway, San Marino, Slovakia, South Korea, Switzerland, United States, Vatican.

Citizens of the following countries may need a visa to enter some EU countries: Argentina, Austria, Bolivia, Bosnia, Brazil, Brunei, Cyprus, Colombia, Costa Rica, Croatia, Ecuador, El Salvador, Guatemala, Honduras, Israel, Jamaica, Kenya, Malaysia, Malawi, Mexico, Nicaragua, Panama, Poland, Singapore, Slovenia, Uruguay, Venezuela.

Source: Immigration Law Practitioners' Association (1995).

[3] A similar subdivision is not available for the other southern European countries, but the total number of work permits is lower in those countries. For example, a large number of foreigners from Europe go to Spain in retirement, so only 30% of the permits are issued for work; this figure rises to 52.3% for non-Europeans (figures for 1995 kindly supplied by the Spanish Ministry of Labor).

Table 5.1. *Residence permits by categories in Italy: 1994, 1996, 1998*

	1994				1996				1998			
	EU residents	%	Non-EU residents	%	EU residents	%	Non-EU residents	%	EU residents	%	Non-EU residents	%
EMPLOYEES	52,927	34.6	467,224	55.9	55,717	36.6	604,328	64.0	55,560	39.2	517,005	58.0
Employed	46,984	30.7	289,398	34.7	49,546	32.6	448,561	47.5	50,984	36.0	396,737	44.5
Awaiting documents	1,752	1.1	16,793	2.0	886	0.6	2,782	0.3	279	0.2	576	0.1
Unemployed	4,190	2.7	134,358	16.1	5,271	3.5	107,053	11.3	4,295	3.0	95,651	10.7
Sailors	0	0.0	59	0.0	0	0.0	16	0.0	0	0.0	0	0.0
Humanitarian reasons with permission to work	1	0.0	26,616	3.2	14	0.0	45,916	4.9	2	0.0	24,041	2.7
SELF-EMPLOYED	8,947	5.8	30,196	3.6	8,487	5.6	24,366	2.6	7,506	5.3	34,421	3.9
Employed	8,434	5.5	23,581	2.8	8,140	5.4	20,858	2.2	7,506	5.3	33,499	3.8
Awaiting documents	513	0.3	6,615	0.8	347	0.2	3,508	0.4	112	0.1	922	0.1
TOTAL EMPLOYED	61,874	40.4	497,420	59.6	64,204	42.2	628,694	66.5	63,178	44.5	551,426	61.9
FAMILY	26,841	17.5	117,569	14.1	30,243	19.9	165,538	17.5	28,940	20.4	222,985	25.0
Study	19,857	12.9	45,528	5.5	15,337	10.1	30,313	3.2	9,048	6.4	20,830	2.3
Political asylum	2	0.0	5,940	0.7	3	0.0	2,809	0.3	2	0.0	3,360	0.4
Asylum request	1	0.0	7,475	0.9	1	0.0	1,093	0.1	–	–	2,793	0.3
Awaiting emigration	0	0.0	5,101	0.6	0	0.0	105	0.0	–	–	11	0.0
Residence	21,263	13.9	24,979	3.0	23,911	15.7	19,153	2.0	24,524	17.3	16,453	1.8
Religious persecution	13,644	8.9	38,469	4.6	14,032	9.2	40,905	4.3	14,197	10.0	40,268	4.5
Tourism	8,450	5.5	55,908	6.7	3,582	2.4	26,368	2.8	1,006	0.7	8,459	0.9
Awaiting adoption	15	0.1	7,661	0.9	9	0.0	7,483	0.8	7	0.0	4,900	0.5
Awaiting foster parents	9	0.1	501	0.1	9	0.0	1,093	0.1	13	0.0	1,785	0.2
Health	448	0.3	2,665	0.3	313	0.2	2,649	0.3	224	0.2	2,613	0.3
Legal proceeding and detention	2	0.0	3,460	0.4	34	0.0	2,963	0.3	12	0.0	1,500	0.2
Not specified	468	0.3	14,131	1.7	348	0.2	4,714	0.5	304	0.2	2,696	0.3
Other reasons	25	0.1	7,479	0.9	66	0.0	9,654	1.0	264	0.2	11,337	1.3
TOTAL	152,954	100	834,451	100	152,092	100	943,530	100	141,819	100.0	891,416	100.0

Source: Caritas, 1994, 1996, 2000

economic objectives.[4] Thus, business owners who have their own capital and skilled workers who are in short supply are given preferential treatment.

There can be various kinds of residence permits. They can be temporary; nonrenewable; renewable every one, two, three, or ten years; or permanent, indicating different kinds of immigrants or different stages of the immigration process. The aim of any immigration policy is to regulate the flow into the country both through the application of rules regarding entry and rules that enable immigrants to extend their stay or make it permanent.

The effectiveness of such policies depends on many factors, especially on the country's ability to control immigration through legal channels: prosecuting illegal immigration and labor and, in some cases, correcting illegal residence with suitable legalization. Immigration policy in exceptional

---

[4] Before the 1967 reform, which introduced a point system, the Canadian system based selection on the potential immigrant's country of origin. If an immigrant came from the United States, France, the United Kingdom, or another Commonwealth country, there were very few requirements. Under the 1967 reform, which is more or less the same as the one now in force, immigrants are chosen according to the number of points they accumulate, 70 out of 100 being the minimum to gain admittance. The points are assigned as follows:

- Education – one point for every school year, up to a maximum of 12
- Special training courses – up to a maximum of 15 points
- Experience – up to 8 points
- Explicit vacancies – up to 10 points if the worker's skills are in short supply
- A definite job offer – 10 points
- Age – up to 10 points for people under 35, one point per year up to the age of 35, after which 1 point is deducted for each year
- Knowledge of French or English – up to 15 points depending on fluency
- Welcome individuals – up to 10 points awarded by an immigration officer according to the potential immigrant's reasons for wanting to emigrate and his or her initiative (Green and Green 1995)

The Canadian system classifies immigrants into seven groups:

1. Independent principal applicant. Such cases are selected on the basis of points.
2. Independent accompanying family. These applicants are not selected with a point system.
3. Entrepreneur principal applicant. These cases are selected on the basis of the relevance of the investment.
4. Entrepreneur's accompanying family. They are not usually included in the point system.
5. Family. Not settled with a point system.
6. A nominated class made up of distant relatives. Candidates are selected on the basis of a point system but are given extra points.
7. Refugees.

The flow of immigrants into the country is decided every year and has fluctuated from 84,000 in 1985 to 245,000 in 1993, with frequent swings. The point system is specifically applied to only two classes, but economic criteria also condition class 3. However, in Canada a large number of those who entered did so for other reasons. Australia has a similar point system, and the number of immigrants who get permits every year is similar – about 100,000 – even though, as in the Canadian case, the effective flow fluctuates from year to year. The United States does not use a point system. Instead, an annual limit is set at a much higher level, about 290,000, with intermediate limits set at about 20,000 for different nationalities. For details see Borjas (1988).

cases can even include offering regular foreign workers in marginal roles incentives to return to their home country.

An immigration policy is defined as *open* if entry into the receiving country is relatively easy. The number of immigrants the country permits is high or even unrestricted; visas are readily granted, and there are few limits to the issuance of residence permits. In contrast, an immigration policy is defined as *restrictive* if it tries to restrict the flow of immigrants by limiting entry – issuing a smaller number of permits than the number of people who want to enter (or even setting the figure at zero) – or by setting exacting requirements for admission.

The most neutral definitions have been considered, at the cost of ignoring theoretical terms such as *liberal* and *protectionist*. But one other definition of immigration policy must be mentioned: *selective*. Such policies combine a given openness with the specification of certain characteristics that allow entry into the country.

To understand the kinds of measures that characterize these policies, it is necessary to consider how relevant the measures are. If an immigration policy is designed to be closed but the regulations are not applied effectively and the controls are limited, it is possible that legal and illegal entry can be relatively easy. Judging an immigration policy on its principles and not on how it is applied is inappropriate because it does not enable us to predict the policy's real impact. Furthermore, opinions can vary as the conditions of the labor supply change. A set of measures can be considered open and sufficient to control a limited flow of immigrants, but if the flow increases it will be considered insufficient or restrictive.

In passing law n.49 in 1990, the so-called Martelli law, Italy decided to fix the number of people to be admitted for work annually. Unfortunately, it was difficult to collect information about job vacancies – there is no jobs register – and as a result the number of new work permits for 1993 and 1994 was set at zero. In this way a measure that was not intended to close borders ended up doing so. A subsequent law passed by Parliament (6 March 1998, n.40) set up a body to decide the number of permits to be issued each year and to specify how they should be distributed among the various classes: family reunification, asylum, and work. About 60,000 work permits were issued in 1998 and 1999.

Spain also decided that the number of admissions for work would be fixed each year. For example, in 1993 the maximum figure was set at 26,000 work permits distributed among agriculture, building, domestic service, and other services (SOPEMI 1995). However, only one-third of those permits were taken up, so in 1995 the figure was reduced to 8,000 (Ministerio de Asunto Sociales 1995). This result suggests three possibilities: that fixing a high number is not necessarily an invitation for additional immigration; that the number of legal immigrants mirrors the negative economic trend; or that the difficulties experienced by employers and employees alike in completing the necessary documents for legal entry discouraged an increase in regular employment, and so informal working arrangements continued.[5] In 1999, 91,000 work permits were issued, 90% of them for wage earners.

In Greece the maximum number of work permits is fixed jointly by the Foreign Office, the Employment Ministry, and the Home Office after consultation with labor boards, trade unions, and employers' organizations. In 1998, 25,000 work permits were issued. Portugal, unlike the other southern European countries, has not set an upper limit for admissions, probably because immigration pressure is not high.

Some of the questions especially relevant to the dynamics of various components of migratory policy are considered in more detail in later sections.

5.1.1 The Effectiveness of Closed Immigration Policies on Entry for Work

The term *restrictive* or *closed* immigration policy has generally been used to define a policy that tries to reduce the entry of people looking for work. As we will see, such a general definition is no longer appropriate because other reasons, such as political asylum, have increased substantially and have led to limits being introduced in those areas, too. Until the end of the 1980s, a restrictive immigration policy meant a policy that limited the entry of people looking for work, and the two terms were used to mean the same thing.

We will examine the evolution of the immigration phenomenon in northern Europe in the mid-1970s so as to analyze how an immigration policy that restricts the entry of people looking for work affects the flow and the stock of immigrants in the receiving country. When immigration *flows* are considered, the reduction of the number of residence permits issued to people looking for work forces workers with temporary permits to stay in the destination country. Those who want to emigrate must use alternative entry channels, such as family reunification or requests for political refugee status, when in fact the real reason is economic. Reducing the number of residence permits also leads to various forms of illegal immigration: workers

[5] According to the Migration Bulletin of the UN Economic Commission for Europe (1996, p. 9), during the same period in Spain there was a decrease in illegal immigration.

with temporary permits who stay in the receiving country after the work permit has expired, people who work even though they hold study permits or tourist permits, or completely illegal immigrants.

Considering the situation in France, Figure 5.1a shows how family re-unification did not mirror the decrease in the flow of permanent workers in 1974 but offset the impact of the restrictive immigration policy. The Swiss case, Figure 5.1b, reveals the same trend. The decrease in the number of people entering for work in 1975 was accompanied by a substantially constant number of inactive people entering the country.

In France the number of requests for political asylum increased from 2,000 in 1972 to 18,000 in 1980, and in Switzerland the number increased from 853 in 1975 to 1,882 in 1982. On the size of illegal flows only estimates exist, but in the case of France the increase in illegal immigration was so large that it forced the government to implement legalization in the 1981–82 period.

The *stock* of foreign residents did not decrease, as was expected, because – in addition to the flow of new immigrants and the fact that fewer immigrants returned to the country of departure than expected – the foreign population in a country has its own dynamics independent of the migration policy. It depends on the birth rate, which is higher for foreigners than it is for natives, and on the naturalization rate.

In Belgium in the 1970s, half of the population inflow was accounted for by foreign births. In France the 1982 census revealed that out of a total foreign population of 3.6 million, about 23% (823,480) were born in France. The fertility rate of immigrants is generally higher than that of natives, it decreases to the national rate only after a long period. In France in 1975 the fertility rate of foreigners was 3.33 and for natives, 1.84; it gradually decreased, reaching 3.05 for foreigners and 1.75 for natives in 1985. Such a trend is common in other European countries, too. In Belgium the fertility rate of foreigners in 1981 was 2.94 and for natives, 1.57; by 1985 it had decreased to 1.82 for foreigners and 1.48 for natives. Germany had a similar falling trend for the two fertility rates (in 1976, 2.57 and 1.36; in 1981, 2.28 and 1.36; in 1985, 1.64 and 1.25). The fertility rate also varies according to the nationality of the immigrant, and it is higher for the most recent waves of migrants.

Naturalization reduces the stock of foreigners. The number depends on the rules regarding citizenship, which differ from country to country, but it also depends on whether foreigners want to use this channel to re-main in the receiving country. Table 5.2 shows that in Germany natural-ization increased immediately after a more restrictive immigration policy

a. France: Inflows of permanent workers and family members (000)

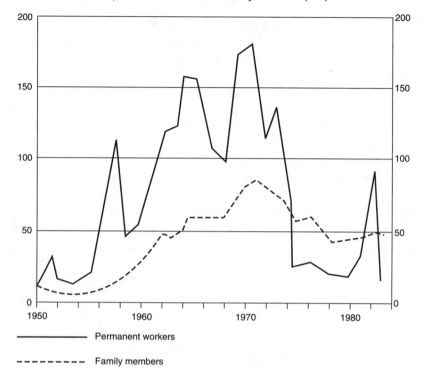

_____ Permanent workers

- - - - - - - - Family members

b. Switzerland: Inflows of active and inactive immigrants (000)

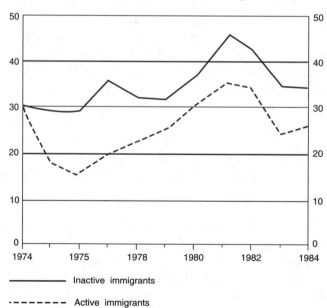

_____ Inactive immigrants

- - - - - - - Active immigrants

Figure 5.1. Trends in immigration flows into France and Switzerland. *Sources:* [a]Penninx (1984), Werner (1985); [b]Data SOPEMI, OCDE, from Maillat (1986)

Table 5.2. *Germany: Population changes, 1971–85 (in thousands)*

Year	Total population 1 January I	German population (including naturalizations) II	Foreign population including naturalizations III	Natural foreign population changes (a) IV	Net migration of foreigners (b) V	(a)+(b) VI	Naturalizations VII	Foreign population net of naturalizations VIII
1971	61,001.2	58,263.2	2,737.9	71.6	+370.5	+442.1	9.0	2,737.9
1972	61,502.5	58,322.5	3,180.0	81.9	+272.7	+354.6	8.2	3,171.0
1973	61,809.4	58,274.8	3,534.6	89.5	+342.3	+431.7	8.5	3,527.4
1974	62,101.4	58,135.1	3,966.3	99.0	−41.9	+57.1	12.3	3,940.6
1975	61,991.5	57,948.0	4,023.5	86.9	−234.0	−147.1	65.6	3,985.4
1976	61,644.6	57,768.3	3,867.3	78.4	−128.1	−49.7	48.6	3,772.7
1977	61,442.0	57,615.4	3,826.6	70.2	−29.2	+41.0	65.4	3,674.4
1978	61,352.7	57,485.1	3,867.6	66.9	+50.4	+117.3	33.7	3,650.0
1979	61,321.7	57,336.8	3,984.9	67.5	+179.2	+246.6	16.4	3,753.6
1980	61,439.3	57,207.5	4,231.5	72.2	+245.6	+317.8	15.4	3,963.8
1981	61,658.0	57,108.7	4,549.3	71.5	+85.6	+157.1	13.6	4,266.2
1982	61,712.7	57,006.3	4,706.4	64.5	−111.6	−47.1	13.3	4,409.7
1983	61,546.1	56,886.8	4,659.3	53.4	−151.6	−98.2	14.3	4,349.3
1984	61,306.7	56,745.6	4,561.1	54.8	−210.0	−155.6	15.0	4,236.8
1985	61,049.3	56,643.8	4,405.5	–	–	–	–	4,066.8

Note: I = II + VIII
Source: Statistiches Boundesamt, Wiesbaden, taken from Tribalat (1986, p. 569)

was introduced because naturalization was perceived as a guarantee that would facilitate the immigrants to stay and work in the destination country. Later, when the economy came out of its recession and the immigration policy became more flexible, the immigration balance became positive and the number of applications for naturalization decreased. Table 5.2 also shows that in Germany between 1971 and 1984 the natural growth of the foreign population was always greater than the number of naturalizations and reduced the effect of any decrease in the stock of immigrants.

The drift of immigration flows due to family reunification and to the difference in the fertility rate varied according to laws that specified who had the right to join their family, and to the nationality of the immigrant. As shown later, immigrants from some countries were more willing than others to use this channel and to have larger families.

5.1.2 The Economic Implications of Family Reunification

Family reunification is an important element in an immigration policy. With a few exceptions, the family members who can join their relatives are spouses, small children (under a certain age), and dependent parents. If the possibility of family reunification is granted to foreign immigrants who have the means to maintain their families, then immigration is not necessarily conceived as being a temporary phenomenon. The countries that want to limit immigration to a certain period of a foreigner's life tend not to authorize family reunification. In some cases they do not even contemplate it, as in the case of Japan[6] and the Arab countries. In contrast, countries that tend to favor permanent settling of foreigners have generous family reunification policies. This is the case for the United States, where brothers and sisters can also benefit from the provision.

Family reunification, however, has three important effects. An initial effect is caused by the creation of an *endogenous dynamic* in the stock of immigrants. A firm that is authorized to bring a foreigner into the country to work sets off a process that – within a given time defined by the laws or by the worker's wish to remain in the country – automatically causes the stock of immigrants to grow through family reunification, thus inducing a flow of foreigners that is higher than it would be for single workers. This type of

[6] For an analysis of the evolution of the immigration policy in Japan, see Gooneratne, Martin, and Sazanami (1994) and Kono (1991).

provision weakens the effectiveness of a restrictive policy, as was shown in the case mentioned earlier of Europe in 1974.

A second effect of family reunification is reflected in the *composition of the stock* of immigrants. This effect is very important in understanding the different degrees of professional and economic integration of foreigners,[7] as in the United States, Canada, and Australia. These three countries are quite similar in that they encourage permanent settlers. This is especially the case for the United States, which, in 1965, with amendments to the Immigration and Nationality Act, introduced the idea of family reunification, a central point of U.S. immigration policy. Canada, with the Immigration Act of 1962, reduced Europeans' privileged entry conditions and centered its new immigration policy on professional requirements. Only in 1976 were amendments introduced that emphasized the role of family reunification in immigration policy. Australia, which only in 1972 abandoned an immigration policy that discriminated according to country of origin,[8] introduced a point system that favors an immigrant's education and professional characteristics; only later, in 1980, was any emphasis given to family reunification.

Because immigrants in the United States were mainly young males and because the relatives joining them were mainly women, children, and old people, there was a general decrease in the quality of the labor force in the 1970s, and this led to decreases in immigrants' average earnings. In the same decade Canada and Australia accepted selected workers who were able to integrate professionally into their respective societies. According to a study by G. Borjas (1988, p. 97), the reduction of wage assimilation of foreigners in the United States in the 1970s and the lack of such reduction in Canada and Australia are due in part to the different regulations that govern entry into the respective countries. And the different regulation is responsible for at least 5% of the reduction of relative wages of immigrants in the United States.

A third effect concerns the *growth of illegal work* done by the family members who join the breadwinner. As has been said, family reunification can be an alternative to entry for work. However, the spouse cannot always enter the labor market immediately, so when he or she does not initially get a legal job, illegal work represents a natural way of increasing family earnings. In fact the arrival of the spouse is often seen as a way of accumulating savings

---

[7] For a definition of what is meant by professional and economic integration, see Section 3.1.2.
[8] In fact it was known as White Australia because the policy excluded immigrants from Asia and Africa.

more quickly, making it possible to return sooner to the country of origin. This explains why the immigrant is not very interested in a permanent job and is willing to look for work wherever it is available.

When governments want to control this flow of immigrants through a more restrictive policy of family reunification, their hands are tied. In the 1970s when France[9] and Germany tried to adopt a more restrictive family reunification policy, the restrictions were fought in the courts on the grounds of defending the rights of the emigrants (Hollifield 1992, p. 35).

It is interesting to note that Italy, Spain, Portugal, and Greece allow family reunification, but only for close relatives: spouses, young children, and parents dependent on the immigrant.

5.1.3 The Economic Implications of the Growth of Asylum Applications

The regulations that govern the procedures for recognizing political refugee status play an increasingly relevant role in migration policy. The policy of granting asylum was originally conceived as the way of solving individual cases or requests by small groups of refugees from countries at war or refugees fleeing political or religious persecution.[10] Thus, there were numerically few cases. However, in the 1980s and 1990s the phenomenon changed so much that its funding and regulations were no longer sufficient to handle the new wave of requests. Figure 5.2[11] shows how requests for political asylum

---

[9] In France a measure restricting family reunification was rejected by the Conseil d'Etat because it included Algerians, and relations with that country could be regulated only through a bilateral agreement. Later, Portuguese were also excluded, and because the two most important groups of immigrants were excluded the whole directive failed. See Moulier-Boutang and Garson (1984).

[10] According to Zolberg (1989), Zolberg, Suhrke, and Aguayo (1989), and Widgren (1991), there are three kinds of persons who ask for protection: activists, who are persecuted for their political activities; the persecuted, who are being victimized because they belong to an ethnic or religious group; and potential victims, who are fleeing from a civil war or other general catastrophe. The first group is covered by asylum law, and very few people are accepted. The second group is covered by the Geneva Convention of Refugees of 1951. The last group is the most important today, and permits to stay on humanitarian grounds are frequently issued.

[11] The data of Figure 5.2 do not match the data in Table 5.3 for the 1980s. The figures, however, are very useful in that they show rapid increases in the late 1980s, when the data are closest. The sources of the two sets of data probably relied on different definitions. It should also be remembered that until recently, information regarding the number of refugees was aggregate and limited. On the one hand, multiple applications were included, and on the other hand, relatives were excluded and only applicants were counted.

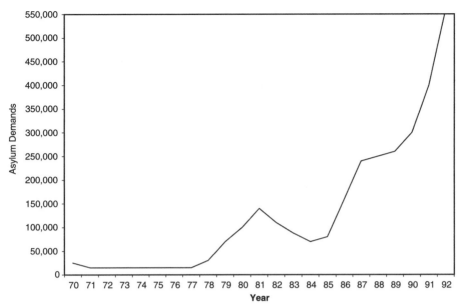

Figure 5.2. Demand for asylum in Europe and North America, 1970–92. *Source:* Widgren (1991, p. 187), data source HCR

increased from 1970 to 1992. The initial jump in requests for political asylum could be interpreted as a response to more restrictive rules for people looking for work. Countries that traditionally welcomed immigrants introduced these rules after the recession in 1974. The even greater demand after 1985 shows that the phenomenon has changed fundamentally.

The southern European countries were not the main "collectors" of these flows, as Table 5.3. shows. Germany was particularly involved in this new phenomenon. Asylum requests were higher for Germany than for the United States and Canada, two countries that have always been the most important countries for this kind of request.

There are three reasons for the general increase in asylum requests: the difficulty of legally entering the labor market in the receiving country, the collapse of the economic and political regimes in eastern Europe, and the gradual growth of fundamentalism in some Islamic countries. Eastern European countries are the most important area of origin, whereas certain African countries (Somalia, Ethiopia, Ghana), Arab countries (Iran, Iraq), and Asian countries (India, Sri Lanka) are the sources of important flows of emigrants.

Table 5.3. *Inflows of asylum seekers into selected OECD countries, 1980–2000*

Country	1980	1985	1987	1989	1991	1993	1995	1996	1999	2000	Average 1990–2000	% asylum of inflows 1998–99[a,1,2]
Greece	1,800	1,400	6,950	6,474	2,800	0,800	1,400	1,560	1,500	3,100	1,594	5,9
Portugal	1,600	100	250	116	0,200	2,090	0,450	0,269	0,300	0,200	0,501	9*
Italy	2,450	5,400	11,050	2,240	27,000	1,300	1,700	0,675	33,400	18,000	11,725	8,3
Spain	1,400	2,350	3,700	3,989	8,000	12,600	5,700	4,730	6,400	7,200	6,376	9,3*
France	18,790	28,809	27,568	61,372	50,000	27,600	20,400	17,405	30,900	38,600	26,415	21,5
Germany	107,800	73,850	57,400	121,318	256,100	322,600	127,900	116,193	95,100	78,600	142,356	31,5
The Netherlands	3,200	5,650	13,450	13,898	21,600	35,400	29,300	22,170	39,300	43,900	27,381	39,5
United Kingdom	9,950	6,200	5,900	16,830	73,400	28,000	55,000	34,800	91,200	97,900	54,329	21
Austria	9,300	5,300	6,000	8,200	15,400	26,500	11,700	6,991	20,100	18,300	14,142	–
Switzerland	3,020	9,700	10,900	24,425	41,600	24,700	17,000	18,001	46,100	17,600	23,572	37,7
Norway[a]	200	800	8,600	4,400	4,600	12,900	1,500	1,800	10,200	10,800	5,971	20
Sweden[a]	3,000	14,500	18,100	30,000	27,400	37,600	9,000	5,800	11,200	16,300	15,329	68,7
United States[a]	26,000	16,600	26,100	101,700	56,300	144,200	154,500	128,217	42,500	52,400	82,588	15
Canada	1,600	8,400	35,000	19,900	32,300	21,100	25,600	26,120	29,400	34,300	24,117	16

[a] For Norway, Sweden, and USA data in the first column refer to 1983.

1. Percentage ratio between average (1990–99) demand of asylum seekers to 1998 or 1999 total inflows

2. For Portugal and Spain estimated inflows. Inflows for Austria not available

Source: OCDE, 2001, Trends in International Migration, Paris.

Asylum applications decreased during the 1990s for a number of reasons:

- The improved economic and political situation in some of the departure countries reduced migratory pressures and led some people to return to their departure country. For example, this has happened for some refugees from Bosnia-Herzegovina.[12]
- The EU's recognition of the governments of some of the refugees has meant that some nationals can no longer apply for asylum.
- The long, drawn-out acceptance procedure hinders smooth integration into the destination societies.
- And last but not least, greater checks have been implemented on illegal immigrants.

The high number of applications has meant that receiving countries have had to adjust their structures and amend their procedures. Thus, they have reduced the time taken to process applications as well as the number of subsequent appeals; in the past, these were ways of remaining in the receiving country while alternative ways of establishing the right to remain were explored.

The rate of acceptance of those who ask for political asylum is very low. In Italy in 1992 and 1999, 83% of the applications were rejected. In other southern European countries – Spain, Portugal, and Greece – an even higher percentage of applications was rejected.[13]

Entering a country as a political refugee is an important channel of immigration and of getting illegal work. An individual can be treated in two ways while waiting to be accepted. One is for the receiving country to issue a temporary work permit while the immigrant awaits the decision. The other is to offer the foreigner subsidies while the application is being processed. The latter reflects the fear that entry into the labor market would make repatriation more difficult. In the past, France and Germany chose different ways of tackling the problem. France initially granted temporary work permits, whereas Germany gave applicants financial assistance. But experience led the two countries to rethink their respective policies and to adopt the alternative procedure, proving that it is not possible to say whether one is better than the other. Italy now guarantees the foreigner a residence permit and financial assistance for forty-five days while he or she waits for asylum

---

[12] To encourage immigrants to return home, the German government offered favorable investment loans to anyone returning home (SOPEMI 1999).

[13] To compare the acceptance rates of various national asylum policies, see Rotte, Vogler, and Zimmermann (1996). The highest values in 1990–94 were for France (23%), Belgium (30%), and the Netherlands (16%).

to be granted.[14] Spain, Greece, and Portugal have similar policies; they do not grant temporary work permits but offer financial support. This suggests that there is a common model for the Mediterranean countries, where illegal work easily permeates the economic system.

The increase in the number of applications for political asylum has been a source of illegal labor, and the presence of illegal foreigners who have fled refugee camps is proof that this channel of entry is being used improperly. To track asylum seekers, the United States has moved the first point of control for asylum applications to the airport, thus confirming the suspicion that many requests are groundless.[15]

5.1.4 How Illegal Immigrants Are Pursued

Now let's consider the phenomenon of illegal immigration in more detail. Figure 5.3, which is an extended version of the table proposed by Tapinos (1994), shows that a foreigner's illegal presence and illegal employment can have various origins.

If an individual enters the country illegally, his or her residence and subsequent employment are illegal, as shown in the flow B-E-L in Figure 5.3. However, this is not the only flow of illegal residents and workers into Europe; it is not even the most important flow. The highest number of illegal residents are those who enter the country legally with a residence permit for study or tourism but become illegal residents[16] when the permit expires (flow A-D in Figure 5.3), and this is often associated with illegal employment (A-D-I).

Irregular residence can be corrected by introducing regularization measures, as in box F in Figure 5.3. This happens when the individual has an expired residence permit (box D) and is in legal or illegal employment. Regularization procedures often require the applicant to have a job, and that links the residence permit closely to the work permit (F-N), creating ambiguity and confusion regarding the objectives of immigration policy.

It is natural to ask whether a part of the migratory policy objective should be to pursue foreigners who hold a valid residence permit but do irregular

---

[14] One exception was the case of the illegal Albanian immigrants in 1997, who were granted temporary work permits while they waited for normal conditions to be restored in their country and democratic elections to be held. Italy played a leading role in the multinational peace force.

[15] *Migration News*, July 1997.

[16] In the specialist literature, the term *illegal* is used for a foreigner who enters the country illegally, and *irregular* for a foreigner who enters the country legally but later, when his or her residence permit expires, does not renew it, thus passing from A to D in Figure 5.3.

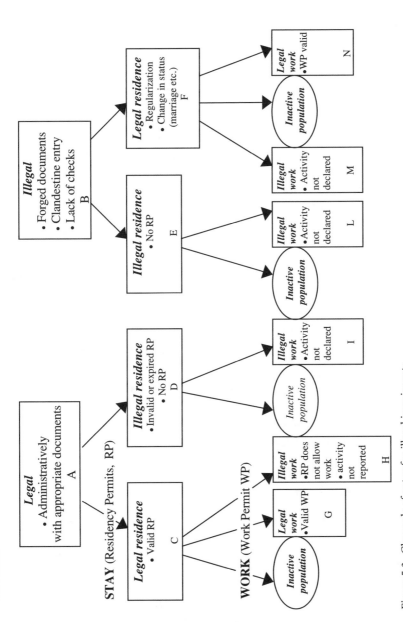

Figure 5.3. Channels of entry for illegal immigrants

work, shown in the figure in the passages from C to H and from F to N. An immigration policy has three main tasks:

- To control entry so as to prevent an illegal flow (B). This is described as a *preventive* policy.
- To pursue illegal residents in the receiving country (D), which is called a policy of *repression*. If illegal entry (B) is prevented, status E does not exist.
- To correct illegal situations (F).[17]

Immigration policy should monitor the creation of illegal jobs due to the shortage of residence permits – as in the cases shown in Figure 5.3, boxes I and L – but it is difficult for a policy to influence a foreigner's illegal activities when his or her residence status is the same as that of natives (N, H).

For selection to be effective, a country must be able to control illegal flows effectively. *Prevention* – that is, border controls – is very costly, considering its effectiveness. Prevention is easier in countries that do not border immigration areas, such as Switzerland and northern Europe, but American studies on border controls show exponential costs with decreasing results.[18] Surprisingly, clandestine Mexican emigrants do not try to cross the border at little-known points that are patrolled infrequently. Instead, they continue to use the more traditional points where patrols are more frequent, reassured by the fact that on average one out of three attempts is successful.

The policy of *repression* in the area can involve the following:

- Only the foreigner. If he or she does not have a residence permit or receives a small conviction, it constitutes an action for deportation, and the person is taken to the border or ordered to leave the country.
- The people who organize clandestine immigration. They are arrested and fined.
- Employers. If they employ illegal workers, they are fined or charged with criminal offenses.

Repressive measures are expensive and not very effective. Deportation, in addition to being expensive, is difficult to apply when the country of origin does not cooperate in identifying forgeries or in cases when foreigners destroy their identity card to make it difficult to ascertain which country

---

[17] It is well known that another basic aim of immigration policy is to achieve economic and social integration, but other objectives are considered under this argument.

[18] Discouraging results can be seen in the simulation of the effectiveness of border controls carried out by Todaro and Maruszko (1987). A general discussion can be found in Chiswick (1986, 1988), Bean et al. (1989), and *Migration News* (1997).

they should be sent to. This is especially true when the departure country is not the country of origin. Bilateral readmission agreements should be drawn up with the immigrants' country of origin so that deportation orders can be executed quickly and support can be provided to discourage illegal immigration.

Employers who take on clandestine workers have been prosecuted for a long time in Europe, and similar measures were introduced in the United States in 1987 (the Immigration Reform and Control Act, or IRCA). Employers can respond to repressive measures in two ways. If they do not wish to risk incurring fines for employing irregular immigrants, they also stop employing regular immigrants; they are afraid of employing people with forged documents. Thus, they practice a perverse form of discrimination. On the other hand, other employers are willing to take the risk and continue to take on foreigners whose documents are obviously forged. Thus, the flow of clandestine immigrants is not affected and regular immigrants are penalized. In southern Europe, such policies have been largely ineffective because there are light sentences and few controls.

When illegal immigration is seen to be widespread and to be the result of a unique situation, the response can be to introduce exceptional measures, such as regularization. This practice helps to correct irregular employment due to clandestine residence in the country or other cases foreseen by the law, such as irregular family reunification and so on. Italy, Spain, and Portugal have adopted such measures (see Table 5.4). There have been five regularization processes in Italy and in Spain, three in Portugal, and two in Greece.

5.1.5 Regularization Procedures

The receiving countries can either adopt a generalized regularization policy aimed at correcting the high number, or assumed high number, of irregular foreigners employed illegally, or they can resort to small, specific regularizations for special cases. A procedure of generalized regularization was adopted by France in 1980–81 and 1988, by the United States in 1988–90, and by the southern European countries Italy, Spain, Portugal, and Greece. The other European countries have never resorted to such measures, and countries such as Switzerland and Germany are strongly against them. They prefer to carry out small ad hoc measures and so keep greater control over the people who live in their country (Garson 1997).

Contrary to the policy in the United States and France, where the question was debated for a long time, the southern European countries passed

Table 5.4. *Recent regularizations in southern European countries by main countries of origin*

Italy

1987–88	a	1990	a	1996	a	1998	a	%	2002[b]
Morocco	21.7	Morocco	49.9	Morocco	42.3	Albania	39.4	18.1%	
Philippines	10.7	Tunisia	25.5	Albania	34.9	Romania	23.4	10.7%	
Sri Lanka	10.7	Senegal	17.0	Philippines	29.9	Morocco	22.4	10.3%	
Tunisia	10.0	Former Yugoslavia	11.3	China	14.9	China	19.1	8.8%	
Senegal	8.4	Philippines	8.7	Peru	14.9	Nigeria	11.6	5.3%	
Former Yugoslavia	7.1	China	68.3	Romania	10.0	Senegal	10.0	5.0%	
Other	50.1	Other	97.1	Other	102.1	Other	91.7	42.4%	
TOTAL	118.1	TOTAL	217.7	TOTAL	249.0	TOTAL	218.7	100	715.0

Spain

1985–86	a	1991	a	1996	a	2000	a	2001	a
Morocco	7.9	Morocco	49.2	Morocco	7.0	Morocco	45.2	Ecuador	48.8
Portugal	3.8	Argentina	7.5	Peru	1.9	Ecuador	20.2	Colombia	36.4
Senegal	3.6	Peru	5.7	China	1.4	Colombia	12.5	Morocco	13.9
Argentina	2.9	Dominican Rep.	5.5	Argentina	1.3	China	8.8	Romania	18.8
United Kingdom	2.6	China	4.2	Poland	1.1	Pakistan	7.3	Ukraine	7.6
Philippines	1.9	Poland	3.3	Dominican Rep.	0.8	Romania	6.9	Bulgaria	6.4
Other	21.1	Other	34.7	Other	7.8	Other	63.1	Other	78.4
TOTAL	43.8	TOTAL	110.1	TOTAL	21.3	TOTAL	163.9	TOTAL	216.4

Portugal						Greece		
1992–93	[a]	1995	[a]	2001	[a]	1997–98	[a]	2000
Angola	12.5	Angola	9.3	Ukraine	42.6	Albania	239.9	
Guinea-Bissau	6.9	Cape-Verde	6.9	Brazil	22.6	Bulgaria	24.9	
Cape-Verde	6.8	Guinea-Bissau	5.3	Moldova	8.5	Romania	16.7	
Brazil	5.3	Brazil	2.3	Romania	7.0	Pakistan	10.8	
San Tomé	1.4	Pakistan	1.7	Cape-Verde	5.2	Ukraine	9.8	
Senegal	1.4	China	1.6	Russia	4.8	Poland	8.6	
China	1.4	San Tomé	1.5	Other	23.2	Other	58.9	
Other	3.5	Other	6.5					
TOTAL	39.2	TOTAL	35.1	TOTAL	120.2	TOTAL	369.6*	TOTAL 350.0[c]

[a] Thousands of immigrants affected
[b] Only demands received by the Ministry, not controlled for duplications
[c] Granted a white card as first step to get a green card in 2001: 148,000.

Source: SOPEMI (2001) and national sources

regularization laws, especially the first one, in response to a wave of unexpected immigration flows that were not suitably controlled. This immigration created an undefined but estimated large stock of illegal immigrants.

Regularization measures are often abused. It is, in fact, difficult to define conditions that favor regularization but cannot be abused. Therefore, clandestine immigrants are often attracted to a country anticipating a regularization measure or during the period it is being applied, and even afterward. Immigrants come in the expectation that further regularization measures will be introduced.

The characteristics of a regularization procedure are as follows:

- The requirements necessary to take advantage of the procedure – for example, residence in the country for a minimum period. It was set at at least $5\frac{1}{2}$ years in the United States, 18 months in France,[19] and about 23 days in Spain and 26 days in Italy for the first legalization. Alternatively, an employer can state that the worker is employed or will be employed.
- The length of the period during which the applications can be made.
- The administrative structure, financing, and advertising of the measure.
- An amnesty for employers.

It was difficult, if not impossible, to foresee all cases, and so the recent regularization measures in southern Europe, like earlier measures in the United States and France, facilitated entry by reducing the necessary requisites. The dilemma is always the same: There is the risk that if the measure is too restrictive it will fail; but if amendments are made they will make the rules governing entry too lax. This does not appear to have been the case with the southern European regularizations, where the number of people registered has always been much less than the estimates of the number of people eligible. The southern European countries have also been forced to extend the expiration date a number of times, and in many cases it reached 18 months. This should not be interpreted as a failure but more as a wrong estimate. In fact, the United States, with a more elaborate structure and more money invested, estimated that the procedure would take between 12 and 18 months depending on the cases. In the southern European countries, such periods have been reached after extensions have been introduced.

All the measures have included specific amnesties for employers of illegal workers (usually fined)[20] so that employers will offer immigrants regular

---

[19] Reference is made only to the first legalization in the French case because more information is available.

[20] Cobb-Clark, Shiells, and Lindsay Lowell (1995) have written an interesting study using U.S. data. They analyze the joint effect on native workers' wages of introducing an amnesty through IRCA

employment and in this way favor their real economic and social integration. The first aim of a regularization measure, however, should be to regularize the presence of foreigners in the country and, only when possible, irregular labor. For this reason regularization measures have included persons looking for jobs or workers falsely declared as self-employed, and so these measures have ended their illegal presence in the country. Temporary residence permits are issued in such cases, and when the permit expires the foreigner often reverts to illegality. For example, in Spain after the second regularization in 1991, which involved 110,000 foreigners, only 82,000 still had a valid permit in 1994. The others had returned to their own countries or had again become illegal residents (Garson 1997).

So that regularization measures do not have an "attraction effect," they should not be announced in advance but instead introduced without prior notice; they should have a very short expiration date, which should never be extended. None of the countries mentioned adopted such a strategy. In the United States and France the regularization was preceded by a long debate, and in the United States the procedure was publicized extensively but not extended. In the other countries the regularization was not given much prior publicity, but the measures were extended many times. The differing situations in Europe and the United States have led to different ways of handling the phenomenon. In the United States an immigrant had to have lived in the country for five years to benefit from the procedure, and therefore it was possible to limit the so-called attraction effect of the measures in spite of the vigorous debate and extensive information campaign.[21] The requisite of only one month's residence in the new immigration countries (Spain and Italy) meant that the measures were not discussed beforehand and that the information campaign was short. Despite the extensions, these two factors probably reduced the number of people who benefited from them. However, if the requisite period is longer, as in the French case of 18 months, there is the risk that few individuals will be able to benefit. This is why the southern European countries chose to introduce the measure without any internal debate and with limited publicity.

One question is whether the measures managed to reduce the number of illegal immigrants and whether those who benefited from the laws managed to remain as legal residents in the receiving country. Empirical research in Italy (Reyneri 1998a) and Spain shows that a high percentage, at least

---

and penalties for employers who take on irregular workers. The effect of sanctions is negative for wages, whereas regularization is positive, but in both cases the effect is very small.

[21] See Durand and Massey (1992) for a survey of Mexican immigration.

30%, of the foreigners who were regularized in the first measure were part of the second and that a substantial share (35%–25%) of the regularized foreigners no longer held a regular residence permit one year later. In other words, they had returned to their country of departure or had again become illegal residents.

The response to the regularization measures clearly shows the wish to reside in the country legally, but for some people it is difficult to maintain that status. How should regularization measures be judged? If only 50% of those who are processed benefit from the law permanently, can it be considered a success? Furthermore, the idea of introducing an amnesty at the same time as a new law regulating migration helps to give illegal immigrants a sense of making a fresh start, but when it happens in a new immigration country, it can help to create a feeling of instability and uncertainty and also can attract more illegal immigrants. As has been stated, the extent of irregular employment is not reduced through regularization because it is fed by family reunification, political refugees, and clandestine immigrants. Therefore, its impact on irregular labor is doubtful or limited. It is even more difficult to estimate the number of illegal residents because there are also those involved in criminal activities, who are difficult to check.

Greece is the only new immigrant country that postponed the regularization of foreigners until 1998. This choice reflected the wish to keep migration limited in time and related to labor (SOPEMI 1995). In fact illegal immigration and irregular employment were considered to be factors that stimulated competition in the economy. But the political system was not ready to accept migration because after immigrants are legalized they call for family reunification and so become permanent immigrants. Despite many doubts, the Greek government also planned to introduce a regularization procedure in 1998 to correct illegal situations that had lasted for many years. Albanians initially were going to be excluded from the regularization procedure so as to avoid a mass exodus, given the political instability in that area; but Albanians made up 60% of the initial 375,000 applications received. A second legalization was approved in 2000, because the problem of illegal immigration had still not been solved.

But what is perhaps most unusual is the repeated use of regularization measures in the southern European countries, especially Italy and Spain. Both the United States and France have used corrective measures, the United States only once and France twice. France has also corrected a limited number of individual cases of illegal immigration each year. Flows of illegal Mexicans to the United States and illegal North Africans to France certainly continued even after the amnesties, but the governments have not thought it necessary to repeat them.

The southern European countries, in the hope of improving their migration policy, have resorted to increasing checks and deportation and to a series of regularizations. Instead of correcting the illegal side of the phenomenon, these policies have had two effects. On the one hand, they have given potential immigrants the general expectation of further legalizations and so have created a continuous flow of illegal immigration. On the other hand, they have given those who employ illegal foreigners the conviction that such behavior will go unpunished. Additionally, citizens have become less tolerant of irregular foreigners, and their call for solidarity goes unheard.

If the amnesties are seen as a means of creating conditions that favor a foreigner's social and economic integration, they attract further illegal immigrants. Therefore, solving the problem for one group creates a bigger one for others.[22]

5.1.6 The Effectiveness of Offering Incentives to Return Home

As mentioned in section 5.1.1, a closed immigration policy has a limited effect on immigration because of its nature and dynamics. All the receiving countries want somehow to influence an individual's movements so that they conform to the country's own economic, political, social, and religious priorities.

Immigrants are accepted when political conditions make it necessary, as in the case of the former colonies of the United Kingdom, France, Portugal, and so on. They are also accepted when democratic pressure, to which the French government is particularly susceptible, makes it appear attractive and when the labor market offers job opportunities. But when political, demographic, and economic conditions change, countries want to change their strategy.

The restrictive policy, as discussed earlier, was aimed at reducing flows of immigrants and making it more difficult to get new permits, and this policy resulted in temporary immigrant workers becoming permanent residents. Thus, the flows of immigrants entering the receiving country were reduced, but the stock of foreigners did not decrease significantly. For example, if the restrictive policies introduced in Europe by Germany, France, Belgium, the Netherlands, and Switzerland in 1974 are considered, only small reductions can be seen. The number of foreigners in Germany was 3,761,100 in 1974 and

[22] See Reyneri (1998a, b).

decreased to 3,711,300 in 1975, and in Switzerland the number decreased from 1,064,526 to 1,012,710 in the same period. In France the decrease occurred later, and only in 1978 was there a reduction (from 4,237,00 in 1977 to 4,170,300) in the total stock of foreigners. In contrast, in Belgium and the Netherlands the change was limited to a slowdown in the rate at which the stock of foreigners increased.

With the failure of the policy of reducing entry and as a way of strengthening the restrictive measures, occasionally governments have adopted policies to encourage immigrants to return home. The incentives are given to help marginal workers. They are often unemployed, but the economic prospects in the departure country are not sufficiently attractive for them to return. Thus, incentives are offered to help stimulate the immigrant's entrepreneurial spirit in the country of departure.

First, there was a disincentive to return to the country of departure because the immigrant risked losing his or her pension contributions. However, this was quickly corrected by introducing measures that authorized foreigners who were leaving the country to capitalize their pension contributions. This procedure was used successfully in Germany at the beginning of the 1980s, when about 181,566 Turks and 16,072 Portuguese decided to return to their home country. Second, incentives to return were offered to immigrants who returned to their home country. These incentives took the form of economic contributions that could be extended to spouses and children.

In Germany, the assisted return policy, introduced in 1983, applied to immigrants who were unemployed or had not been in full-time employment for at least six months, together with members of their family. Such immigrants who returned to their departure country were given a sum of 10,500 Marks, with an additional amount of 1,550 Marks for each child. This measure was in force until June 1984, and 13,716 applications were approved, 12,016 of them from Turkish workers. The government considered the program successful because provision had been made for about 19,000 cases. However, the offer has not been repeated.

In June 1977, French Prime Minister Raymond Barre launched a "million" campaign for those who returned to their home country (a contribution of 10,000 French francs). An unemployed foreign worker would receive 10,000 FF, along with 5,000 FF for a spouse who did not work. The sum of 10,000 francs was paid to a spouse who worked, and 5,000 francs for each child who held a residence permit. The following month, Secretary of State Lionel Stoleru, who was responsible for immigrant workers, sent a letter to the 23,842 foreigners registered as unemployed proposing assisted return. By September only 3,601 people had applied for help, so the offer was extended to people who had been employed for five or more years. Some 93,999 people (mostly family members), along with only 13,354 unemployed workers, took advantage of this measure, which ended in December 1981. The measure might seem to have been a success, considering that it involved 100,000 people. However, during the same period 190,000 foreigners entered the country to join their families, and about 100,000 new permanent workers came in (Verhaeren 1986, p. 5).

Toward the end of 1979, Stoleru tried unsuccessfully to negotiate the return of 500,000 Algerians. Equally unsuccessful was the Bonnet Law, passed on 10 June 1980, which extended deportation to people who did not have a residence permit.[23]

Although the incentive policy does not appear to have been effective, the French government perseveres with it. In 1984, a new policy to help repatriation was introduced for foreign workers threatened by layoff. It was foreseen that employers would underwrite an agreement with OMI (Organization pour les Migrations Internationales). In 1987, the scheme was extended to unemployed workers who were receiving benefits, and in 1989 it was further extended to workers older than 45 whose employers had agreed with OMI to guarantee them a quarterly income until the age of 60. The measure seems to have been successful, especially during the first five years; from 1984 to 1990, 70,936 people (30,936 of them workers) benefited from the program. Algerians, Portuguese, Turks, and Moroccans benefited most from the measure. Fewer people took advantage of the scheme in the years that followed. At the end of 1994, the total reached 72,302 people, of whom 32,050 were workers.

Unfortunately, there is only a tenuous link between immigrants' activities in France and what they do in the country of origin. Some 78% of the workers in France worked in industrial sectors, whereas in the home country, 52% went into commerce and 27.7% into agriculture (Lebon 1995). This shows that the skills gained in France were not always easily transferred to the country of departure, perhaps because the growth of overall human capital, language, and communication experience is exploited much more in the commercial sector of the home country.

Another measure introduced in 1991 was a scheme of voluntary return for asylum applicants whose requests had not been accepted. A contribution was offered of 1,000 francs for an adult and 300 francs for a child in addition to the cost of the journey back. The response was very poor. From 1991 to

---

[23] See Cansot and Vialle (1988) for a more detailed description.

1994, only 3,944 people – out of a total of 30,746 who had been identified by the OMI office – returned home. Immigrants from Romania, Turkey, and the south of Sahara were most interested in the offer.

This overview of European return incentive policies shows how difficult it is to control and influence waves of immigrants. It is surprising that in Germany more people returned when it became possible to get back their pension contributions than when they were offered financial incentives. This confirms that an incentive policy is effective only if the immigrants have a good chance of finding work in the country of departure and if they already have plans to return. In sum, we can say that there is no single measure that is better than the others. The conditions in the goods and labor markets in the country of origin determine whether the policy is a success or a failure. The conditions in the destination country also are important. For example, access to unemployment benefits discourages immigrants from returning home, as was found in the Dutch case (Muus 1996).

5.2 CITIZENSHIP AND NATURALIZATION

In addition to immigration policy in its strictest sense, there are many other norms that affect the dynamics of migration. Citizenship and naturalization rights play an important role; the legal principle on which citizenship is granted strongly influences immigration. If citizenship is based, as in Germany, on the principle of *jus sanguinis*, all those who can claim to have German blood, or rather to descend from Germans, can obtain German nationality; and being German, they can enter the country and immediately enjoy all the political and civil rights of the nationals, no longer appearing as immigrants in the statistics.

This rule is based on the idea of nationhood that existed before the birth of the modern state (Stalker 1994) (as in the case of "German Volk") or on the wish to maintain a link with citizens who have emigrated, as happens in the northern European countries (for example, Norway and Sweden). This principle prevails in many European countries, and Italy, Spain, Portugal, and Greece guarantee citizenship to persons who can demonstrate that they descend from citizens who emigrated abroad.

In contrast, the principle of *jus solis*, according to which nationality is granted to those who are born in that country, is the form chosen mainly by settlement countries, such as the United States, Canada, and Australia. These countries did not have a strong sense of nationality before colonization and have built up a heterogeneous population during the great waves of immigration. If the *jus solis* principle (also applied in France) facilitates the control of the growth of nationals through immigration, the *jus sanguinis* principle means that economic and political changes in national communities abroad can create uncontrollable immigration pressures. There are millions of ethnic Germans – that is, *Aussiedler* – living abroad who could claim German citizenship. In fact, when there was a potential threat of immigration from the German communities in Russia, the German government, having no other means to control immigration, decided to review the regulations concerning nationality (1 July 1993).

Reserving special treatment for descendants of national emigrants is widespread. Italy guarantees special status to Argentinean citizens of Italian origin. However, the Italian government has not felt it necessary to review the special treatment it reserves for Italian emigrants because there are relatively few of them and there is a limited flow of immigrants from that region. Greece offers special reception treatment, including language teaching, to ethnic Greeks coming from Albania, Romania, Bulgaria, and so on, not to mention Pontus Greeks.

Another interesting case is that of the countries that have guaranteed different levels of citizenship to citizens of their colonies or former colonies. Thus, these people, who are not nationals, cannot be considered to be foreigners, either. The United Kingdom is one of the most interesting cases because there are three kinds of flows:

- The citizens from Commonwealth countries who are considered to be British citizens and as such are not subject to any restrictions.
- EU citizens, who, despite being classified as "aliens," have the right of movement within the Union. On entering the country they are not asked to register, although they are not citizens.
- Non-EU foreigners, who must have a residence permit as well as a work permit and in some cases a visa.

In the United Kingdom there are about 2.6 million people who are considered immigrants, and most of them can be classified as British citizens (Stalker 1994, p. 62).

5.3 INTEGRATION POLICIES: LINGUISTIC PROFICIENCY

The policy of economic and social integration adopted by the receiving country is another kind of policy that influences immigration. Generally, receiving countries try to gradually extend to immigrants the rights enjoyed by nationals.

Table 5.5. *Rates of unemployment for natives and foreigners according to age in France, Germany, the Netherlands, and Sweden, 1983–94*

	France				Germany				The Netherlands				Sweden			
	Natives		Foreigners		Natives		Foreigners		Natives		Foreigners		Natives		Foreigners	
	Total[a]	<25	Total[a]	<25	Total[a]	<25	Total[a]	<25	Total[a]	<25	Total[a]	<25	Total[a]	<25	Total[a]	<25
1983	7.4	19.1	14.5	30.0	6.0	10.1	11.3	18.2	11.3	20.5	23.7	33.7	–	–	–	–
1984	9.0	23.8	16.6	34.3	6.3	9.8	11.3	17.1	–	–	–	–	–	–	–	–
1985	9.6	24.8	18.5	39.1	6.4	9.3	12.0	17.4	9.9	16.9	25.6	33.7	–	–	–	–
1986	9.7	23.2	18.6	36.8	6.1	7.3	12.0	14.8	–	–	–	–	–	–	–	–
1987	10.2	22.8	19.0	34.0	6.3	6.9	12.5	15.4	9.4	16.4	23.5	32.5	1.8	4	4.4	8.1
1988	9.6	21.7	18.5	30.0	5.9	6.4	10.9	12.7	8.8	13.7	24.9	27.3	1.5	3.2	3.8	6.0
1989	9.0	19.0	17.8	27.9	5.4	5.2	9.3	9.9	8.1	12.5	25.8	32.7	1.2	2.8	3.4	5.2
1990	8.8	19.2	17.0	29.0	4.5	4.3	8.6	7.0	7.1	10.5	23.9	28.1	1.4	3.2	4.0	7.3
1991	8.7	19.4	16.7	25.8	3.7	3.2	8.0	7.1	6.6	10.4	24.0	31.7	2.4	5.7	6.6	11.5
1992	9.7	21.2	18.8	28.8	3.6	3.4	8.9	10.1	5.1	7.7	16.4	16.3	4.3	10.4	12.8	17.8
1993	10.8	25.2	20.6	32.3	4.9	4.8	12.7	14.1	5.7	9.8	19.6	25	7.8	18.0	20.8	27.8
1994													7.6	16.2	21.0	30.6

[a] Thousands of people

Source: Böhning (1995, p. 6)

It is easy to explain the gradual extension of political rights (voting in local elections) and social rights (access to free health care, social services, unemployment benefits, and so on) to immigrants. On the one hand, immigrants need time to gather information and learn the rules and culture of the receiving country, which they can accept temporarily or permanently. On the other hand, if rights, especially social rights, are granted to foreigners as soon as they arrive, situations similar to a poverty trap can be created: Foreigners are attracted by the benefits and are satisfied with poverty-level subsidies and social benefits. In this way the transformation of temporary immigration into permanent immigration is encouraged, and efforts to achieve real economic and social integration are discouraged. For example, in the Netherlands, where benefits are high, the unemployment rate in 1995 among Turks and Moroccans was 41% and 27%, respectively, whereas the activity rate was 42% and 40% (Muus 1996). This means that in the case of the Turks only 1% were employed, and in the case of the Moroccans, 13%.

Various reception and integration activities are offered to immigrants on their arrival, and literacy courses in the receiving country's language are among the most important. These courses are organized at a local level by various organizations such as reception centers, local community groups, trade unions, and the Ministry of Education, and they can help foreigners to overcome their diffidence, but they are poorly attended. Foreigners consider such courses to be a waste of time because most immigrants intend to stay only temporarily and consider their stay to be a way of accumulating savings. Therefore, the time invested in education represents time taken away from possible earnings or from their free time. As the immigration phenomenon becomes more mature and family reunification begins, course attendance increases, but usually by members of the family, especially female members.

The importance of literacy and language courses becomes more evident when unemployment rates for foreigners and second-generation immigrants are compared to those of natives. Table 5.5, which refers to the period before the wave of migration from eastern Europe, shows that in all European countries involved in immigration during the postwar period, unemployment was higher for foreigners than for natives. This trend can be explained by the transformation of production during the 1990s. Employment decreased in the industrial sector, where foreigners were concentrated, and increased in the tertiary sector, where the specific experience of a foreign worker cannot be used and where the human capital that has been accumulated since arrival is not enough to find work. Such reasoning, however, cannot explain why the level of unemployment for foreigners who are less than 25 years old is higher than that for natives of the same age. It does not explain why it is more difficult for immigrant children – those in the second generation – to find work. Specific studies (Maurin 1991; Lebon 1994; Böhning 1995) show that unemployment is higher and finding a job is more difficult for foreigners than natives with the same qualifications and skills because they received less linguistic knowledge from their parents even though they gained literacy skills by attending school in the receiving country. In the case of first-generation immigrants, Maurin (1991) emphasizes that in France one immigrant out of three knows very little French. Linguistic ability is also an important way for political refugees to gain economic and social integration (Muus 1996).

5.4 CONCLUSIONS

An analysis of the complexity of immigration policies in their strictest sense and the other measures that define a foreigner's status and rights after immigration highlights the myriad aspects of the migratory phenomenon and the difficulty of controlling it institutionally. Because receiving countries want to manage immigration and not simply passively accept it, numerous difficulties regarding the control of the flow of immigrants will have to be resolved.

A receiving country must overcome many difficulties if it wants to control entry. It is hard to choose who can enter the country and look for a job because the "rights" already acquired by foreigners, such as family reunification and political asylum, contradict the aim both to choose immigrants and to limit their number. Similarly, limiting the growing number of immigrants who want political asylum is impossible, although many of these requests are from people who do not qualify for recognition as refugees but only want to leave the country of origin. Preventing illegal immigration is also difficult because of the exponential costs of border controls that are not very effective.

Similarly, it is difficult for the receiving countries to reduce the number of unwelcome immigrants. There are many technical difficulties in carrying out deportation orders, and deportation is costly, both in absolute terms compared with its effectiveness and as a deterrent to future illegal immigrants. Incentive policies designed to encourage immigrants to return to the country of departure are no more effective in managing the flows of immigrants because they are efficient only when the foreign workers themselves want to return.

In addition to immigration policy in its strictest sense, other measures – such as reviewing the procedures to obtain citizenship, naturalization, and the regulations regarding nationality – all define who a foreigner is and in this way affect the evolution of immigration. However, foreigners often use such regulations to counter the restrictive aims of an immigration policy, and thereby its effectiveness is weakened.

Various examples taken from European experience reveal all the difficulties that the receiving countries face in applying an immigration policy. These difficulties do not depend on the international agreements that Italy, Spain, Portugal, Greece, and the other European countries have signed. The Schengen agreement aims at establishing two regimes: one for free circulation within the Union, and one of limited entry for people who come from outside the Union. When the system is fully implemented, it may favor the southern European countries, which at least initially paid the cost of the restrictive immigration policies adopted by the northern European countries in the mid-1970s, in the best tradition of a "beggar thy neighbor" policy. Improved international coordination and more homogeneous measures would reduce the undesirable effects of individual policies.

It is more difficult for the southern European countries (Italy, Spain, Portugal, and Greece) than the other European countries to adopt effective prevention policies because it is more difficult for them to control their borders, especially their coastlines. In addition, their unofficial labor market attracts individuals and workers whose main interest in immigration is to get some form of income. These immigrants come from countries where there is little or no social security, and so they are not aware of the economic consequences of accepting irregular work.

But the biggest and most common difficulty that the southern European countries share in controlling the migratory phenomenon is revealed by the characteristics of the productive system and the labor market, where there is a high level of irregular employment. The migratory policies must take such facts into account.

A foreigner's irregular activity is not spread uniformly among the sectors of the economy; rather, it is higher in agriculture, building, services, and certain industrial sectors. However, in Italy, although foreigners account on average for 3% of regular employment, they account for 23% of non-regular employment. The data for agriculture in Greece (Lianos et al. 1996) confirm this trend, as does research done by M. Baganha (1996) in Portugal.

The dangers of illegal employment for the immigrant and for the receiving country are well known. The immigrant is exploited and has no rights; the receiving country does not know exactly who is in the country, and illegality facilitates recruitment into organized crime. The immigration policies of the southern European countries must take into account the uniqueness of the situation, and therefore they must counter both clandestine entry and irregular employment.

To do this, the receiving countries must first adopt a clear-cut foreign policy toward the countries of origin that offers them commercial agreements, foreign aid, and migration policies within a single framework. This framework must give the country of departure more direct control over its own economic growth, which depends on three factors: goods, capital, and labor. Uncertainty regarding the foreign policy of the receiving country has often created confusion, and this has enabled immigrants to avoid deportation and border checks. Instead, it is necessary for countries of departure to collaborate with the receiving countries so that it is possible to control the number and quality of immigrants.

Second, the effectiveness of an immigration policy depends on the organizations that are available to manage the phenomenon, and so it is necessary to provide sufficient funding and qualified staff. The unexpected recent transformation of the southern European countries into destination countries for immigrants must now be met by the creation of a permanent organization that can handle the immigration phenomenon, which, it is estimated, will last for the next thirty to forty years. Voluntary organizations often handle the reception of new immigrants, but migration must be the responsibility of a permanent organization, as is the case in countries with a long tradition of immigration.

Third, countries subject to high immigration pressures must use a mix of incentives and controls. Checks and deportations must be credible and rapid and must be carried out in collaboration with the immigrant's country of origin. This can be done only if legal entry for those who are looking for work is guaranteed.

Fourth, the receiving country has everything to gain from such a guarantee, which will be determined by the demand for regular labor in the country. In this way workers can be selected according to the needs of the national labor market, but the departure countries must be involved in a clear relationship of collaboration, with immigration favored from the countries that collaborate in limiting clandestine immigration. The receiving countries must decide how many workers are needed, which skills and professions they should have, and which countries they should come from. The countries of departure could be involved in drawing up some parts of the list. An "open the front door and close the back door" policy is the only possible choice for the countries subject to immigration pressures from neighboring countries, such as the United States and Mexico, Mediterranean Europe and Africa, and the northern European and eastern European countries.

Fifth, all-embracing amnesties should no longer be passed. They regularize some cases of irregular workers, but they encourage further illegal flows in expectation of the measure being repeated. Countries whose borders are difficult to control and that have a significant irregular labor market must rely mainly on incentives to achieve their immigration policy objectives and so discourage illegal immigration.

Sixth, the importance of adopting a clear immigration policy seems to be underestimated in the present debate. Although it is believed that immigrants have access to sufficient information about the help available in the receiving country through word of mouth networks, some groups of immigrants are less fortunate. They enter the country illegally, and their hopes cannot be achieved. On arrival they are immediately marginalized and so can easily be recruited by organized crime. These groups are the most difficult to help, and they arouse among natives feelings of intolerance that often spread to other groups. Thus, it is important to ensure that sufficient information is available about the real possibilities of finding work and accommodation in the receiving countries.

Seventh, arguments are often put forward to explain why there is clandestine entry and irregular employment even when it is possible for foreigners to find regular employment. These arguments suggest that employers need to get to know individuals through a trial period before actually employing them. In other words, employers are reluctant to employ someone they do not know. This argument may be true for certain jobs and in certain sectors – such as in the services and domestic help – but not in agriculture or the building industry. The difficulties of bringing demand and supply together may be one of the real causes of clandestine immigration. If that is so but it is not the most important cause, then clandestine entry must be stopped and replaced by a procedure that enables a foreigner looking for work to enter the country legally. For example, this was the case before in Italy, where the law passed in 1998 provided for legal entry sponsored by regularly employed foreigners and by professional associations (abrogated by the last law in 2001). The illegal trial period – which in the case of domestic work is often followed by the worker returning to the country of origin and then being employed regularly – could be avoided, and clandestine immigration could thus be reduced. If the economic system really needs certain skilled workers, then an attempt should be made to create a supply from which an employer could choose. In this way, there would be no reason for immigrants looking for work to enter the country illegally.

Finally, there must be a clear and strong response to the involvement of organized crime in the illegal traffic of immigrants and those who recruit the marginalized.

The southern European countries must send a clear and unequivocal message to the countries of departure that it is not possible to legalize irregular entry and that only regular entry is conceivable. This can be achieved only with the collaboration of the countries of departure. They must sign bilateral agreements that establish joint arrangements that make it easier for immigrants to gain legal entry, thereby discouraging illegal entry.

The receiving countries can defend themselves against uncontrolled immigration, but the measures they can adopt vary in effectiveness depending on the economic and social situation, and when such measures are most needed, their effectiveness is much weaker. Therefore, there should be some form of permanent collaboration among the parties involved so that a common project of development and growth can be devised.

References

WORKS CITED

Abowd, J. M., and R. B. Freeman. 1991. *Immigration, Trade, and the Labor Market.* Chicago: University of Chicago Press.

Adams, R. H. 1994. Remittances, inequality and asset accumulation: The case of rural Pakistan. Paper presented at the OCDE Workshop on Development Strategies, Employment and International Migration, Paris, July.

Adelman, I., and J. E. Taylor. 1990. Is structural adjustment with a human face possible? The case of Mexico. *Journal of Development Studies* 26: 387–407.

Adelman, I., and J. E. Taylor. 1991. Multisectoral models and structural adjustment: New evidence from Mexico. *Journal of Development Studies* 28(1): 154–63.

Akbari, A. H. 1989. The benefits of immigrants to Canada: Evidence on tax and public services. *Canadian Public Policy* 15: 424–35.

Albert, M., and H. J. Vosgerau. 1989. Mobility: A theoretical analysis of the key factors of structural differences. In *Wage Differential in the European Community*, edited by W. Molle and A. Van Mourik. Aldershat: Ashgate Publishing.

Altonji, J. G., and D. Card. 1991. The effect of immigration on the labour market outcomes of less-skilled natives. In *Immigration, trade and the labour market*, edited by J. M. Abowd and R. Freeman. Chicago, IL: Chicago University Press.

Amrhein, C. G., and R. D. MacKinnon. 1985. An elementary simulation model of the job matching process within an interregional setting. *Regional Studies* 19(3): 193–202.

Antolin, P. 1992. Labour market and international migration flows: The case of Spain 1960–1988. IVIE Working Paper n.92-09.

Atchinson, J. 1988. Immigration in two federations: Canada and Australia. *International Migration Review* 36(1): 5–32.

Baganha, M. 1996. Immigrant insertion in the informal economy: The Portugal case: CE-TSER-Program. Project: Migrants insertion in the informal economy deviant behavior and the impact on receiving societies. First Portuguese report. Unpublished.

Baganha, M. 1998. Immigrant involvement in the informal economy: The Portuguese case. *Journal of Ethnic and Migration Studies* 24(2): 367–85.

Baganha, M. I., J. Ferrao, and J. M. Malheiros. 1998. Immigrants and the labour market: The Portuguese case. In *Metropolis*, Metropolis International Workshop. Lisbon: Luso-American Foundation.

Baganha, M. I., and P. Perreira. 2000. Portuguese migration. Unpublished.

Baker, M., and D. Benjamin. 1994. The performance of immigrants in the Canadian labor market. *Journal of Labor Economics* 12(3): 369–405.

Baldacci, E., L. Inglese, and S. Strozza. 1999. Determinants of foreign workers' wages in two Italian regions with high illegal immigration. *Labour* 13(3): 675–710.

Barsotti, O., ed. 1988. *La presenza straniera in Italia. Il caso della Toscana.* Milan: F. Angeli.

Barisik, A., A. Eraydin, and A. Gedik. 1990. Turkey. In W. J. Serow, C. B. Nam, D. F. Sly, and R. H. Weller. *Handbook on International Migration.* New York: Greenwood Press.

Bauer, T. 1997. Do immigrants reduce natives' wages? Evidence from Germany. Munchener Wirtschaftswissenschaftliche Discussion Paper n. 97-5.

Bauer, T., and K. Zimmermann. 1997. Integrating the east: The labour market effects of immigration. In *Europe's economy looks east: Implications for Germany and the EU,* edited by S. W. Black. Cambridge University Press.

Bauer, T., and K. Zimmermann. 1999. Assessment of possible migration pressure and its labour market impact following EU enlargement to central and eastern Europe. IZA Research Report n.3.

Bean, F. D., B. L. Lowell, and L. J. Taylor. 1988. Undocumented Mexican immigrants and the earnings of other workers in the United States. *Demography* 25(1): 35–52.

Bean, F., G. Vernez, and C. Keely. 1989. *Opening and closing the doors: Evaluating immigration reform and control.* Washington, DC: The Urban Institute Press.

Beine, Michel, Frédéric Docquier, and Hillet Rapoport. 2001. Brain drain and economic growth: Theory and evidence. *Journal of Development Economics* 64: 275–89.

Bentolila, S., and J. J. Dolado. 1991. Mismatch and internal migration in Spain 1962–1986. In *Mismatch and Labour Mobility,* edited by F. Padoa Schioppa. Cambridge University Press.

Beretta, C. 1995. Occupazione immigrata nel Bresciano e nella Bergamasca. Unpublished.

Bevelander, P., and K. Scott. 1996. The employment and income performance of immigrants in Sweden, 1970–1990. *Yearbook of Population Research in Finland* 33: 157–72.

Bhattacharyya, B. 1985. The role of family decision in internal migration. *Journal of Development Economics* 18: 51–66.

Bianchi, F. 1993. Un'analisi dei flussi migratori intraeuropei alla luce del principio gravitazionale. *Economia e Lavoro* 27(1): 133–42.

Bird, E. J., H. Kaiser, and J. R. Frick. 1999. The immigrant welfare effect: take-up or eligibility? IZA Discussion Paper n.66.

Blanchard, O., F. J. Jimeno et al. 1995. *Spanish unemployment: Is there a solution?* London: C.E.P.R.

Blanchet, D. 1988. Immigration et régulation de la Structure par age d'une population. *Population* 2: 249–66.

Blau, F. 1984. The use of transfer payment by immigrants. *International Labor Relations Review* 37: 222–39.

Boeri, T., G. Hanson, and B. McCornick, eds. 2002. *Immigration Policy and the Welfare System.* With A. Venturini, H. Brüker, G. Epstein, B. McCornick, G. Saint-Paul, and K. Zimmermann. Oxford: Oxford Economic Press.

Bloom, D. E., G. Grenier, and M. Gunderson. 1995. The changing labour market position of Canadian immigrants. *Canadian Journal of Economics* 28(4b): 987–1005.

Böhning, R. W. 1984. *Studies in International Labour Migration.* London: MacMillan.

Böhning, R. W. 1995. Labour market integration in western and northern Europe: Which way are we heading? In *The integration of migrant workers in the labour market: Policies and their impact*, edited by R. W. Böhning and R. Zegers de Beijl. I.L.O. Employment Department, International Migration Papers, n.8.

Bonjour, D., and L. Pacelli. 1998. Wage formation and gender wage in Italy and Switzerland. UCL Discussion Paper 12/98.

Borjas, G. 1983. The substitutability of black, Hispanic and white labor. *Economic Inquiry* 21(1): 93–106.

Borjas, G. 1985. Assimilation, changes in cohort quality, and earnings of immigrants. *Journal of Labor Economics* 4: 463–89.

Borjas, G. 1986. The sensitivity of labor demand functions to choice of dependent variable. *Review of Economics and Statistics* 68(1): 58–66.

Borjas, G. 1987. Immigrants, minorities, and labor market competition. *Industrial and Labor Relations Review* 40(3): 382–92.

Borjas, G. 1988. *International differences in the labor market performance of immigrants.* Kalamazoo, MI: W. E. Upjohn Institute for Employment Research.

Borjas, G. 1990. *Friends and Strangers.* New York: Basic Books.

Borjas, G. 1994. The economics of immigration. *Journal of Economic Literature* XXXII(4): 1667–1717.

Borjas, G. 1999a. Immigration and welfare magnets. *Journal of Labor Economics* 17(4): 607–37.

Borjas, G. 1999b. *The Heaven Door.* Princeton, NJ: Princeton University Press.

Borjas, G. and R. Freeman, eds. 1992. *Immigration and the Workforce.* NBER. Chicago: University of Chicago Press.

Borjas, G., R. Freeman, and L. F. Katz. 1992. On the labor market effects of immigration and trade. In *Immigration and the Workforce*, edited by G. Borjas and R. Freeman. NBER. Chicago: University of Chicago Press.

Borjas, G., and L. Hilton. 1996. Immigration and the welfare state: Immigrant participation in means-tested entitlement programs. *The Quarterly Journal of Economics* 111: 575–604.

Borzaga, C., M. Carpita, and L. Covi. 1995. Gli immigrati ed il lavoro in Trentino. Un tentativo di interpretazione dell'evoluzione piu' recente del fenomeno. Working Paper, Department of Economics Trento University.

Briggs, V. M., and M. Tienda, eds. 1984. *Immigration: Issues and policy.* Salt Lake City, UT: Olympus Publishing.

Brown, R. P. C. 1997. Estimating remittance functions for Pacific Island migrants. *World Development* 25(4): 613–26.

Bruni, M., ed. 1994. *Attratti, Sospinti, Respinti.* Milan: F. Angeli.

Bruni, M., and A. Venturini. 1995. Pressure to migrate and propensity to emigrate. *International Labour Review* 134(3): 377–400.

Burda, M. C. 1993. The determinants of East-West German migration: Some first results. *European Economic Review*, Papers and Proceedings 37: 452–61.

Butare, T., and Ph. Favarger. 1995. Analyse empirique de cas de la Suisse. In *Main d'Oeuvre Etrangere: Une analyse de l'économie Suisse*, edited by B. Burgenmeier. Paris: Economica.

Callovi, G. 1988. Prospective des flux des migrations internationaux dans l'Europe Communaire à l'aube d'une traisitionne millenaire, Coloque internationale sur le viellissement demografique. Paris: Futurible International.

Calvanese, F., and E. Pugliese. 1983. Emigrazione ed. immigrazione in Italia: tendenze recenti. *Economia & Lavoro* 1: 147–58.

Calvanese, F., and E. Pugliese. 1988. Emigration and immigration in Italy: recent trends. *Labour* 2(3): 181–99.

Cansot, M., and A. Vialle. 1988. Les dispositifs d'aide à la reinsertion dans le pays d'origine: un bilan raisonne. *Revue Française d'administration publique* 47: 71–80.

Card, D. 1990. The impact of Mariel boatlift on the Miami labor market. *Industrial and Labour Relations Review* 43(2): 245–57.

Caritas diocesana di Roma. 1994. *Immigrazione, Dossier Statistico '94*. Rome: Anterem Edizioni Ricerca.

Caritas diocesana di Roma. 1996. *Immigrazione, Dossier Statistico '96*. Rome: Anterem Edizioni Ricerca.

Caritas diocesana di Roma. 1999. *Immigrazione, Dossier Statistico '99*. Rome: Anterem Edizioni Ricerca.

Caritas diocesana di Roma. 2000. *Immigrazione, Dossier Statistico 2000*. Rome: Anterem Edizioni Ricerca.

Caritas diocesana di Roma. 2001. *Immigrazione, Dossier Statistico 2001*. Rome: Anterem Edizioni Ricerca.

Carrington W., and P. De Lima. 1996. The impact of 1970's repatriates from Africa on the Portuguise labour market. *Industrial and Labour Relations Review* 49(2): 330–47.

Cerase, F. 1967. Su una tipologia di emigrati ritornati: il ritorno di investimento. *Studi Emigrazione* IV(10): 327–49.

Chillemi, O., and B. Gui. 1977. Fattori determinanti le rimesse dei lavoratori migranti: uno schema metodologico ed. una applicazione al caso dei lavoratori italiani nella Repubblica federale tedesca (1964–1975). *Rivista di Politica Economica* year LXVII, series III, fold.XII, Dic.

Chiswick, B. 1978. The effect of Americanisation on the earnings of foreign-born men. *Journal of Political Economy* 86: 897–921.

Chiswick, B. 1980. The earnings of white and coloured male immigrants in Britain. *Economica* 47: 81–7.

Chiswick, B. 1986. *Illegal aliens: Their employment and employers*. Kalamazoo, MI: WE Upjohn Institute for Employment Research.

Chiswick, B. 1988. Illegal immigration and immigration control. *Journal of Economic Perspectives* 2: 101–15.

Chiswick, B. 1991. Speaking, reading, and earnings among low-skilled immigrants. *Journal of Labor Economics* 9(2): 149–70.

Cinnari, P. 1975. La questione meridionale e l'emigrazione mediterranea in Europa. *Quaderni Mediterranei* 1 (Nov.): 73–88.

Cobb-Clark, D., C. R. Shiells, and B. Lindsay Lowell. 1995. Immigration reform: The effects of employer sanctions and legalization wages. *Journal of Labour Economics* 13(3): 472–98.

Coda, F. 2001. The effects of immigrants' inflows on the italian welfare state sustainability: A generational accounts perspective study. CeRP, Working Paper n.5.

Collado, M. D., I. Iturbe-Ormaetxe, and G. Valera. 2002. Quantifying the impact of immigration on the Spanish welafre state. Paper presented at the 2002 ESPE Annual Conference in Bilbao.

Collectivo IOE e Perez Molina. 1995. La Discimination laboral a los trabajadores immigrantes en Espana. ILO International Migration Paper n.9, Geneva.

Conti, C., M. Natale, and S. Strozza. 2003. Le rimesse degli immigrati: determinanti, modalita' di invio e aspettative di impiego. In *Movimenti di popolazione e movimenti di capitale in Europa*, edited by N. Acocella and E. Sonnino. Bologna: Il Mulino.

Courbage, Y. 1988. L'offre de Travail en Egypte en Perspective. Comunicazione Seminario Internazionale di Sorrento, Italy. Unpublished.

Courbage, Y. 1990. Effetti dell'Emigrazione Internazionale sul Mercato del Lavoro dei Paesi della Riva Sud del Mediterraneo. In *Migrazioni Mediterranee e Mercato del Lavoro*, edited by G. Ancona. Bari, Italy: Cacucci Editore.

D'Amore, N., E. D'Andrea, and M. Scuderi. 1977. Bilanci familiari e rimesse degli emigranti meridionali, in *Studi Emigrazioni*, XIV 45: 3–37.

Daneshvary, N., H. W. Herzog, R. A. Hofler, and A. M. Schlottmann. 1992. Job search and immigrant assimilation: An earning frontier approach. *The Review of Economics and Statistics* 74(3): 482–92.

Daveri, F., and R. Faini. 1999. Where do migrants go? Risk-aversion, mobility costs and the locational choice of migrants. *Oxford Economic Papers* 51(4): 595–622.

Daveri, F., and A. Venturini. 1993. Gli effetti economici dell'immigrazione sul paese di destinazione. *Economia & Lavoro* 1: 93–105.

Davies, J. B., and I. Wooton. 1992. Income inequality and international migration. *The Economic Journal* 102: 789–802.

De Castro, V. H. 1994. Financial strategies for collecting and employing the saving of Portuguese emigrants and regional development prospects. In *Migration et Dévelopment: un nouveau partenariat pour la coopération*, pp. 288–292. Paris: OCDE.

Dell'Aringa, C., and F. Neri. 1987. Illegal immigrants and the informal economy in Italy. *Labour* 1(2): 107–26.

De New J. P., and K. Zimmermann. 1994. Native wage impacts of foreign labor: A random effects panel analysis. *Journal of Population Economics* 177–192.

Dixit, A. 1992. Investment and hysteresis, *Journal of Economic Perspectives* 6: 107–32.

Djajic, S. 1989. Migrants in a guest-worker system. *Journal of Development Economics* 31: 327–39.

Djajic, S., and R. Milbourne. 1988. A general equilibrium model of guest-worker migration. *Journal of International Economics* 25: 335–51.

do Céu Esteves, M., ed. 1991. *Portugal, Pais, de Imigraçao*. Lisbon: Instituto de Estudos para o Desenvolvimento.

Dolado, J., A. Goria, and A. Ichino. 1994. Immigration and growth in the host country. *Journal of Population Economics* 7(2): 193–215.

Dolado, J., J. F. Jimeno, and R. Duce. 1996. The effects of migration on the relative demand of skilled versus unskilled labour: Evidence from Spain. CEPR Discussion Paper n.1476.

Domenicich, T., and D. McFadden, 1975. *Urban travel demand: A behavioural analysis*. Amsterdam: North Holland.

Durand, J., and D. S. Massey. 1992. Mexican migration to the United States: A critical review. *Latin American Research Review* 27(2): 3–42.

Durand, J., E. A. Parrado, and D. S. Massey. 1996. Migradollars and development: A reconsideration of the Mexiacan case. *International Migration Review* 30(114): 423–44.

Dustmann, C. 1993. Earnings adjustment of temporary migrants. *Journal of Population Economics* 6: 153–86.

Dustmann, C. 1994. Return intentions of migrants: Theory and evidence. CEPR Discussion Paper series n.906.

Ekberg, J. 1983. Inkomsteffekter av invandring. Wäxjö: Acta Wexionensia.

Elbadawi, I. A., and R. de Rezende Rocha. 1992. Determinants of expatriate workers' remittances in Norh Africa and Europe. World Bank W.P. Unpublished.

Eurostat. 1993. *Demographic statistics.* Luxembourg.

Eurostat. 1994a. *Demographic statistics.* Luxembourg.

Eurostat. 1999. *Demographic statistics.* Luxembourg.

Eurostat. 1995a. *Migration statistics.* Luxembourg.

Eurostat. 1995b. *Regional statistics.* Luxembourg.

Faini, R. 1994. Workers remittances and the real exchange rate. *Journal of Population Economics* 7: 235–45.

Faini, R., G. Galli, and F. Rossi. 1996. Mobilita' e disoccupazione in Italia: Un'analisi dell'offerta di lavoro. In *La mobilita' della sociata' italiana,* edited by G. Galli. Rome: SIPI.

Faini, R., G. Galli, P. Gennari, and F. Rossi. 1997. An empirical puzzle: Falling migration and growing unemployment differentials among Italian regions. *European Economic Review* 41: 571–9.

Faini, R., and A. Venturini. 1993. Trade, aid and migration: Some basic policy issues. *European Economic Review* 37: 435–42.

Faini, R., and A. Venturini. 1994a. Migration and growth: The experience of southern Europe. CEPR Working Paper n.964.

Faini, R., and A. Venturini. 1994b. Italian emigration in the pre-war period. In *Migration and the international labour market, 1850–1913,* edited by T. Hatton and J. Williamson. London: Routledge.

Ferri, J., A. G. Gomez-Plana, and J. Martin-Montaner. 2000. General equilibrium effect of increasing immigration: The case of Spain. Paper presented at the 2000 ESPE Annual Conference in Bonn, 2001. University of Valencia, Departamento de Analisis Economico, Working Paper 01–02.

Fertig, M., and C. M. Schmidt. 2001. First- and second-generation migrants in Germany: What do we know and what do people think? In *Migration policy and the economy: international experience,* edited by R. Rotte. Studies and Comments 1 series. Munich: Hanns Seidel Stiftung.

Filer, R. 1992. The effect of immigrant arrival on migratory patterns of native workers. In *Immigration and the work force,* edited by G. J. Borjas and R. Freeman. Chicago: University of Chicago Press.

Frey, L. 1991a. Il dibattito sugli effetti dell'integrazione economica europea: gli effetti occupazionali. *Quaderni di Economia del Lavoro* 39: 11–135.

Frey, L. 1991b. I fattori determinanti dei movimenti migratori ed i mercati del lavoro europei. *Quaderni di Economia del Lavoro* 44: 11–56.

Gang, I., and F. Rivera-Batiz. 1994. Labor market effects of immigration in the United States and Europe. *Journal of Population Economics* 7: 157–83.

Garson, J-P. 1994. The implications for the Maghreb countries of financial transfers from emigrants. In *Migration et dévelopment: un nuveaou partenariat pour la coopération.* Paris: OCDE.

Garson, J-P. 1997. Corporative analysis of regularization experience in France, Italy, Spain and the United States. Paper presented at the CEPR Conference on the Economics of Illegal Migration, Athens.

Garson, J-P., Y. Moulier-Boutang, R. Silberman, and T. Magnac. 1987. La Substitution des Autochtones aux Etrangers sur le Marche' du Travail dans la CEE, rapport pour la CEE, Direzione Generale pur l'emploi. Affair Sociale et de l'Education e Groupe de Recherche et d'Analyse des Migrations Internationales. Unpublished.

Garson, J-P., and G. Tapinos. 1981. *L'argent des immigrés.* Paris: Presses Universitaires de France.

Gavosto, A., A. Venturini, and C. Villosio. 1999. Do immigrants compete with natives? *Labour* 13(3): 603–22.

Gesano, G. 1994. Nonsense and unfeasibility of demographically-based immigration policies. *GENUS* L(3–4): 47–63.

Gesano, G. 1995. Mobilita' e strutture demografiche, *Continuita' e Discontinuita' nei Processi Demografici.* Proceedings Annual Conference of the Italian Demographic Society, 20–21 April.

Giubilaro, D. 1997. Les Migrations en provenance du Maghreb et le pression migratoire: Situation actuelle et prévisions. International Migration Papers n.15, Geneva: I.L.O.

Glytsos, P. N. 1988. Remittances in temporary migration: A theoretical model and its testing with the Greek-German experience. *Weltwirtschaftliches Archiv* 124(3): 524–49.

Glytsos, P. N. 1993. Measuring the income effects of migrant remittances: A methodological approach applied to Greece. *Economic Development and Cultural Change* 131–68.

Glytsos, P. N. 1995. Problems and policies regarding the socio-economic integration of returnees and foreign workers in Greece. *International Migration* XXXIII(2): 155–76.

Golini, A. 1978. Presupposti e conseguenze demografiche dell'emigrazione. In *Tendenze dell'emigrazione italiana: Ieri, oggi.*, edited by A. Dell'Orefice. Geneva: Libraire Droz.

Golini, A., and S. Strozza. 1998. The impact of migration on population growth and its interplay with social and political issues. Proceedings of the Joint IASS/IAOS Conference Statistics for Economic and Social Development.

Gooneratne, W., P. L. Martin, and H. Sazanami, eds. 1994. *Regional development impacts of labour migration in Asia.* UNCRD Research Report Series n.2.

Gordon, I., and R. Vickerman. 1982. Opportunity, preference and constraint: An approach to the analysis of metropolitan migration. *Urban Studies* 19: 247–61.

Goria, A., and A. Ichino. 1994. Flussi Migratori e Convergenza fra le Regioni Italiane. *Lavoro e Relazioni Industriali* 3: 3–38.

Gould, J. D. 1979. European inter-continental emigration, 1815–1914: Patterns and causes. *Journal of European History* 8: 593–679.

Gould, J. D. 1980a. European inter-continental emigration. The road home: return migration from USA. *Journal of European History* 9: 41–112.

Gould, J. D. 1980b. European inter-continental emigration: The role of 'diffusion' and green. *Journal of European History* 9: 267–315.

Gowa, J., and E. Mansfield. 1993. Power politics and international trade. *American Political Science Review* 87: 408–20.

Grammenos, S. 1982. Migrant labour in western Europe. European Centre for Work and Society, Maastrich Studies n.3.

Granier, R., and J. P. Marciano. 1975. The earnings of immigrant workers in France. *International Labour Review* 111(2): 143–65.

Green, A. G., and D. A. Green. 1995. Canadian immigration policy: The effectiveness of the point system and other instruments. *Canadian Journal of Economics* 28(4b): 1006–41.

Gross, D. M. 1999. Three million foreigners, three million unemployed? Immigration and the French labour market. IMF Working Paper n.124.

Grossman, J. B. 1982. The substitutability of natives and immigrants in production. *Review of Economics and Statistics* 64(4): 596–603.

Gustafsson, B. 1990. Public sector transfers and income taxes among immigrants and natives in Sweden. *International Migration* 28: 181–99.

Haisken–De New, J. P., and K. Zimmermann. 1995. Wage and mobility effects of trade and migration. CEPR Discussion Paper n.1318.

Haisken–De New, J. P., and K. Zimmermann. 1999. Wage and mobility effects of trade and migration. In *Trade and jobs in Europe: Much ado about nothing?* edited by M. Dewatripont, A. Sapir, and K. Sekkat. Oxford: Oxford University Press.

Hamilton, C., and A. Winter. 1992. Trade with eastern Europe. *Economic Policy* April: 77–116.

Hansen, B., and S. Radwan. 1982. *Employment opportunity and equity in Egypt.* Geneva: ILO.

Harris, J. R., and M. Todaro. 1970. Migration, unemployment, and development: A two-sector analysis. *American Economic Review* 60: 126–42.

Hart, R. A. 1975. Interregional economic migration: Some theoretical considerations, part II. *Journal of Regional Science* 15(5): 289–305.

Hatton, T. 1995. A model of U.K. emigration, 1870–1913. *The Review of Economics and Statistics* 407–15.

Hatton, T. 2001. Why has UK net immigration increased? Unpublished.

Hatton, T., and J. Williamson, eds. 1994. *Migration and the international labour market, 1850–1913.* London: Routledge.

Hatzius, J. 1994a. The unemployment and earnings effect of German immigration. Applied Economics Discussion Paper series n.165, University of Oxford.

Hill, J. K. 1987. Immigration decisions concerning duration of stay and migratory frequency. *Journal of Development Economics* 25: 221–34.

Hollifield, J. 1992. *Immigrants, markets and the state: The political economy of post-war Europe.* Cambridge, MA: Harvard University Press.

Hunt, J. 1992. The impact of the 1962 repatriates from Algeria on the French labor market. *Industrial and Labour Relations Review* 45(3): 556–72.

Hunt, J. 2000. Why do people still live in East Germany? IZA Discussion Paper n.123.

Immigration Law Practitioners' Association. 1995. Information for members, Nov. Unpublished.

ILO. 1976. Migration of workers as an element in employment policy. Quaderni dell'Istituto di Demografia dell'Universita' di Roma.

INE. 1995. *Annuario statistico, Portugal.*

INE. 1993. *Annuario statistico, Spain.*

Jensen, L. 1988. Pattern of immigration and public assistance utilization, 1970–80. *International Migration Review* 22: 51–83.

Jensen, L., and M. Tienda. 1988. Nativity differentials in public assistance receipt: A research note. *Sociological Inquiry* 58: 306–21.

Jimeno, J. F., and S. Bentolila. 1998. Unemployment persistence and regional unadjustment, Spain 1976–94. *Labour Economics* 5(1): 25–51.

Jimeno, J. F., and L. Toharia. 1992. The productivity and wage effects of fixed-term employment contracts. FEDEA Working Paper, pp. 92–4.

Jimeno, J. F., and L. Toharia. 1994. *Unemployment and labour market flexibility: The case of Spain.* Geneva: ILO.

Johnson, G. E., and W. E. Whitelaw. 1974. Urban-rural income transfers in Kenya: An estimated remittances function. *Economic Development and Cultural Change* 22: 473–9.

Kakwani, N. 1986. *Analysing redistribution policies: A study using Australian data.* New York: Cambridge University Press.

Katseli, L., and P. N. Glytsos. 1989. Theoretical and empirical determinants of International labour mobility: A Greek-German perspective. In *European factor mobility: Trends and consequences,* edited by I. Gordon and A. P. Thirlwall. London: MacMillan.

Katz, E., and O. Stark. 1986. Labor migration made asymmetric information with moving and signaling costs., *Economic Letters* 21: 88–94.

Kee, P. 1994. Native-immigrant employment differentials in the Netherlands: The role of assimilation and discrimination. *International Review of Applied Economics* 8(2): 174–96.

Kindelberger, C. 1967. *Europe's postwar growth: The role of labor supply.* Cambridge, MA: Harvard University Press.

Kohli, U. 1999. Trade and migration: A production-theory approach. In *Migration: The controversies and the evidence,* edited by R. Faini J. De Melo, and K. Zimmermann. Cambridge University Press.

Kono, S. 1991. International migration in Japan: A demographic sketch. *Regional Development Dialogue* 12(3): 37–52.

Kuncu, M. E. 1989. The savings behaviour of migrant workers: Turkish workers in W. Germany. *Journal of Development Economics* 30: 273–86.

LaLonde, R., and R. Topel. 1992. The assimilation of immigrants in the U.S. labor market. In *Immigration and the workforce,* edited by G. Borjas and R. Freeman. NBER. Chicago: University of Chicago Press.

Langley, P. C. 1974. The spatial allocation of migrants in England and Wales. *Scottish Journal of Political Economy* XXI(3): 259–77.

Layard, R., O. Blanchard, R. Dornbusch, and P. Krugman. 1992. *East-West migration: The alternatives.* Cambridge, MA: The MIT Press.

Lebon, A. 1994. *Situation de l'immigration et présence étrangère en France 1993–1994.* Direction de la Population et des Migrations, Ministère de l'Amenagement du Territoire, de la Ville et de l'Intégration.

Lebon, A. 1995. *Migrations at Nationalité en France en 1994.* Direction de la Population et des Migrations, Ministère de l'Amenagement du Territoire, de la Ville et de l'Intégration.

Le Bras, H. 1991. L'Impact Déemographiques des Migrations d'Après-Guerre dans Quelques Pays de l'OCDE. In *Les Migrations, Aspects démographiques.* Paris: OCDE.

Lesthaeghe, R., H. Page, and J. Surkyn. 1991. Are immigrants substitutes for births? [Sind Einwanderer ein Ersatz fur Geburten?] *Zeitschrift fur Bevolkerungswissenschaft* 17(3): 281–314.

Lewis, A. W. 1954. Economic development with unlimited supplies of labor. *The Manchester School of Economic and Social Studies* 22: 139–91.

Lianos, T. 1997. Factors determining migrant remittances: The case of Greece. *International Migration Review* 31(1): 72–87.

Lianos, T. P., A. H. Sarris, and L. T. Katseli. 1996. Illegal immigration and local labour markets: The case of northern Greece. *International Migration Quarterly Review* 34(3): 449–84.

Linnemann, H. 1966. *An economic study of international trade flows*. Amsterdam: North-Holland.

Livi-Bacci, M., and F. Martuzzi Veronesi, eds. 1990. *Le risorse Umane del Mediterraneo*. Bologna, Italy: Il Mulino.

Lucas, R. 1988. On the mechanics of economic development. *Journal of Monetary Economics* 22: 3–42.

Lucas, R. E. B., and O. Stark. 1985. Motivation to remit: Evidence from Botswana. *Journal of Political Economy* 93: 901–18.

Lutz, V. 1961. Some structural aspects of the southern problem: The complementarity of immigration and industrialism. *Quarterly Review* Banca Nazionale del Lavoro 367–402.

Maccheroni, C., and A. Mauri. 1989. *Le migrazioni dall'Africa Mediterranea verso l'Italia*. Milan, Italy: Giuffré.

Mackay, D. F., and M. J. White. 1995. Occupational segregation and the immigrant worker in the U.K.: An ordered probit approach. Paper presented at the Annual EALE Conference, Lyon, Sept.

Maillat, D. 1986. The experience of European receiving countries. OCDE Conference, Paris.

Mankiw, G. N., D. Romer, and D. N. Weil. 1992. A contribution to the empirics of economic growth. *Quarterly Journal of Economics* 107: 407–37.

Marie, C. V. 1994. L'immigration en France dans les années quatre-vingt dix: nouvelle donne pour l'emploi et nouveaux enjeux de société. *Sociologie du travail* 2: 143–63.

Markusen, J. R. 1983. Factor movement and commodity trade as complements. *Journal of International Economics* 13: 341–56.

Markusen, J. R., and S. Zahniser. 1999. Liberalisation and incentives for labor migration: Theory with applications to Nafta. In *Migration: The controversies and the evidence*, edited by R. Faini, J. DeMelo, and K. Zimmermann. Cambridge University Press.

Martin, Ph. 1991. *The unfinished story: Turkish labour migration to western Europe*. Geneva: ILO.

Martin, Ph., and E. Midgley. 1994. Immigration to the United States: Journey to an uncertain destination. *Population Bulletin* 49(2): 1–47.

Massey, D. S., J. Arango, G. Hugo, A. Kouaouci, A. Pellerino, and J. E. Taylor. 1993. Theories of international migration: A review and appraisal. *Population and Development Review* 19(3): 431–66.

Massey, D. S., and E. Parrado. 1994. Migradollars: The remittances and savings of Mexican migrants to the U.S.A. *Population Research and Policy Review* 13: 3–30.

Maurin, E. 1991. Les étrangers: une main-d'oevre à part? *Economie et Statistique*, INSEE 242: 39–50.

Melotti, U. 1990. L'immigrazione straniera in Italia: da caso anomalo a caso exemplare. In *Stranieri in Italia*, edited by G. Cocchi. Bologna, Italy: Misure/Materiali Istituto Cattaneo.

Merkle, M., and K. Zimmermann. 1992. Savings, remittances, and return migration. *Economics Letters* 38: 77–81.

Miegel, M. 1984. *Arbeitsmarkpolitik auf Irrwegen*, Bonn. Cited in Straubhaar and Weber (1994).

Ministero de Asuntos Sociales. 1995. *Anuario de migraciones*. Madrid: Direction General de Migrationes.

Ministero de Asuntos Sociales. 1999. *Anuario de migraciones*. Madrid: Direction General de Migrationes.

Miyagiwa, K. 1991. Scale economies in education and the brain drain problem. *International Economic Review* 32(3): 743–60.

Mohammad, A., W. R. Butcher, and C. H. Gotsch. 1973. Temporary migration of workers and return flow of remittances in Pakistan. Economic Development Reports n. 234, Center for International Affairs, Harvard University.

Molle, W., and A. van Mourik. 1987. A static explanatory model of international labour migration to and in western Europe. In *European factor mobility: Trends and consequences*, edited by I. Gordon and A. P. Thirlwall. London: MacMillan.

Moreno, J. L. 1995. Le donne in banca: rimesse e famiglie di emigranti meridionali in Argentina prima del 1930. *Studi Emigrazioni* XXXII(118): 289–320.

Moulier-Boutang, Y., and J.-P. Garson. 1984. Major obstacles to control of irregular migrations: Prerequisites to policy. *International Migration Review* 18(67): 579–92.

Mountford, A., 1997. Can brain drain be good for growth in the source economy? *Journal of Development Economics* 53: 287–303.

Muller, T., and T. J. Espenshade. 1985. *The fourth wave*. Washington, DC: Urban Institute Press.

Munz, M., and G. Rabino. 1988. Italy. In *Interregoinal migration, dynamic theory and comparative analysis*, edited by W. Weidlich and G. Haag. Berlin: Springer Verlag.

Muus, Ph. 1996. *Migration, immigrants and policy in the Netherlands: Recent trends and developments*. (SOPEMI-Netherlands-1996). ERCOMER publication, Utrecht University, The Netherlands.

Nascimbene, B. 1988. *Lo straniero nel diritto italiano*. Milan: Giuffre'.

Nielson, H. S., M. Rosholm, N. Smith, and L. Husted. 2001. Qualifications, discrimination, or assimilation? An extended framework for analysing immigrant wage gaps. IZA Discussion Paper n. 365.

Niesing, W., B. van Praag, and J. Veenman. 1994. The unemployment of ethnic minority groups in the Netherlands. *Journal of Econometrics* 61: 173–96.

Nickell, S. 1981. Biases in dynamic models with fixed effects. *Econometrica* 49: 1417–26.

NSSG. 1995. *Monthly statistical bulletin*. Nov., Athens.

OECD. 1990. *Employment outlook*. Paris: OECD.

OECD. 1991. *Migration: The demographic aspects*. Series Demographic Change and Public Policy. Paris: OECD.

OECD. 1993. *Migrationes Internationales: le tournent.* Paris: OECD.

OECD. 1998. *Migrations, Libre-Echange et Integration Régionale dans le Bassin Méditerranéen.* Paris: OECD.

Ohlin, B. 1933. *Interregional and international trade.* Cambridge, MA: Harvard University Press.

Paine, S. H. 1974. *Exporting workers: The Turkish case.* Cambridge University Press.

Palaskas, B. T., and D. Christopoulos. 1997. Technological progress, returns to scale and capital-labour substitution in Greek industries: Further results. Development Studies Working Papers, n.111, Centro Studi Luca d'Agliano.

Penninx, R. 1984. Immigrant populations and demographic development in the member states of the Council of Europe. Strasbourg: Council of Europe.

Penninx, R., J. Schoorl, and C. van Praag. 1994. *The impact of international migration on receiving countries: The case of the Netherlands.* NIDI, The Hague, Report n.37.

Pereira, P. T. 1994. Portuguese emigration 1958–1985. *Empirical Economics* 19: 647–57.

Piras, R. 1995. Flussi Migratori, Capitale Umano e Convergenza tra le Regioni Italiane. Working Paper Dipartimento di Economia, Universita' di Cagliari.

Pischke, J. S. 1993. Assimilation and the earnings of guest-workers in Germany. Unpublished.

Pischke, J. S., and J. Velling. 1994. Wage and employment effects of immigration to Germany: An analysis based on local labour markets. CEPR Discussion Paper n.935.

Pischke, J. S., and J. Velling. 1997. Employment effects of immigration to Germany: An analysis based on local labor markets. *Review of Economics and Statistics* 79(4): 594–604.

Portes, A. 1978. Toward a structural analysis of illegal (undocumented) immigration. *International Migration Review* 12(4): 469–84.

Razin, A., and E. Sadka. 1992. International migration and international trade. NBER Working Paper n.4230.

Rempel, H., and R. A. Lobdell. 1978. The role of urban-to-rural remittances in rural development. *Journal of Development Studies* 324–41.

Reyneri, E. 1979. *La catena migratoria.* Bologna: Il Mulino.

Reyneri, E. 1998a. Addressing the employment of migrants in an irregular situation: The case of Italy. Paper presented at the Technical Symposium on International Migration and Development, UN, Den Hagen.

Reyneri, E. 1998b. The role of the underground economy in irregular migration to Italy: Cause or effect? *Journal of Ethnic and Migration Studies* 24(2): 313–31.

Riphahn, R. 1998. Immigrant participation in the German welfare program. *Finanzarchiv* 55: 163–85.

Rodriguez, E. R. 1996. International migrants' remittances in the Philippines. *Canadian Journal of Economics.* April: S427–S432.

Rosenzweig, M. R., and O. Stark. 1989. Consumption smoothing, migration, and marriage: Evidence from rural India. *Journal of Political Economy* 97(4): 905–26.

Rosholm, M., K. Scott, and L. Husted. 2000. The times they are a-changin': Organisational change and immigrant employment opportunities in Scandinavia. Centre for Labour Market and Social Research, W.P. n.7.

Rotte, R., M. Vogler, and K. F. Zimmermann. 1996. Asylum migration and policy coordination in Europe. SELAPO. Unpublished.

Russel, S. S. 1992. Migrants remittances and development. *International Migration* XXX(3/4): 267–88.

Salt, J., and H. Clout, eds. 1976. *Migration in post-war Europe: Geographical essays.* New York: Oxford University Press.

Salt, J., A. Singleton, and J. Hogarth. 1994. *Europe's international migrants.* London: HMSO.

Samuel, T. J. 1988a. Family class immigrants to Canada, 1981–1984: Part 1: Labour force activity aspects. *International Migration* 26(2): 171–86.

Samuel, T. J. 1988b. Family class immigrants to Canada, 1981–1984: Part 2: Some aspects of social adaptation. *International Migration* 26(3): 287–99.

Sartor, N., ed. 1997. Finanza Pubblica e sviluppo demohgrafico: un'analisi basata sui conti generazionali. Working Paper, G. Agnelli Foundation, Torino, Italy.

Sarris, A., and S. Zografakis. 1999. A computable general equilibrium assessment of the impact of illegal immigration on the Greek economy. *Journal of Population Economics* 12(1): 155–82.

Sassen, S. 1988. *The mobility of labor and capital: A study in international migration and labor flow.* Cambridge University Press.

Schmidt, C. 1993. The earnings dynamic of immigrant labour. CEPR Discussion Paper n.763.

Schmidt, C., A. Stilz, and A. Zimmermann. 1994. Mass migration, union and government intervention. *Journal of Public Economics* 55: 185–201.

Schneider, F., and D. H. Enste. 2000. Shadow economies: Size, causes, and consequences. *Journal of Economic Literature* XXXVIII: 77–114.

Signorelli, A., M. C. Tiriticco, and S. Rossi. 1977. *Scelte senza potere: Il ritorno degli emigranti nelle zone dell'esodo.* Rome: Officina Edizioni.

Simon, J. 1984. Immigrants, taxes, and welfare in the United States. *Population and Development Review* 10: 55–69.

Simon, J. 1989. *The economic consequences of immigration.* Oxford: Basil Blackwell.

Sjaastad, L. A. 1962. The costs and returns of human migration. *Journal of Political Economy* 86: 80–93.

SOPEMI. 1995. *Trends in international migration, annual report 1994.* Paris: OECD.

SOPEMI. 1999. *Trends in international migration, annual report 1998.* Paris: OECD.

SOPEMI. 2000. *Trends in international migration, annual report 1999.* Paris: OECD.

SOPEMI. 2001. *Trends in international migration, annual report 2000.* Paris: OECD.

Sori, E. 1979. *L'emigrazione italiana dall?unita' alla seconda guerra mondiale.* Bologna: Il Mulino.

Speare, A. 1974. Residential satisfaction as an intervening variable in residential mobility. *Demography* 11(2): 173–88.

Stalker, P. 1994. *The work of strangers: A survey of international labour migration.* Geneva: ILO.

Stark, O. 1984. Migration decision making: A review article. *Journal of Development Economics.* 14: 251–9.

Stark, O. 1991. *The migration of labor.* Cambridge: Basil Blackwell.

Stark, O. 2002. The economics of brain drain turned on its head. ABCDE World Bank Conference, Oslo.

Stark, O., and D. Bloom. 1985. The new economics of labor migration. *American Economic Review* 75: 173–8.

Stark, O., C. Helmenstein, and A. Prskawetz. 1997. A brain gain with a brain drain. *Economic Letters* 55: 227–34.

Stark, O., C. Helmenstein, and A. Prskawetz. 1998. Human capital depletion, human capital formation, and migration: A blessing or a "curse"? *Economic Letters* 60: 363–7.

Stark, O., and D. Levhari. 1988. Labor migration as a response to relative deprivation. *Journal of Development Studies* 1: 57–70.

Stark, O., and E. Taylor. 1989. Relative deprivation and international migration. *Demography* 26: 1–14.

Stark, O., and E. Taylor. 1991. Migration incentives, migration types: The role of relative deprivation. *The Economic Journal* 101: 1163–78.

Stark, O., E. Taylor, and S. Yitzhaki. 1986. Remittances and inequality. *The Economic Journal* 96: 722–40.

Stark, O., E. Taylor, and S. Yitzhaki. 1988. Migration, remittances, and inequality: A sensitivity analysis using the extended Gini index. *Journal of Development Economics* 28: 309–22.

Straubhaar, T. 1986. The determinants of workers' remittances: The case of Turkey. *Welwirtschaftliches Archiv* 122: 728–39.

Straubhaar, T. 1988. *On the economics of international labor migration*. Bern: Haupt.

Straubhaar, T., and R. Weber. 1994. On the economics of immigration: Some empirical evidence for Switzerland. *International Review of Applied Economics* 8(2): 107–29.

Strozza, S., G. Gallo, and F. Grillo. 2002. Gender and labour market among immigrants in some Italian areas: The case of Moroccans, former Yugoslavians and Poles. In the Proceedings of the IUSSP Conference on *Women in the Labour Market in Changing Economies: Demographic Issues*. New York: Oxford University Press.

Subramaniam, R. 1994. A theory of remittances. Discussion Paper n.9406, University of St. Andrews.

Summers, L., and A. Heston. 1988. A new set of international comparisons of real product and prices: Estimates for 130 countries, 1950–85. *The Review of Income and Wealth* 1.

Swamy, G. 1988. Population and international migration. World Bank Staff Working Paper n.689.

Swan, N., et al. 1991. *Economic and social impacts of immigration*. Ottawa, Canada: Economic Council of Canada.

Tapinos, G. 1994. *Elementi di demografia*. Milan: EGEA.

Tapinos, G., and A. de Rugy. 1993. The macroeconomic impact of immigration: Review of the literature published since the mid-1970s. In *Trends in International Migration, Annual Report*, SOPEMI. Paris: OEDC.

Taylor, A. M., and J. Williamson. 1994. Convergence in the age of mass migration. NRER Working Paper n.4711.

Termote, M. 1996. Causes et conséquences économiques de la migration. *Demografia: Analisi e Sintesi*, Dipartimento di Scienze Demografiche. Rome: La Sapienza.

Tienda, M., and L. Jensen. 1986. Immigration and public assistance participation: Dispelling the myth of dependency. *Social Science* 15: 372–400.

Todaro, M. 1969. A model of labor migration and urban unemployment in less-developed countries. *The American Economic Review* 59: 138–48.

Todaro, M. P., and L. Maruszko. 1987. Illegal migration and US immigration reform: A conceptual reform. *Population and Development Review* 13(1): 101–14.

Tribalat, M. 1986. Croniques de l'immigration. *Population* 1: 131–52.

Tribalat, M. 1988. Croniques de l'immigration. *Population* 1: 181–206.

Tribalat, M., J.-P. Garson, Y. Moulier-Boutang, and R. Silberman. 1991. *Cent Ans d'Immigration, Etrangers d'hier Français d'Aujourd'hui.* Paris: PUF, INED.

Tsamourgelis, Y. 1995. The impact of migration on employment, wages and unemployment of the host country: The case of Greece and Portugal. Paper presented at CEPR Workshop, Halkidiki.

Ulrich, R. 1992. Der Einfluss der Zuwanderung auf die staatlichen Einnahmen und Ausgaben In Deutschland. *Jahrestagung des Ausschusses für Bevölkerunsökonomie des Vereins für Socialpilitik* 31: 1–2. Cited in Straubhaar Weber (1994).

United Nations Economic Commission for Europe. 1979. *Labour supply and migration in Europe: Demographic dimensions, 1950–1975 and prospects.* Geneva: United Nations.

United Nations Economic Commission for Europe. 1996. Highlights. *International Migration Bulletin*, n.9.

Urbani, G., and E. Granaglia. 1991. Introduction, Conferenza nazionale sull'immigrazone. *Immigrazione e diritti di cittadinanza.* CNEL. Rome: Editalia.

Urga, G. 1992. The econometrics of panel data: A selective introduction. *Ricerche economiche* XLVI(3–4): 379–96.

Venturini, A. 1988. An interpretation of Mediterranean migration. *Labour* 2: 125–54.

Venturini, A. 1999. Do immigrants working illegally reduce the natives's legal employment in Italy? *Journal of Population Economics* 12(1): 135–54.

Venturini, A. 2001. *Le migrazioni ed i paesi del Sud Europa.* Torino, Italy: Utet.

Venturini, A., and C. Villosio. 1999. Foreign workers in Italy: Are they assimilating to natives? Are they competing against natives? An analysis by the S.S.A. dataset. *Einwanderungsregion Europa*? n.33. Arbaitstagung der Deutschen Gesellschaft fur Bevolkerungswissenschaft in Zusammenarbeit mit dem Istitut fur Migrationsforschung und Interkulturelle Studien der Universitat Osnabruck.

Venturini, A., and C. Villosio. 2000. Are immigrants assimilating in the Italian labour market? The role of big town. CHILD W.P.11/2000.

Venturini, A., and C. Villosio. 2002a. Are immigrants competing with Natives in the Italian labour market? The employment effect. IZA Discussion Paper n.467.

Venturini, A., and C. Villosio. 2002b. Immigrazione extracomunitaria in Italia ed integrazione economica. In ISFOL Report for the EU Commission, La politica del lavoro italiana negli anni recenti: valutazione e impatto.

Venturini, A., and C. Villosio. 2002c. Trade and migration in Italy. CHILD Working Paper. Unpublished.

Verhaeren, R. H. 1986. Politiques d'immigration en Europe. *Revue Problemes Politiques et Sociaux* 530: 1–40.

Vijverberg, W. P. M. 1993. Labour market performance as a determinant of migration. *Economica* 60: 143–60.

Wadensjö, E. 1973. Immigration och samhällsekonomi. Lund, Studentlitteratur. Cited in Straubhaar and Weber (1994).

Wang, Z. K., and A. L. Winters. 1991. The trading potential of eastern Europe. CEPR Discussion Paper n.610.

Weber, R. 1993. *Einwanderung und staatliche Umverteilung: Eine ökonomische Wirkungsanalyse für die Schweiz.* Zürich: Rüegger.

Wehrmann, M. 1989. Auswirkungen der Ausländerbeschäftigung auf die Volkswirtschft der Bundesrepublik Deutschland in Vergangenheit und Zukunft. Diiseration Universitata Bochum, Baden-Baden.

Weintraub, S. 1984. Illegal immigrants in Texas: Impact on social services and related considerations. *International Migration Review* 18: 733–47.

Werner, H. 1985. On international migration and international relations. *Population and Development Review* 11(3): 441–55.

Whiteford, P. 1991. Are immigrants overrepresented in the Australian social security system? *Journal of the Australian Population Association* 8(2): 93–109.

Widgren, J. 1991. I movimenti dei rifugiati e dei richiedenti asilo politico: Recenti tendenze in una prospettiva comparata. Presidenza del Consiglio dei Ministri and OCDE. Atti della Conferenza Internazionale sulle migrazioni, Roma, 13–14 marzo 1991. Rome: Editalia.

Winter-Ebmer, R., and K. Zimmermann. 1999. East-west trade and migration: The Austro-German case. In *Migration: The controversies and the evidence*, edited by R. Faini, J. De Melo, and K. Zimmermann. Cambridge University Press.

Winter-Ebmer, R., and J. Zweimuller. 1996. Immigration and the earnings of young native workers. *Oxford Economic Papers* 48: 473–91.

Winter-Ebmer, R., and J. Zweimuller. 1999. Do immigrants displace young native workers: The Austrian experience. *Journal of Population Economics* 12(2): 327–40.

Withers, G. 1986. Migration and the labour market: Australian analysis. CEPR Discussion Paper No. 144.

Wolpert, J. 1966. Migration as an adjustment to environmental stress. *Journal of Social Issues* 22: 92–102.

Zimmermann, K. 1994. European migration: Push and pull. *Proceedings of the World Bank Annual Conference on Development Economics.*

Zimmermann, K. 1995. Tackling the European migration problem. *Journal of Economic Perspectives* 9(2): 45–62.

Zlotnik, H. 1991. The role of international migration in population. OCDE, International Conference on Migration, Rome.

Zolberg, A. 1989. The next moves: Migration theory for a changing world. *International Migration Review* 23(3): 403–30.

Zolberg, A. R., A. Suhrke, and S. Aguayo. 1989. *Escape from violence, conflict and refugee crisis in the developing world.* New York: Oxford University Press.

WORK CONSULTED

Abeilla, M., ed. 1994. Turning points in labor migration. *Asian and Pacific Migration Journal,* Special Issue 3(1).

Actis, W. 1993. Foreign immigration in Spain: Its characteristics and differences in the European context. In *Recent Migration Trends in Europe: Europe's New Architecture,* edited by M. B. Rocha-Trindade. Lisbon: Universidade Aberta.

Adams, R. H. 1991. The economic uses and impact of international remittances in rural Egypt. *Economic Development and Cultural Change* 39: 695–722.

Adams, R. H. 1992. The effects of migration and remittances on inequality in rural Pakistan. *Pakistan Development Review* 31(4): 189–206.

Amor, M. B. H. 1992. International aid to reduce the need for migration: The Tunisian case. International Labor Organization. Migration section. Working Paper n.MIG-ILO WP.92-66.

Ancona, G., ed. 1990. *Migrazioni Mediterranee e Mercato del Lavoro.* Bari, Italy: Cacucci Editore.

Angrist, J. D., and A. D. Kugler. 2001. Protective or counter-productive? European labor market institutions and the effect of immigrants on the EU natives. NBER Working Paper n.w8660.

Antolin, P., and O. Bover. 1993. Regional migration in Spain: The effect of personal characteristics and unemployment, wage and house price differentials using pooled cross-section. Bank of Spain W.P. n.9318.

Arditis, S. 1986. Migration de retour an Europe du Sud. I.L.O. Migration Section, internal report. Unpublished.

Baganha, M., J. C. Marques, and G. Fonseca. 2000. Is an ethclass emerging in Europe? The Portuguese case. Lisbon: Luso-American Foundation.

Baldwin-Edwards, M. 1997. The emerging European immigration regime: Some reflections on implications for Southern Europe. *Journal of Common Market Studies* 35(4): 497–519.

Barros, L., and J-P. Garson. 1998. Migrations et integration regionale: L'Union Europeenne face aux pays tiers du Bassin Mediterraneen. In *Migrations, libre-echange et integration régionale dans le bassin Méditerranéen*. Paris: OCDE.

Bean, F. D., E. E. Telles, and B. L. Lowell. 1987. Undocumented migration to the United States: Perceptions and evidence. *Population and Development Review* 13(4): 671–90.

Bentolila, S., and J. J. Dolado. 1994. Labour flexibility and wages: Lessons from Spain. *Economic Policy* 18: 53–99.

Bergstrand, J. H. 1985. The gravity equation in international trade: Some microeconomic foundations and empirical evidence. *Review of Economics and Statistics* LXVII: 474–91.

Berninghaus, S., and H. G. Seifrt-Vogt. 1991. A temporary equilibrium model for international migration. *Journal of Population Economics* 4(1): 13–36.

Bhagwati, N. J., K. W. Schatz, and K. Y. Wong. 1984. The West German gastarbeiter system of immigration. *European Economic Review* 23: 277–94.

Birindelli, A. M., and C. Bonifazi, eds. 1993. *Italy*. Published in the series Impact of migration in the receiving countries, edited by L. A. Kosinski. Committee for International Co-operation in National Research in Demography (CICRED) and International Organization for Migration (IOM).

Böhning, R. W. 1970. The differential strength of demand and wage factors in intra-European labour mobility: With special reference to West Germany 1957–1968. *International Migration* 3(4): 193–202.

Böhning, R. W. 1975. Some thoughts on emigration from the Mediterranean basin. *International Labour Review* III(3): 251–77.

Böhning, R.W., P. V. Schaeffer, and T. Straubhaar. 1991. *Migration pressure: What is it? What can one do about it?* October. World Employment Programme Working Paper. Geneva: ILO.

Böhning, R.W., and R. Zegers de Beijl. 1995. The integration of migrant workers in the labour market: Policies and their impact. ILO Employment Department, International Migration Papers, n.8.

Borjas, G. 1995a. Immigration and welfare, 1970–1990. *Research in Labor Economics* XIV: 251–80.

Borjas, G. 1995b. Assimilation and changes in cohort quality revisited: What happened to immigrant earnings in the 1980s? *Journal of Labor Economics* 13(2): 201–45.

Borras, A. 1995. *Diaz Anos de la Ley de Extranjeria: Balance y perspectivas.* Madrid: Fundacion Paulino Torras Domenech.

Borzaga, C. 1992. Immigrazione e domanda di lavoro: evidenze recenti e possibili linee evolutive. *Politiche del lavoro,* Special Isssue on Immigration (21): 5–18.

Borzaga, C., and M. Frisanco. 1993. L'evoluzione della partecipazione e della disoccupazione giovanile. In Ministry of Labour, *Report '91–'92 on Labour and Employment Policies in Italy.* Rome.

Borzaga, C., E. Renzetti, and L. Covi. 1993. L'immigrazione extracomunitaria in provincia di Trento: dimensioni ed aspetti secondo i risultati di un'indagine sul campo. *Studi Emigrazioni* 30(110): 194–218.

Brown, R. P. C. 1994. Migrants' remittances, savings and investment in the South Pacific. *International Labour Review* 133(3): 347–67.

Bruni, M. 1988. A stock-flow model to annualise and forecast labour market variables. *Labour* 1.

Bruni, M. 1989. An integrated accounting for firms, job positions and employment. *Labour* 3: 73–92.

Burda, M. C., and C. Wyplosz. 1992. Human capital, investment and migration in an integrating Europe. *European Economic Review* 36: 677–84.

Burgenmeier, B., ed. 1992. *Main d'Oeuvre Etrangère. Une analyse de l'économie Suisse.* Paris: Economica.

Bussery, H. 1976. Incidence sur l'économie française d'une réduction durable de la main-d'oeuvre immigrée. *Economie et statistique,* INSEE, 37–45.

Callovi, G. 1992. Regulation of immigration in 1993: Pieces of the European Community jig-saw puzzle. *International Migration Review* 26(2): 353–72.

Caritas Espanola. 1987. Los Immigrantes en Espana. *Documentation social* 66.

Castles, S., and G. Kosac. 1973. *Immigrant workers and class structure in Western Europe.* London: Oxford University Press.

Castles, S., and M. J. Miller. 1993. *The age of migration: International population movements in the modern world.* New York: Guilford Press.

C.C.E. 1994. *On immigration and asylum policies.* Communication from the Commission to the Council and European Parliament, Brussels.

Cerase, F. P. 1993. Strategic issues in migration policies in the 90's: A glance at the Italian scene. In *Recent Migration Trends in Europe. Europe's New Architecture,* edited by M. B. Rocha-Trindade. Lisbon: Universidade Aberta.

Céu Esteves, do M., Carlos L. Palma, V. Franci, Gomes T. Ferreira, P. Guibentif, R. Pena Pires, and A. Saint-Maurice. 1991. *Portugal, Pais de Imigraçao.* Lisbon: Instituto de Tstudos para o Desenvolvimento.

Chesnais, I. C. 1986. *La transition démographique.* Parigi: Ined.

Chesnais, I. C. 1987. Le poids de la démographie. *RAMSES 1987–8,* IFRI, Paris.

Chiswick, B. 1982. *The gateway: U.S. immigration issues and policies.* Washington: D.C.: American Enterprise Institute.

Cocchi, G., ed. 1990. *Stranieri in Italia. Caratteri e tendenze dell'immigrazione dai paesi extracomunitari.* Bologna Italy: Misure/Materiali dell'Istituto di Ricerca Cattaneo.

Cole, E. W., and R. D. Sanders. 1985. International migration and urban employment in the third world. *American Economic Review* 75(3): 481–94.

Conseil de l'Europe. 2000. Evolution demographique recente in Europe. Strasbourg: Edition du Conseil de l'Europe.

Cornelius, W. A., Ph. L. Martin, and J. F. Hollifield, eds. 1992. *Controlling immigration: A global perspective.* Stanford, CA: Stanford University Press.

Covi, L. 1992. L'immigrazione extracomunitaria nel sistema economico trentino: da fenomeno emergente a realta' consolidata. *Politiche del lavoro,* Special Issue on Immigration 21: 19–38.

Daboussi, R. 1991. Economic evolution, demographic trends, employment and migration movements. International Labour Office [ILO], International Migration for Employment Branch, Geneva, Switzerland.

De Grazia, R. 1984. *Clandestine employment.* P.I.A.C.T. study, I.L.O., Geneva.

Dewatripont, M., A. Sapir, and K. Sekkat, eds. 1999. *Trade and jobs in Europe, much ado about nothing?* Oxford: Oxford University Press.

Del Boca, D., and A. Venturini. 2001. Italian migration. CHILD WP.26/2001, forthcoming in *European migration,* edited by K. Zimmermann. Oxford: Oxford University Press.

Djajic, S. 1987. Illegal aliens, unemployment and immigration policy. *Journal of Development Economics* 25: 235–49.

Espenshade, T. J., L. F. Bouvier, and W. B. Arthur. 1982. Immigration and the stable population model. *Demography* 19(1): 125–33.

Esposito, G. 1990. L'economia sommersa nelle statistiche di Contabilita' nazionale. n.41–42, 147–56.

Ethier, W. J. 1985. International trade and labor migration. *American Economic Review* 75: 691–707.

Ethier, W. J. 1986a. Illegal immigration. *American Economic Review* 76(2): 258–62.

Ethier, W. J. 1986b. Illegal immigration the host country problem. *American Economic Review* 76(1): 56–71.

Eurostat. 1992. *Demographic statistics.* Luxembourg.

Eurostat. 1994b. *Maghreb countries 1994.* Luxembourg.

Evers, G. H., and A. Van der Veen. 1985. A simultaneous non-linear model for labour migration and commuting. *Regional Studies* 19(3): 217–29.

Faini, R. 1995. Stesso lavoro, diverso salario? In *Le nuove frontiere della Politica Economica,* edited by F. Galimberti, F. Giavazzi, A. Penati, and G. Tabellini. Il Sole 24 Ore Libri.

Faini, R. 1996. Increasing returns, migrations and convergence. *Journal of Development Economics* 49: 121–36.

Faini, R., J. De Melo, and K. Zimmermann. 1999. *Migration: The controversies and the evidence.* Cambridge University Press.

Faini, R., and A. Venturini. 2001. Home bias and migration. CHILD WP:27/2001.

Fargues, P. 1986. Un siecle de transition demographique en Afrique Mediterraneenne 1885–1985. *Population* 2: 205–32.

Fassman, H., and R. Munz. 1994. *European migration in late twentieth century.* London: Elgar.

Ferri, J., A. G. Gomez-Plana, and J. Martin-Montaner. 2002. Internal immigration and mobility across sectors: An exploration of alternative scenarios for Spain. Presented at the 2002 ESPE Annual Conference in Bilbao, Spain.

Frey, L. 1990. Il mercato del lavoro sommerso: aspetti di continuita' e nuove tendenze. *Quaderni di Economia del Lavoro* 41.42: 157–66.

Frey, L. 1992. Fattori determinanti dei flussi di immigrazione dal lato dell'offerta. *Quaderni di Economia del Lavoro* 43: 41–76.

Frey, L., and R. Livraghi. 1996. Jobs refused by nationals, with special reference to Italy. In *The jobs and effects of migrant workers in Italy: Three essays*, edited by L. Frey, R. Livraghi, A. Venturini, A. Righi, and L. Tronti. International Migration Papers n.11, I.L.O., Geneva.

Funkhouser, E. 1992. Mass emigration, remittances, and economic adjustment: The case of El Salvador in the 1980s. In *Immigration and the Workforce*, edited by G. Borjas and R. Freeman. NBER. Chicago: University of Chicago Press.

Gallino, L. 1900. Doppio lavoro ed economia informale. *Quaderni di economia del lavoro* 41–42: 167–80.

Garson, J-P. 1989. Comparative analysis of regularisation experience in France, Italy, Spain and the United States. From SOPEMI Report 1989.

Glytsos, P. N. 1998. Le Migration comme Moteur de l'Integration Réegionale: l'example des Transferts de Fonds. In *Migrations, Libre-Echange et Integration Régionale dans le Bassin Méditerranéen*. Paris: OECD.

Glytsos, P. N., and L. Katzeli. 2001. Greek migration: The two faces of Janus. Presented at the CEPR Conference "European migration: What do we know?" Munich. Forthcoming in *European migration: What do we know?*, edited by K. Zimmermann. Oxford: Oxford University Press.

Golini, A. 1974. Distribuzione della Popolazione, Migrazioni Interne e Urbanizzazione in Italia. Collana dell'Istituto di Demografia della Facolta' di Scienze Statistiche Demografiche ed Attuariali dell'Universita' di Roma, n.27.

Golini, A., and A. M. Birindelli. 1990. Italy. In *Handbook on International Migration*, edited by W. J. Serow, C. B. Nam, D. F. Sly, and R. H. Weller. Westport, CT: Greenwood Press.

Golini, A., and C. Bonifazi. 1987. Demographic trends and international migration. *Future of Migration*. Paris: OCDE.

Grazioglu, S. 1994. Assimilation: Compensating differences and job disamenities by using life-cycle adjustment income. *International Review of Applied Economics* 8(2): 157–73.

Greenwood, M. 1975. Research on internal migration in the United States: A survey. *Journal of Economic Literature* 13: 397–433.

Greenwood, M. 1985. Human migration: Theory, models and empirical evidence. *Journal of Regional Science* 25: 521–44.

Greenwood, M., G. L. Hunt, and J. M. McDowell. 1986. Migration and employment change: Empirical evidence on the spatial and temporal dimensions of the linkage. *Journal of Regional Science* 26(2): 223–34.

Gustafsson, B. 1986. International migration and falling into the income safety net: Social assistance among foreign citizens in Sweden. *International Migration* 24: 461–83.

Hamermesh, D. 1986. The demand for labor in the long run. In *Handbook of Labor Economics*, edited by O. Ashenfelter and R. Layard. Amsterdam: Elsevier Science Publishers.

Hamermesh, D. 1993. *Labor demand*. Princeton, NJ: Princeton University Press.

Hammar, T. 1985. *European immigration policy: A comparative study*. Cambridge University Press.

Hammar, T., S. Oberg, G. Brochmann, and K. Tamas. 1994. Migration, population and poverty: A theoretical and empirical project on south-north migration and the immigration control policies of industrialised countries. CEIFO paper.

Hanson, G. H., and A. Spilimbergo. 1999. Illegal immigration, border enforcement, and relative wages: Evidence from apprehensions at the U.S.-Mexico border. *American Economic Review* 89(5): 337–57.

Hartog, J., and N. Vriend. 1990. Labour market analysis of allocation and earnings. *Oxford Economic Papers* 42: 379–401.

Hatton, T., and J. Williamson. 1998. *The age of mass migration.* New York: Oxford University Press.

Hatzius, J. 1994b. Regional migration, unemployment and vacancies: Evidence from West German microdata. Applied Economics Discussion Paper series n.164, University of Oxford.

Hill, J. K., and J. A. Mendez. 1984. The effect of commercial policy on international migration flows: The case of United States and Mexico. *Journal of International Economics* 17: 41–53.

Hodges-Aeberhard, J., and P. Morgenstern. 1996. Problems of discrimination against women migrant workers and possible solutions. ILO, Interdepartmental Project on Migrant Workers.

Hoffmann, E., and S. Lawrence. 1996. Statistics on international labour migration: A review of sources and methodological issues. ILO Bureau of Statistics working paper.

Hufbauer, G., and J. Schott. 1992. *North American free trade: Issues and recommendations.* Washington, D.C.: Institute for International Economics.

Husted, L., H. S. Nielsen, M. Rosholm, and N. Smith. 2000. Employment and earnings assimilation of male first generation immigrants in Denmark. Centre for Labour Market and Social Research, W.P. n.6.

ILO. 1988–92. *Yearbook of labour statistics.* Geneva.

ILO. 1986. *Economically active population, 1950–2000.* Geneva.

International Monetary Fund. 1950. *Balance of payments statistics yearbook.*

International Monetary Fund. 1981. *Balance of payments statistics yearbook.*

International Monetary Fund. 1991. *Balance of payments statistics yearbook.*

International Monetary Fund. 1995. *Balance of payments statistics yearbook.*

International Monetary Fund. 1999. *Balance of payments statistics yearbook.*

International Monetary Fund. 2000. *Balance of payments statistics yearbook.*

ISMU. 1997. *Terzo Rapporto sulle Migrazioni.* Milan: Franco Angeli.

ISTAT. 1993. *The Underground Economy in Italian Economic Accounts.* Annali di statistica, anno 122, serie X, vol. 2.

ISTAT. 1995. *Contabilita' Nazionale.* Collana Informazione, n.19.

ISTAT. 1994. *Contabilita' Nazionale.* Collana Informazione, n.20.

ISTAT. 1991. *Contabilita' Nazionale.* Collana Informazione. n.42.

ISTAT. many years. *Conti Economici Nazionali.*

Izquierdo Escribano, A., and F. Munoz-Perez. 1989. L'Espana pays d'immigration. *Population* 2: 257–89.

Jackman, R., and S. Savoouri. 1992. Regional migration in Britain: An analysis of gross flows using NHS Central Register data. *The Economic Journal* 102: 1433–50.

Karafolas, S. 1998. Migrant remittances in Greece and Portugal: Distribution by country of provenance and the role of the banking presence. *International Migration* 36(3): 357–81.

Karras, G., and C. U. Chiswick. 1999. Macroeconomic determinants of migration: The case of Germany 1964–1988. *International Migration* 37(4): 657–77.

Katz, E., and O. Stark. 1987. Migration, information and the costs and benefits of signalling. *Regional Science and Urban Economics* 17: 323–31.

Kee, P. 1993. Immigrant wages in the Netherlands: The valuation of pre- and post-immigration human capital. *The Economist* 141(1): 96–111.

Keyfitz, N. 1988. Some demographic properties of transfer schemes: How to achieve equity between the generations. In *Economics of changing age distributions in developed countries*, edited by R. D. Lee, W. B. Arthur, and G. Rodgers. International Studies in Demography. Oxford: Clarendon Press.

King, R., ed. 1986. *Return migration: A regional economic problem*. London: Croom Helms.

King, R., ed. 1993. *The new geography of European migrations*. London: Belhaven Press.

King, R., and K. Rybaczuk. 1993. Southern Europe and the international division of labour: From emigration to immigration. In *The new geography of European migrations*, edited by R. King. London: Belhaven Press.

Klassen, L. H., and P. Drewe. 1973. *Migration policy in Europe: A comparative study*. Farnborough, UK: Saxon House/Lexington Books.

Kopits, G. 1987. Structural reform, stabilization, and growth in Turkey. World Bank, Occasional Paper n.52.

Kritz, M. M., C. B. Keely, and S. M. Tomasi, eds. 1983. *Global trends in migration: Theory and research on international population movements*. New York: Center For Migration Studies.

Lebon, A. 1996. *Rapport sur l'immigration et la présence étrangère en France 1995–1996*. Direction de la Population et des Migrations, Ministère de l'Amenagement du Territoire, de la Ville et de l'Intégration.

Lebon, A. 2000. *Rapport sur l'immigration et la présence étrangère en France 1999–2000*. Direction de la Population et des Migrations, Ministère de l'Amenagement du Territoire, de la Ville et de l'Intégration.

Lewis, J., and A. Williams. 1985. Portugal's retornados: Reintegration or rejection? *Iberian Studies* XIV (1–2).

Lewis, J., and A. Williams. 1986. The economic impact of return migration in Central Portugal. In *Return migration: A regional economic problem*, edited by R. King. London: Croom Helms.

Licht, G., and V. Steiner. 1994. Assimilation, labor market experience and earnings profiles of temporary and permanent immigrant workers in Germany. *International Review of Applied Economics* 8(2): 130–56.

Lippman, S. A., and J. J. McCall. 1976. The economics of job search: A survey. *Economic Inquiry* 14: 155–89.

Lutz, W., ed. 1994. *The future population of the world: What can we assume today?* London: Earthscan.

MacMillen, J. M. 1982. The economic effects of international migration: A survey. *Journal of Common Market Studies* XX(3): 245–67.

Macura, M., and D. Coleman, eds. 1994. *International migration: Regional processes and responses*. Geneva: United Nations Economic Commission for Europe, United Nations Population Fund, Economic Studies n.7.

Malfatti, E. 1976. Le Migrazioni meridionali alla luce delle fonti statistiche ufficiali (1951–1975). *Studi Emigrazioni* XIII(42): 148–58.

Manion, J. R., M. Nunez, and P. Sandoval. 1994. *Anuario de Migraciones*. Ministerio de Asuntos Sociales, Direction General de Migraciones.

Martin, Ph. 1993. *Trade and migration: NAFTA and agriculture*. Policy Analysis in International Economics, n.38.

Martin, Ph. 1995. NAFTA and labor migration. Paper presented at the EUI Immigration Workshop, Florence, Italy.

Maruani, M., E. Reynaud, and C. Romani, eds. 1990. La flessibilita' del lavoro in Italia. *Quaderni di Economia del Lavoro* 41–42.

Mayer, E. 1990. Immigration: Some issues for discussion. Discussion Paper 90/05, Australian Government Publishing Service, Camberra, September.

Migration News, various issues and years.

Miller, M. J. 1988. Les regularisations de la population clandestine dans les democraties industrielles: un bilan comparatif. *Revue françaises d'Administration Publiques* 47: 61–9.

Mingione, E. 1988. Old and new areas of "travail noir," EEC, *Underground economy and irregular forms of employment*, study n.87929.

Mingione, E. 1995. Labour market segmentation and informal work in southern Europe. *European Urban and Regional Studies* 2(2): 121–43.

Ministero de Trabajo y Asunto Sociales. 2000. *Anuario de migraciones*, Subirection General de Publicationes, Madrid, Spain.

Mitra, S. 1983. Generalization of the immigration and the stable population model. *Demography* 20(1).

Molho, I. 1984. A dynamic model of interregional migration flows in Great Britain. *Journal of Regional Science* 317–37.

Molho, I. 1986. Theories of migration: A review. *Scottish Journal of Political Economy* 33(4): 396–459.

Montanari, A. 1995. Skilled migrations from Italy. *Studi Emigrazioni* XXXII(17): 42–53.

Mottura, G., ed. 1992. *L'arcipelago immigrazione. Caratteristiche e modelli migratori dei lavoratori stranieri in Italia*. Rome: Ediesse.

Mouhoud, E. M. 1991. Enterprise relocation, north/south economic relations, and the dynamics of employment. OCDE, International Conference on Migration, Rome.

Moulier-Boutang, Y., J. P. Garson, and R. Silberman. 1986. *Economie Politique des Migrations Clandestines de main-d'oeuvre*. Paris: Publisud.

NSSG. 1991. *Labour force survey*, Athens.

Oberai, A. S. 1993. International labour migration statistics: Use of censuses and sample surveys. ILO-WEP working paper n.75.E.

OECD. 1994. *Migration and dévelopment: un nuveau partenariat pour la coopération*. Paris: OECD.

OECD. 1995. *Country studies: Greece*. Paris: OECD.

OECD. 1995. *Country studies: Portugal*. Paris: OECD.

OECD. 1995. *Country studies: Spain*. Paris: OECD.

OECD. 1996. *Country studies: Italy*. Paris: OECD.

OECD. 1990–1998. *Labour force statistics*. Paris: OECD.

O'Rourke, K. 1992. Why Ireland emigrated: A positive theory of factor flows. *Oxford Economic Papers* 44: 322–40.

Papademetriou, D. G. 1985. Emigration and return in the Mediterranean Litoral. *Comparative Politics* 18(1): 22–39.

Papademetriou, D. G. 1989. Uncertain connection: Labor migration and development. Commission Working Paper, No. 9. Washington, DC: Commission for the Study of International Migration and Cooperative Economic Development.

Pena Pires, R. 1993. Immigration in Portugal: A typology essay. In *Recent Migration Trends in Europe: Europe's New Architecture*, edited by M. B. Rocha-Trindade. Lisbon, Portugal: Universidade Aberta.

Penninx, R. 1986. International migration in Western Europe since 1973: Developments, mechanisms and controls. *International Migration Review* 20(4): 951–72.

Piore, M. 1979. *Bird of passage: Migrant labour and industrial societies.* Cambridge University Press.

Picard, L. 1996. *Conventions Internationales du Travail et législations nationales sur les Travailleurs Migrats: Convergences et Divergences.* ILO Interdepartmental Project on Migrant Workers.

Pope, D. 1981. Modelling the peopling of Australia: 1900–1930. *Australian Economic Papers* Dec.: 258–82.

Portes, A. 1989. Unauthorised immigration and immigration reform: Present trends and prospects. Working Papers Commission for the Study of International Migration and Cooperative Economic Development, n.7, Washington, D.C.

Portes, A. 1995. *The economic sociology of immigration.* New York: Russell Sage Foundation.

Portes, A., and R. Bach. 1985. *Latin journey, Cuban and Mexican immigrants in the United States.* Berkeley: University of California Press.

Pugliese, E. 1992. The new international migrations and the changes in the labour market. *Labour* 6(1): 165–79.

Quibria, M. G. 1988. A note on international migration, non-traded goods and economic welfare in the source country. *Journal of Development Economics* 28: 377–87.

Quibria, M. G. 1989. International migration and real wage. *Journal of Development Economics* 31: 177–83.

Rauch, J. E. 1991. Reconciling the pattern of trade with the pattern of migration. *The American Economic Review* 81(4): 775–96.

Razin, A., and E. Sadka. 1997. International migration and international trade. In *Handbook of population and family economics*, edited by Mark R. Rosenzweig and O. Stark. Amsterdam: Elsevier Science Publishers.

Reyneri, E. 1998c. Immigrazione ed economia sommersa. *Stato e Mercato* 53: 287–317.

Reyneri, E. 2000. Integrazione nel mercato del lavoro. In *Primo rapporto sull'integrazione degli immigrati in Italia*, edited by G. Zincone. Bologna, Italy: Il Mulino.

Ricca, S. 1984. L'administration du travail de l'immigré en situation irreguliere en Espagna, en Grece et en Italie. I. L. O. Migration Section, Document de Travail. Unpublished.

Ricci, R. 1990. Rapporti e scambi economico-sociali. In *Le risorse umane del Mediterraneo*, edited by M. Livi-Bacci and F. Martuzzi Veronesi. Bologna, Italy: Il Mulino.

Rivera-Batiz, F. L. 1983. Trade theory, distribution of income and immigration. *American Economic Review* 73(2): 183–87.

Rivera-Batiz, F. L. 1989. The impact of international migration on real wages. *Journal of Development Economics* 31: 185–92.

Rivera-Batiz, F. L. 1986. International migration, remittances and economic welfare in the source country. *Journal of Economic Studies* 13(3): 3–20.

Robin, S. 1996. The provision of services and the movement of labour in the countries of the European Union. OECD International Migration and Labour Market Policies Occasional Papers n.2, OCDE/GD(96)63.

Rocha-Trinidade, M. B. ed. 1993. *Recent migration trends in Europe: Europe's new architecture*. Lisbon, Portugal: Edition Universidade Aberta.

Rotte, R., M. Vogler, and K. F. Zimmermann. 1997. South-north refugee migration: Lessons for development cooperation. *Review of Development Economics* 1(1): 99–115.

Russel, S. S., and M. Teitelbaum. 1992. International migration and international trade. World Bank Discussion paper n.160, Washington, D.C.

Sassen, S. 1993. Economic internationalization: The new migration in Japan and the United States. *International Migration* XXXI(1): 73–102.

Sassen, S. 1995. *Cities in a world economy*. Thousand Oaks, CA: Pine Forge Press.

Schaeffer, P. V. 1991. A definition of migration pressure based on demand theory. In *Migration Pressure: What is it? What can one do about it?*, edited by W. R. Böhning, P. V. Schaeffer, and T. Straubhaar. Geneva, ILO, October, World Employment Programme Working Paper, 10–33.

Serow, W. J., C. B. Nam, D. F. Sly, and R. H. Weller, eds. 1990. *Handbook on international migration*. New York: Greenwood Press.

Simon, J., S. Moore, and R. Sullivan. 1993. The effect of immigration on aggregate native unemployment: An across-city estimation. *Journal of Labor Resources* 14(3): 299–316.

Simon, R. J. 1993. Old minorities, new immigrants: Aspirations, hopes, and fears. *Annals of the American Academy of Political and Social Science* 530: 61–73.

SOPEMI. 1993. *Trends in international migration, annual report 1992*. Paris: OECD.

SOPEMI. 1994. *Trends in international migration, annual report 1993*. Paris: OECD.

SOPEMI. 1997. *Trends in international migration, annual report 1996*. Paris: OECD.

SOPEMI. 1998. *Trends in international migration, annual report 1997*. Paris: OECD.

Stark, O., and D. Levhari. 1982. On migration and risk in LDCs. *Economic Development and Cultural Change* 31: 191–6.

Stark, O., and S. Yitzhaki. 1988. Labor migration as a response to relative deprivation. *Journal of Population Economics* 1: 57–70.

Straubhaar, T. 1986a. The causes of international migration: A demand determined approach. *International Migration Review* 20(4): 835–55.

Straubhaar, T. 1991. Migration pressure. In W. R. Böhning, G. P. Tapinos, and C. B. Keely. Two views on international migration. ILO MIG Working Paper 68.

Straubhaar, T. 1992. The impact of international labor migration for Turkey. In *Migration and Economic Development*, edited by K. Zimmermann. Berlin: Springer-Verlag.

Straubhaar, T., and R. Weber. 1996. Immigration and the public transfer system: Some empirical evidence for Switzerland. *Welwirtschaftliches Archiv* 132(2): 330–55.

Straubhaar, T., and M. Wolburg. 1999. Brain drain and brain gain in Europe: An evaluation of the East-European migration to Germany. *Jahrbücher für Nationalökonomie und Statistik* 218(5–6): 574–604.

Strozza, S., and A. Venturini. 2002. Italy is no longer a country of emigration: Foreigners in Italy, how many, where they come from and what they do. In *Migration policy and the economy: International experiences*, edited by R. Rotte and P. Stein. Studies and Comments 1 series. Munich: Hanns Seidel Stiftung.

Tapinos, G. 1996. *Europe Méditerranéenne et Changements Démographiques*. Paris: Forum International.

Tapinos, G. 1997. Illegal migration. Institut d'Etudes Politiques de Paris. Unpublished.

Tapinos, G. P., D. Cogneau, P. Lacroix, and A. de Rugy. 1994. Libre-echange et migration internationale au Maghreb. Fondation Nationale des Sciences Politiques, research commissioned by EEC, G.D.1.

Tapinos, G. P., P. Lacroix, and A. de Rugy. 1996. *Les methodes d'evaluation de l'immigration clandestine dans certains pays etrangers*. Paris: Fondation Nationale des Sciences Politiques.

Todaro, M. 1976. *International migration in developing countries*, Geneva: I.L.O.

Todisco, E., ed. 1995. *Immigrazione: dai bisogni ai diritti, dall'emarginazione all'integrazione*. Universita' degli studi "La Sapienza," Facolta' di Economia.

Tribalat, M. 1987. Croniques de l'immigration. *Population* 1: 129–52.

Tribalat, M. 1989. Croniques de l'immigration. *Population* 1: 113–52.

United Nations Organization. 1988. *World demographic estimates and projections*. New York: ONU Publications.

Uygur, E. 1992. Foreign aid as a means to reduce emigration: The case of Turkey. MIG-ILO WP.92-64.

Venturini, A. 1990a. I mercati del lavoro nel bacino del Mediterraneo: Andamenti e possibili evoluzioni di fronte a crescenti flussi migratori. In *Le risorse umane del Mediterraneo*, edited by M. Livi Bacci and F. Martuzzi Veronesi. Bologna: Il Mulino.

Venturini, A. 1990b. Il ruolo delle immigrazioni nelle societa' industrializzate: complementarita', sostituzione o trasformazione. In *Migrazioni Mediterranee e Mercato del Lavoro*, edited by G. Ancona. Bari, Italy: Cacucci Editore.

Venturini, A. 1990c. Italy in the European migratory contest. In Ministero del lavoro e della Previdenza Sociale, *Report '89 on Labour and Employment Policies in Italy*.

Venturini, A. 1996. Extent of competition between and complementarity among national and third-world migrant workers in the labour market: An exploration of the Italian case. In L. Frey, R. Livraghi, A. Righi, L. Tronti, and A. Venturini, The jobs and the effects of migrant workers in Italy. I.L.O., International Migration Papers, n.11.

Venturini, A. 2003. Immigration is a problem in Italy, but it isn't an economic one. In *Controlling immigration: A global perspective*, edited by W. Cornelius, P. L. Martin, and J. F. Hollifield. Stanford, CA: Stanford University Press.

Venturini, A., H. Brücker, G. Epstein, B. McCornick, G. Saint-Paul, and K. Zimmermann. 2002. Managing Migration in the European welfare state. In *Immigration policy and the welfare system*, edited by T. Boeri, G. Hanson, and B. McCornick. Oxford: Oxford Economic Press.

Verhaeren, R. H. 1988. *Une theorie economique des migrations internationales*. Grenoble: Les Cahiers du Criss.

Wahba, S. 1991. What determines workers' remittances. *Finance & Development* 41–4.

Wattelar, C., and G. Roumans. 1991. Simulations of demographic objectives and migration. In OECD, *Migration: The demographic aspects*. Paris: OECD.

Weidlich, W., and G. Haag, eds. 1988. *Interreginal migration, dynamic theory and comparative analysis*. Berlin: Springer Verlag.

Weintraub, S. 1990. The Maquiladora industry in Mexico. Working Papers Commission for the Study of International Migration and Cooperative Economic Development, n.39, Washington, DC.

Winegarden, C. R., and L. B. Khor. 1991. Undocumented immigration and unemployment of U.S. youth and minority workers: Econometric Evidence. *Review of Economics and Statistics* 73(1): 105–12.

World Bank. 1988, 1990, 1992. *World development report 1988, 1990, 1992.* Washington, DC: Oxford University Press.

World Bank. 1999, 2000, 20001. *World development indicators.* Washington, DC.

Zegers de Beijl, R. 1995. Labour market integration and legislative measures to combat discrimination against migrant workers. In R. W. Böhning, and R. Zegers de Beijl, The integration of migrant workers in the labour market: Policies and their impact. I.L.O. Employment Department, International Migration Papers, n.8.

Zimmermann, K., ed. 1992. *Migration and economic development.* Berlin: Springer-Verlag.

Zincone, G. 1992. *Da sudditi a cittadini.* Bologna: Il Mulino.

Zincone, G. 1997. The powerful consequences of being too weak: The impact of immigration on democratic regimes. *Archives Européennes de Sociologie* XXXVII(1): 104–38.

Zincone, G., ed. 2000. *Primo rapporto sull'integrazione degli immigrati in Italia.* Bologna: Il Mulino.

Zincone, G., ed. 2001. *Secondo rapporto sull'integrazione degli immigrati in Italia.* Bologna: Il Mulino.

Zlotnik, H. 1993. Le role des migrations internationales dans l'equilibre démographique. OCDE, *Migrations Internationales Le Tournant.* Paris: OCDE.

Zlotnik, H. 1994. Migration to and from developing regions: A review of past trends. In *The Future population of the world: What can we assume today?*, edited by W. Lutz. London: Earthscan.

Zucchetti, E., ed. 1997. Il risparmio e le rimesse degli Immigrati. Quaderni ISMU, n.5.

Index

Note: Italicized pages refer to notes, tables and illustrations